SHALINI

A LIFE EXTRAORDINAIRE

BY

COLONEL HARPREET SINGH KOHLI

AS NARRATED BY

LT GEN AJAI KUMAR SINGH

PVSM, AVSM, YSM, SM, VSM, PHD (RETD)

INDIA • SINGAPORE • MALAYSIA

ISBN
Paperback 979-8-89699-500-5
Hardcase 979-8-89724-550-5

Dedicated to the unsung families of The Armed Forces,

who shoulder the onerous responsibility of taking care

of the ones who safeguard our Nation.

"WALK THE LINE"

"Here's to the ones
Who play the part
With a smiling face
But an aching heart."

"Who ride the wave
But all the while
They hide the pain
Behind a smile."

"Walk the Line"

"This is to those

Who face the rain

When the tide is high

And the days are gray."

"Who walk the line

To pave the way

To a better life

And brighter days."

FOREWORD

I am overjoyed to hold in my hands this aptly titled book ***Shalini – A Life Extraordinaire***, just five years after Shalini left us. I knew Shalini for nearly three decades through our husbands, who were course mates and frequently reunited during their military careers. When I think of how to describe Shalini, I realise that no words can do justice to her charming, thoughtful, kind, ever-smiling persona, which brought joy to everyone around her.

Shalini embodied not only the qualities of an amazing lady but also how an ideal human being would look like in a perfect world. She effortlessly balanced her multiple roles - mother, daughter, sister, daughter-in-law, Regimental Lady, mentor, wife, friend and companion. However, the persona I came to admire most **was that of a fighter**, especially in her final years.

My husband and I lived next door to Shalini and General Ajai in Mhow when she was diagnosed with critical medical issues. I still recall the moment vividly—our husbands were away, and the news hit us hard. I watched Shalini grapple with her diagnosis, virtually a death-warrant due to the disease ravaging her kidneys, but soon rise with fierce determination. She transformed her battle against the disease into a powerful testament of will, choosing to live life on her own terms. To this day, her story fills me with awe and inspiration...

Lt Gen Ajai Kumar Singh's narration brilliantly captures the quintessence of Shalini in its entirety, and I am truly grateful that her story, through this book, will now inspire many more to be fighters. Ajai and Shalini made an exceptional couple, walking hand in hand for three decades and creating a beautiful journey filled with love and support. Their bond left indelible footprints in the hearts of everyone fortunate enough to witness it. This book ensures that their heartening and powerful story will reach and touch the lives of many. It is a magnificent tribute to a soul-mate from someone now navigating life alone, yet forever connected to her **essence** like a guardian angel. General Ajai captures their story in a way that only a true partner would. His anecdotes take readers on an emotional roller coaster, filled with joy, heartbreak, excitement, sadness and everything in between. ***Shalini – A Life Extraordinaire*** is a testament to true love–a remarkable narrative encapsulated in just a few hundred pages in the book that you hold in your hands.

The book beautifully reveals that despite her travails, Shalini never ever complained or lost the radiant smile that defined her.

She was indeed a woman on a mission who faced life's trials with stoicism, refusing to let them hinder her from living on her own terms. Before she departed, she ensured all her responsibilities were fulfilled, once again, acting on her own terms. The very title of the first chapter – ***अब मैं जा रही हूँ... (I am leaving now)*** – as derived from her last words to her husband, just about sums up the immensely proud woman that Shalini was...

I have been looking forward to this book since General Ajai often mentioned his mission to publish Shalini's memories for posterity. I am honoured to contribute the foreword, allowing me to be among the first to read the manuscript. After reading, I can confidently say that the book accurately and authentically captures the sinusoidal journey of one of the strongest willed women I have had the pleasure of being friends with. She lived an inspiring life until the very end, departing content and free from worldly attachments–an ideal we should all strive to emulate.

This book will take its readers on highs and lows that will resonate deeply with them and I am sure that those who read through the story of Shalini will be better versions of themselves by the time they finish this wonderfully written book. In the end, I offer my best wishes to Lt Gen Ajai Kumar Singh and his family as they bring this labour of love to fruition. ***There could be no better tribute to the truly blessed soul that Shalini was...***

Mrs. Sunita Dwivedi

President Army Wives Welfare Association

ODE TO OUR MOTHER

Beneath the shadow of life's cruel decree,

You stood, a beacon, unyielding, free.

Through battles fierce and storms untamed,

Your spirit soared, forever unmaimed.

A warrior clad in strength and grace,

You faced each trial with a smiling face.

The knife of surgeries, the test of pain,

You bore it all, yet love remained.

Ode to our Mother

The gift of a kidney, a fragile reprieve,

You cherished each breath, each moment to weave.

Through years of struggle, through every strain,

Your courage shone like sunlight through rain.

When infection darkened the hopeful skies,

And your body faltered, we said our goodbyes.

But never your spirit, your laughter, your light–

They remain, like stars in the deepest night.

Loved by all, your heart so true,

A treasure to us, a universe to you.

Now in peace, beyond the strife,

You live in our hearts, eternal life.

Oh Mother, brave, with a smile that stayed,

In memory's garden, your love is laid.

Forever cherished, forever near,

In every tear, in every cheer.

– Abhinav Chauhan

My mumma, Shalini, was my best friend, my soulmate, and the mirror to my soul. We shared an unspoken connection, a bond so deep that words often felt unnecessary. She was my safe space, and the constant in my ever-changing world. For 14 years, she fought a relentless battle with kidney failure, a battle that eventually took her physical presence from us in 2020. But even in her frailty, she showed me what it truly means to be strong–not by denying her weaknesses but by embracing them with grace.

She was deeply involved in my childhood, ensuring every moment was magical. She made me believe in tooth fairies. Whenever my tooth broke she used to ask me to put it under the pillow and the next day there was a gift for me and invariably it was exactly what I wanted. She loved with her whole heart–fiercely and unconditionally–and scolded me with the same intensity, always wanting the best for me. She loved dressing me up, helping with school projects, and patiently guiding me through life's little challenges. Her love was my anchor and her positivity, my guiding light.

Every time life knocked her down, she allowed herself to feel the pain, to cry, to question–yet she always rose again, a little stronger, a little braver. Her body may have been weak, but her heart held an infinite reservoir of resilience. She faced every challenge with a smile that could light up the darkest room, hiding her struggles not out of vanity but out of her immense love for those around her.

She never pretended to be invincible; instead, she taught me that it's okay to be vulnerable, to falter, and to lean on those who love you. It was through her honesty, her ability to keep moving forward despite her fears and breakdowns, that she unknowingly taught me how to live.

Her positivity wasn't born from ignorance of her suffering but from her decision to cherish life even when it seemed unbearably hard.

When she left, a part of me went with her, but she left behind an indelible mark on my soul. She taught me to find strength in my weaknesses, to smile through my tears, and to embrace life's imperfections with open arms. Her golden heart taught me the value of compassion and kindness, while her passion for life inspired me to pursue my dreams fearlessly. She was not just a mother but a mentor, guiding me with love, wisdom, and an unyielding belief in my potential, leaving an indelible mark on my character and outlook on life. She was my hero, not because she was unbreakable but because she faced her challenges with unimaginable courage. My mother was the bravest soul I have ever known, and her essence will forever be a part of me.

– Sanjana Shalini Singh

In the short spell of time I got to spend with my mother in law, what Struck me the most was her zest for life and courage.

I saw how sometimes it meant that she rested all week in order to gather the energy to function with family on the weekends. Other times, it was more of pushing through the week and spending the weekend in recovery. She always said she was fine and never complained even when she went through the toughest of days.

I learnt that courage isn't only fighting your circumstances but accepting and making peace with one's circumstances requires more courage. This is something that I admired about her and will stay with me as an important life lesson.

Dear Mom, wherever you are, may you be happy and at peace. We all miss you!!

– *Sukriti Sah Chauhan*

She was a remarkable lady. The brief time I spent with her taught me the importance of wearing a smile, no matter how big the challenges I might face. A lover of dogs with a joyful spirit, she understood that her time was limited. Rather than allowing her illness to confine her, she chose to enjoy every moment in whatever way she could. From traveling to going out to the movies, she managed it all. Her mental strength was impressive. The situation she faced could break even the bravest, yet she handled it all with remarkable calmness.

I realized the severity of her health condition when I lifted her up from the bed to the vehicle which was waiting to take her for what would be her final visit to the hospital. At that moment, I understood just how weak she had become, as she had never shown her vulnerability before. I later learned that for the past 14 years, she had never allowed anyone to pick her up and assist her into a vehicle. I truly believe I was just meant to be there for that moment.

I have spent some great times with you, filled with fun, excitement, drama, and even anxiety—everything was there. I miss you, and I want you to know that the last promise I made to you will be fulfilled to the best of my ability.

– *Akshat Randev*

REFLECTIONS

'Meeting Shalini was probably one of the most important and absolute necessity in my life. I was going through a lot with my own life, the ups and downs with aged parents and my own daughter's health issues. And then Shalini came along, happy and cheerful, not a care in the world, getting a hold on everything in her frail yet strong hands. You actually needed to know her to see where she "was", where her life was "leading" her, but where she herself "steered" her life......

Every time I was with her, I came back a stronger and positive person. Every time I met her, her zest for life always rubbed off on me. She never complained, never let you know what havoc was happening within her, never once forgot to share a smile or laugh heartily to my silly jokes or escapades......

Here was a true woman of strength. She has fought and was still bravely fighting all odds when I met her last. I was in tears seeing her in bed, almost shrunken beyond recognition, managing her dialysis and her medication. But nothing could stop her!......my mind was distraught but she was softly pressing my hand. That squeeze told a hundred tales ......a tale to let go, a story that began with " It's fine, this too shall pass", a beautiful documentary on doing what has to be done in life despite everything, a comforting climax that she had fought right till the end, and won over it all. And majestically'

- Aparna Ananth

The image of Shalu that will remain etched in my memory will be her ever-smiling face. She found joy and cheer wherever possible. The memories of the chats and laughter shared are still so vivid. I can still feel the excitement in her voice when she called me up to inform me about Sanjana's marriage being fixed, the moment that she had long awaited.

What struck a chord in me about her was her ever smiling countenance and the never complaining indomitable spirit. Shalu, your memories will linger on bringing forth tears and smiles... You are missed badly and remembered fondly forever.

– Swapna Nair

'I have been full of admiration for her. The fact that she was always so warm towards everyone she met, gave attention to people.........and most of all carrying out her duties with indomitable strength and a sweet smile. She will always be remembered as one of the most wonderful people I have come across in my life'

- Poonam Chaudhary

'I found her graciously silent and thoughtful. Hardly I knew that there has been an enormous amount of endurance being so bravely shouldered by her, as I could know it only after her demise. And after I read about her brave fight against all her health issues, I could relate her meaningful silence and thoughtfulness to her dignified battle against a very beautiful but ruthless adversary called life'

- *Anayat, Watergam, Rafi Abad*

'Little did I know that I am meeting an angel who was sent by God to spread kindness here. She was a motivator. Simply knowing her exposed one to some great virtues of grit, calmness, selflessness and above all a smiling face though she was enduring great pain. She was a symbol of Sacrifices and selfless attitude. In a world where there is a bitter fight for one's survival she sacrificed her own well-being by foregoing the kidney meant for her for a strange person who needed it more'

- *Maj Gen VC Chitravanshi*

'Our good fortune to know a person with such indomitable spirit and warmth. A very friendly and affectionate person, she made a charming hostess'

- *Vijay and Nandita*

'Our memory sees Mrs Shalini Singh as a Commanding Officer's wife who had a very positive and pleasant demeanour. An ever smiling lady who was gracious and filled with regimentation and pride. She very passionately carried a very happy and cheerful ladies team under her wings...... one person who was full of life and was ever smiling. She radiated the charm of her smile among the people around'

Never got into the spree of any one upmanship or making any loose remark against anyone.

Infact her aura of grace and positivity was something that all younger ladies spoke about and those in the impressionable age into the Olive Greens did look forward to imbibe. One always heard the ladies of First Eleven Gorkha Rifles boast about her as Hamare CO ki wife as a proud possession. She was more of a friend, philosopher and a guide rather than a Senior Lady amongst the team. Even we saw her doing the things with her own hands instead of bossing around. Her humane way of talking to troops in a respectful manner was again worth emulating'

– Ritu Kala

Her warmth and her welcoming smile is etched in my memory forever....... She indeed was an epitome of love and warmth – a legacy that she has left behind in her beautiful children as she has moved on to rest in eternal peace. I feel fortunate to have met her and experience her blissful warmth'

- Guneet Sethi

'To a beautiful woman inside out........The way she was, the way she always has been can be defined as "valiant". Her caressing me in the ambassador staff car as I felt ill would be one of the most beautiful moments I remember. A resilient person who always greeted everyone with warm hugs and positivity........always laughing, smiling. An approachable, friendly and loving woman who radiated good vibes all the time. Ageless her, beautiful her. The best mother, wife, daughter and my idol.

She was gods favourite and he better take care of an ageless angel like her'

- *Daksha*

'A pillar of strength, always calm, composed and large hearted. Had the grit, patience and an innate desire to live a full life.

She lived a full life, she completed her responsibilities as a mother, she gave you the support and balance to reach one of the highest ranks, never burdened you with her illness, gave you the freedom to dedicate your time to the sensitive appointments you held. What else could be expected from a person. She went with grace, balance, full of zest and in control of things'

– Samar & Ritu

'Few occasions I met her left a profound impression.......She would talk about her children with great pride. She taught me that being a mother is not about just asking your children to do your will, but embracing their dreams as your own and being their rock, in letting them fulfil their desires.......But I will always be grateful that I had the pleasure & good fortune to have met this angel – Shalu'

- Monica.

'We remember her as an enthused person, spreading happiness and positivity. One could never make out that She was struggling for her life because she had an effervescent smile and was a very warm host...... held her responsibilities with aplomb and in style'

- Harman, Rannvijay, Lt Gen Ike Singha & Ballie Singha.

'Just learnt one thing from her, no matter what life and destiny throws at you.....Don't allow any thing in this world to take off smile from your face.......so that the most difficult phase of your life even turns out to be a lesson of your life'

- Major Kunal, SM (Retd)

'That ever smiling face, cheerful always........ the never-ending energy in you was always like a magic, a miracle which keeps people around you strong'

- Col Satheesh

'Truly her life is ever inspiring....... the way you both have lived your lives together has very few parallels. The way you live life now and the love, compassion and empathy you have for all those who are in need of it is a testimony of the beautiful life you and Shalini have shared and she continues to be with you at every moment of your life'

- Anonymous

'An exceptional person- energy, enthusiasm, strength, and the list extends endlessly .... You both made such a fabulous couple. She lives palpably in every nook and corner of your house and persona'

- Suman and Vijay

'She put not just my knowledge, but also my patience to test with her complete insistence on not undergoing dialysis ever. I was partly frustrated and mostly amazed at the willpower and stubbornness of this petite lady, who was fast deteriorating and really needed to be initiated on haemodialysis to survive. In the process, we forged an unseeming bond of friendship, laced with friendly banter and gentle sarcasm,

but always respectful. By June 2009, when her condition deteriorated to such an extent that she did not have the energy to object, and the basic instinct of self-preservation kicked in, that she finally consented to initiating haemodialysis. In a few more months, we managed to obtain a donor from the extended family and conducted her kidney transplantation successfully in Sep 2009. From then on she was my ideal patient! Always compliant, taking her medicines on time, coming for her follow-up regularly, and it was heartening to note the way the colour returned to her cheeks and the sparkle in her dark expressive eyes grew stronger. I was struck by the deep and enduring bond shared by her with her husband. There was an unspoken thread that joined the two of them, that made his eyes light up whenever she was around, or even discussed. He put up with all her tantrums in the early days with an understanding smile and then listened to my frustrated rants with an equally equanimous attitude. It was when I met them in Lucknow in Nov 2013, when I realized how their roles were reversed at home, where he stayed silent and smiled and she did all the talking!

She taught me to respect my patient's wishes and be patient with them. My interactions with her have made me a better doctor and human being. And watching the couple, taught me how an ideal husband should be. Theirs was truly a bond which transcends life on this earth'

– Brig Ranjith Nair

आप करुणामयी, सहनशील , धैर्यवान ,बुद्धिवान , संतोषी और सुंदर महिला थी । मैं आप के पास 2006 मैं आया था । जब से मैं आपके पास आया तब से मैं आपसे कुछ न कुछ सीखता रहा । यह शायद उनके ही व्यक्तित्व का प्रभाव मुझ पर है की में किसी भी कार्यों को पूरा करने मैं पीछे नहीं हटता हूँ ।

उन्होंने मेरे कार्य को करने मै दक्षता लाने वाले तरीक़े सिखाए । इसके लिए मैं उनका जीवन भर उनका आभारी रहूंगा । और मेमसाब मुझसे कहा करते थे कि मेरे दो पुत्र है एक आशु और आप । और मुझे भी कभी यह एहसास नहीं हुआ कि मैं अपनी माँ और घर परिवार से दूर हूँ । इसलिए मैं भी उनके घर के सभी कार्य को नि स्वार्थ भाव से किया करता था । मेमसाब मेरे सुख दुख में मैरा साथ देते थे ।अपनी सुख दुख की बातें भी मुझसे किया करते थे। और अपना समझकर डांटे भी थे। अपने बच्चों के भविष्य के बारे में बहुत चिंतित रहते थे । (जब आशु भैया की शादी थी तब हम लोग चादनी चौक शॉपिंग के लिये गए थे और उस दिन मेमसाहब ने अपने दोनों पैरों में अलग अलग चपल पहनी थी मैं और सूची हँस रहे थे और बोल रहे थे लड़के की शादी करने में ऐसा ही होता हैं) इस तरह से जीवन की चुनौतियो का सामना करने वाली महिला मैंने पहली बार देखी । अपने दुख को उन्होंने अपने चेहरे पर कभी भी प्रदर्शित नहीं होने दिया । और न ही दूसरों से अपनी दुख की बातें करते थे । और कहते थे ऊपर वाले से मेरी लड़ाई है कि वह ज़्यादा बलवान है या मैं ।स्वर्गवास होने के एक सप्ताह पहले । उन्होंने मुझसे कहा कि मैं अब जीना नहीं चाहती हूँ अब में जाना चाहती हूँ । भगवान मुझे अपने पास बुला ले । मैं उनके साथ में 14 वर्षों तक रहा ऐसी बातें उन्होंने कभी नहीं बोली । शायद उन्हें अपने जाने का आभास हो गया था।

– Gopal Singh Bisht

CONTENTS

PRAY FOR HER

(Transcript of WhatsApp message sent by Lt Gen Ajai Kumar Singh on 01 Apr 2020 at 5 PM asking family & friends to pray for Shalini in her last moments)

Shalini is admitted in Army Hospital (Research & Referral) for the last few days. She was put on a ventilator but true to her fighting spirit, she regained consciousness. May be, only to summon me & state very clearly "अब मैं जा रही हूँ" (I am leaving now) in a way assuring me that she has done what she had to do, the purpose is accomplished. And she is breaking free to merge with the cosmic consciousness. Not only that, she asked me the date and said, let's celebrate our daughter Sanjana's birthday, which falls on 19 April. I helped her to sit, massaged her back. She tried to clap as a mark of birthday celebration.

I have read somewhere that one of the barometers of a person's spiritual evolution is how they face death. Death, invariably is something which is feared. Now here is she, absolutely calm, composed, in control of her emotions in the last stage of her physical gross life. And informing her life partner that she is leaving and yet celebrating her daughter's birthday.

My mind reflects on our conversation in the last couple of months as the writing on wall becomes clearer to us. She is running out of options. Despite all efforts, modern medicine may not be able to help her beyond a point. For fourteen years, she faced such trials & tribulation smilingly & valiantly. Yet the physical body had taken a toll. Now she is reaching a point of no return. Often, I would tell her that when the moment comes, break free. Don't worry about us. You have done much more than what you could possibly do.

This is TAPAS, which she had done for Fourteen Years. Prince Ram returned after fourteen years of exile as Maryada Purshottam Ram, Prince Siddharth after seven years of TAPAS got self-realization and became The Buddha. Even Shalu has done TAPAS for fourteen years undoubtedly for the sake of her loved ones. In my assessment her sacrifice & TAPAS is also of the same league. And she must break free without any incumbrance to attain a higher realm of existence.

Possibly she remembered that and is now assuring her life partner that she is ready to shed this mortal body. This is the highest state of empathy and compassion, demonstrated while staring into the face of Death.

Shalini is an epitome of courage, grit, patience, determination & resilience. The spirit with which she faced all odds is unparalleled. Despite the vicissitudes of her medical condition, she not only did full justice but excelled in all her roles as a Mother, Wife, Daughter, Sister and a Regimental & Service Lady.

As she lay on her hospital bed in ICU, her smile is intact and her face has the radiance of peace. Her organs may be failing and her breath weak, yet her spirit is palpable. Let us all pray for her and salute her indomitable spirit and resilience.

She may cast off her mortal body but her spirit will shine forth and be a guiding beacon for us to chart the course of our lives. She will continue to live in spirit, in our memories as a guardian angel inspiring us.

"Adieu Shalini, you lived a complete life. And you will continue to live in us"

01

अब मैं जा रही हूँ...
(I AM LEAVING NOW)

"He knew it was time for the inevitable to happen."

She had been in and out of hospitals for better part of the past 14 years. But never before had she said these words. In any case, together, the family had delayed it much much beyond what was to be generally expected, given her condition.

Because there were matters to be resolved .. dreams to be fulfilled .. kids to be raised up ..

Much of that was already done, or visible on the horizon.

She had done her bit.

She knew it.

As did he.

They both knew.

So much so that he had in their conversation, even assured her a few days before this latest hospital admission that if she decided to finally go, she may do so without worrying about him or the kids.

And now, she had decided that it was time to move on.

Shalini's journey has been extraordinary, one of resilience, perseverance, sacrifice, love, care, compassion, empathy and steadfastness.

Major General Ajai Kumar Singh had been a very busy man lately. It was the month of March 2020 and India, just like the rest of the world, was just about coming to terms with the rapidly spreading COVID-19 Pandemic. And it just so happened that he was occupying a key position in the branch that the Indian Army had decided to be the nodal agency for coordinating the operations against this deadly virus.

To say that he was a busy soul would be an understatement.

In the midst of this, the health of his wife, Shalini, who had been suffering from renal and later, liver related issues for the past 14 years, had been deteriorating again.

During the last week of the month, she was increasingly unable to eat any food. Even if she ate, her body would end up vomiting it out. Finally, Ajai decided to take her to the renowned R&R Hospital of the Indian Army where she had been undergoing treatment for the past many years.

Unsurprisingly, she declined and instead told him that she would try and have lunch.

It was almost as if she was trying to steal a few more moments at home before leaving for good ..

Anyhow, not only did she eat a bit but even summoned some energy from the deepest depths of her being to walk a few steps in the drawing room of the ground floor flat that the couple were occupying in a military enclave in Dhaula Kuan.

At night, she vomited out the contents of her stomach yet again.

Ajai suggested she have some *Nariyal Pani*, but she declined again and said she just wanted to sleep. She specifically mentioned that she did not want to be disturbed while she slept.

Next morning she finally had that *Nariyal Pani* but threw up yet again.

This time she agreed to go to the hospital.

However, Shalini's 47kg body was so weak that Akshat, who was soon to marry her daughter Sanjana, had to carry her to the car. This being the only time that she was carried to the car while on the way to the hospital. Gritty and resilient that she was, she always walked to the car irrespective of her medical condition.

She had never been *this* weak before.

Headed straight to the ward, she was quickly hooked up with an IV line and critical medicines started getting pumped into her system. With his wife in good hands, Ajai headed out to his office at the Army Headquarters with a promise to come back during the lunch break in the afternoon.

If not for the rampaging Corona Virus, he wouldn't have bothered going to the office at all. However, national duty couldn't wait, and in any case she was in the best possible medical care in the country, with Sanjana and Akshat right next to her.

So off he went and was soon neck deep in work, coordinating the Indian Army's efforts against this latest, invisible enemy besides his other multifarious operational duties.

Lunch too was soon forgotten. There just wasn't time, thanks to the continuously ringing phones.

It was about 3 p.m. when he got a call from one of the doctors at the hospital. Shalini had been shifted to the ICU due to low blood pressure.

He left office 15 minutes later, letting his staff know that he would be available on mobile and once at the hospital, on a secure army line as well.

The date that day was 27th March 2020 and with the first lockdown underway at that point in time, it took him less than 10 minutes to reach the hospital and by 3:30pm he was right outside the ICU.

In the ICU, Ajai didn't enter the cubicle because Shalini was surrounded by doctors, nurses and other support staff trying to get her blood pressure to go up.

Even at that moment he had hope that she will pull through, just as she had done so many times in the past.

For a while it seemed that he was right. Doctors were ultimately able to stabilize her, as well as start an emergency dialysis to offset the compromised transplanted kidney.

Yet, she continued to be in the ICU, hooked on to a ventilator.

Ajai finally went home, even as Sanjana insisted to stay in a family room next to the ICU. Little did she know that this would be her home for the next four days, since she just refused to leave her mother's side.

The next day Ajai got a call from the Military Secretary of the Indian Army.

'You are going to be commanding the 33 Corps', he told him.

Despite the gloomy events of the past few days, this brought a momentary smile on his face.

'She had been right', he mused, going over one of their many conversations when times were a bit better!

Major General Ajai Kumar Singh had recently been approved for promotion to the next rank of Lieutenant General. It would be a few months before a vacancy for promotion opened up.

Upon promotion, his first appointment would be that of a Corps Commander. He had already calculated that there would be 3-4 options for where he goes to command his Corps, based on when the tenures of the then incumbents were getting over. The options that seemed likely to open up included Jalandhar, Bhopal, Bhatinda and Sukna.

As always, he shared these with his wife, Mrs Shalini Singh. He also told her that he was keen to go to Jalandhar since the local hospital there had a Nephrologist who could look after her.

However, Shalini said she wasn't too keen on Jalandhar.

Bhatinda too was ruled out by her.

Bhopal option was a 'maybe'. But this is what seemed to be the most likely option to Ajai, based on the timelines when vacancies would be created. It also helped that Bhopal was fairly well connected to New Delhi and if needed, Shalini could quickly reach the R&R Hospital.

The last option he had told his wife that day was Sukna. And it was an immediate and enthusiastic YES by her!

Today, after all those months, she was proven right!

However, he couldn't share the news with her just yet. For one, he was still in office and busy as could be. And Shalini was still on a ventilator.

Somehow, even the doctors didn't seem to have very optimistic prognosis on when that might happen, even if it happened at all.

But she was a strong-willed woman. At 5:30 a.m. on 31st March 2020, Sanjana got a message that her mother was off ventilator.

She rushed to her.

Shalini, though breathing on her own, was still very weak and unable to talk. So she was communicating with her daughter by scribbling letters of the alphabet on her hand instead.

So the mother and daughter got talking after a long break!

Her first message had been to send for Ajai, which was duly communicated to him back home, before she got busy talking with Sanjana.

Ajai rushed to the hospital and was soon with his wife of 32 years.

Happy to see him, she asked him to help her sit up on the ICU bed. He gently helped her sit up. And then he told her about the impending move to Sukhna, that was likely to happen a few months later. She was visibly happy to hear about that.

She willed herself to stay lucid.

She had to, because there was a very important message she wanted to give to him.

'*अब मैं जा रही हूँ*', she told him.

He took it with all the calmness and composure that he could muster.

Somehow, it seemed that he too knew.

They had already discussed this distinct possibility.

And he had told her that when it was time, she must break free and should go happily and without any worry about him or her kids.

He was quite right on that aspect. Both their kids had grown up to be good human beings and were well settled in their respective careers. Their son Abhinav, was already married a few years ago to Sukriti while Sanjana too was engaged to Akshat.

Moreover, Ajai too was well on his path to reach further heights in an already well-accomplished military career. If things went well, he would at the very least, reach the rank of an Army Commander. For that too, Shalini had already made preparations by purchasing a set of Army Commander's *Gorget Patches* and placed them in the Mandir at her home for him to wear when the day came.

Lieutenant General Ajai Kumar Singh took over as the Commander of Southern Army on 1st November 2022, wearing the Gorget Patches that his wife had already procured for him.

It was time for this couple to let go, so that Shalini could finally be free from the pain and suffering which she had so stoically endured for almost two decades, with the last 14 years after her kidney ailment was discovered, being especially challenging.

She repeated her assertion that she is leaving now.

Ajai said that he understood.

Some time later, she went back to sleep, unable to communicate due to the sheer weakness that had overwhelmed her body.

However, before that she had still managed to tell Sanjana that her father was going to command a Corps in Sukna!

Meanwhile, Abhinav too rushed from Dehradun to Delhi on the 29th. He met her on the same day. Shalini being herself, the only thing she could ask him was have you eaten anything. She was always concerned whether he has had his fill, before dozing off again. This was the last time the mother and son conversed. Ajai decided to give a call to Sukriti who was in Haldwani at that moment with her mother, and made preparations for her to come back to Delhi. They both knew that it would be a challenge to travel during the lockdown. But regardless, she rushed to be back in Delhi with her Mother-in-Law. Her husband, Abhinav was already there with his mother, having left behind a nascent business venture in Dehradun.

Shalini didn't communicate any further with anyone. Her frail body seemed to have finally overcome even her strong willpower and on the morning of 1st April 2020, she was put back on a ventilator.

In a befitting testimony to her indomitable spirit, the doctors treating her told Ajai later that they themselves were surprised that she had come out of the ventilator and stayed without it for so long.

1st April 2020 happened to be an *Ashtami* day of Navratri. Every *Ashtami,* Shalini's mother would do a pooja for her ailing daughter at their home in Dehradun. That day, just as she was about to settle down for the prayer, she received a call from Ajai.

He said that they should come over to Delhi.

She quickly finished her prayer and along with her husband, started for Delhi soon thereafter. Ajai's staff had already obtained necessary permissions for them to travel during the lockdown.

They and Sukriti would reach R&R Hospital at about 7 p.m., completing the gathering of the nearest family members by Shalini's bedside.

At about 8 p.m., Shalini's heart stopped beating.

It was a heart that was made of sheer gold .. a heart that was filled with compassion and understanding .. a heart that kept on beating despite tremendous odds, just so that Shalini could fulfill her obligations in this mortal realm.

What follows is the story of Shalini - A woman who lived life to the fullest, come what may .. a woman whose ordinary heroism touched so many lives .. a woman who lives on in so many other hearts.

02

LAKSHMI

"I shall forever be thankful that I was blessed with such a daughter"

– Suresh Pundir (Shalini's Mother)

Third week of December 1970: Advocate Yash Pal Singh Pundir was a worried young man, as he raced to Coronation Hospital in Dehradun.

He had good reasons to be anxious.

His wife was in labour, about to give birth to their first child shortly.

But far from being a joyous occasion, it was causing him immense worries.

Having just taken his first steps in his chosen career, he wasn't in the best of financial health. His monthly income was barely Rs 100, which was simply *not* enough to start a family.

In fact, if not for a Govt Hospital nearby, he wouldn't even have been able to afford critical medical care for his wife and soon to be born child.

However, divine plans were in place and the Pundir Couple were soon blessed with a daughter at 2 a.m. on 20th Dec 1970.

But the new parents only saw more despair come their way.

Yes, it was still a time when a daughter, that too a first-born, was not a very welcome addition to many families. Yet, it wasn't the birth of a girl that was causing despair.

On the contrary, Yash Pal Pundir and his wife Suresh, were ecstatic at the birth of their tiny little daughter!

It was her health that was the cause of despair.

Something was very wrong with their daughter.

So wrong, in fact, that the doctors had immediately put her on ventilator support, pumping in much needed oxygen into her tiny lungs.

Hooked to a ventilator was how she began her journey in that lifetime, and ironically, it was how she concluded it as well.

Something was seriously wrong with their little girl, and the helpless Pundir couple could only look at her from afar, unable to do anything to make her better. All that they could do was look at her from a distance and pray for a miracle.

Yash Pal was also silently keeping track of the mounting bill. Despite his daughter being in a Govt hospital due to his financial condition.

She would stay on a ventilator for nine days.

'It was almost as if she was taking her own time to decide whether she wanted to stay or not', muses Mr Yash Pal Singh Pundir, who is now one of the top lawyers in Dehradun.

Thankfully, she chose to stay!

It would appear that as soon as she made up her mind to stay, she became the true epitome of Goddess Lakshmi for her family. It manifested even before she left the hospital when her father came across an unexpected windfall and was able to pay off his dues to the hospital comfortably.

Thus, the *Lakshmi* came home in form of this little girl.

Now came the immediate issue of giving her a formal name. After the traditional pooja and preparation of her *janampatri*, it was decided that her name should start with the letter 'म'.

Yash Pal's father came up with the name Manju for his eldest grandchild.

But there was an issue with his suggestion. His son and daughter-in-law weren't keen on naming their daughter as Manju. But being from a traditional family in an era where the word of the elders was the law, they didn't quite know how to put across their hesitation to the head of the family.

Apparently, their *Lakshmi* too didn't want to be called Manju and hence found a way out for her parents, with the help of her Bombay based Mausi!

Some time during the efforts to name the child, the phone rang at the Pundirs' household. It was the sister-in-law of Mr Pundir calling from Bombay.

'Yash Pal ki ladki ka naam Shalini rakhna', she said.

It wasn't a suggestion, mind you, but a direct and somewhat forceful order!

Her reason for suggesting this name?

She had just seen the movie *Jewel Thief* and *Vyjayanthimala's* character in it was named Shalini!

The name stuck and thus the little *Lakshmi* came to be known as Shalini to the world at large.

However, her parents continue to call her their Lakshmi to this day.

As life unfolded, it soon became apparent that Shalini was perhaps what best describes the kind of person that she was right from the very beginning.

Over the next five years, two younger brothers – Atul and Amit – too joined the family but despite that, Shalini continued to be the favourite child of her parents. Mr Yash Pal maintains that she being his eldest child and the only daughter, it was natural for him and his wife to have that much more of a soft corner for her.

That said, it might not be wrong to say that very nearly having lost her, right in the beginning, would have made her that much more precious to her parents.

So much so, that even as they packed off both their sons to study in Mussoorie, they chose to put Shalini in a convent school within Dehradun itself. They just couldn't bear to let her be away from them.

Of course, another reason may be that ever since Shalini came into their lives, their circumstances had taken a drastic turn for the better.

Mr Yash Pal's legal practice was booming and the days when he didn't know how he could afford even critical medical care for his loved ones were long gone. His income grew by leaps and bounds and he never looked back thereafter.

Shalini was truly their Lakshmi. So much so, that once she left home after marriage, his practice even saw a dip! Ever so often, he would implore his daughter to come stay with him for a few days so that he could make some recovery. Even though it might just have been a ploy to get his daughter back home for a while, Mr Yash Pal maintains that with Shalini back home, he would almost always get an unexpected windfall!

Shalini had another medical scare when she was about 18 months old. Her legs had stopped working and a local doctor had declared that she was afflicted with Polio.

Yash Pal and his wife were stunned.

After all the difficulties that they had experienced at the time she was born, they had thought that the worst was already past.

And now there was a doctor telling them that their kid was in the grip of yet another deadly disease.

They did what any parent would have done in such a circumstance – they rushed her to Delhi for specialized medical care. Enroute, they halted at the renowned *Daat Kaali Mandir* in order to seek the blessings of the Divine Mother.

Overwhelmed with emotion, Shalini's mother placed her little child at the feet of the Mother Goddess and told her that she was to take care of her.

Thankfully, divine intervention soon manifested when the *Mahant* of the temple came up to the distraught mother with an oil and asked her to apply it to her daughter's legs.

Yash Pal took it upon himself to keep massaging his infant daughter's legs with that oil throughout the journey to Delhi and by the time they reached their destination, Shalini had regained the use of her legs!

The doctor who saw Shalini in Delhi also ruled out Polio and said that the child would soon be fine.

In fact, whenever her health deteriorated, especially in her last days, this same oil from the Daat Kali Mandir would help revive her, at times even instantaneously.

A scientific mind may attribute this 'miracle' to any number of different, rational reasons, but Shalini's entire life was too full of these 'miracles' to firmly establish the presence of a divine hand keeping her safe.

Shalini had come to this lifetime with a mission.

A mission to make a positive and happy change in any and every life that she touched.

A mission that could not be brought to a premature halt by illness.

Thus, Shalini continued on her path in this particular lifetime. She was a happy, content, shy and a quiet child, her mother reminisces fondly, her eyes brimming with tears and her smiling face full of warm glow.

Shalini was never one to say or talk anything out of line to anyone. She had absolutely no demands whatsoever. She was always happy with what she had or what her parents brought for her.

In fact, her lack of any demands would often make the job of parenting a bit difficult for her parents, since they had to work extra hard to think of what their favourite child wanted!

She was truly a blessing that had come their way, who had nothing but love to give to all whom she came across.

As the fortunes of the Pundir family kept growing, so did the size of the family. Two years after Shalini, they welcomed their son, Atul, and another three years later came the youngest child of the family, another son named Amit.

With each new arrival, Shalini's ocean of love too expanded appropriately and she was soon half a parent to both her siblings. Each received her love in a different way, but Amit was the one that attached himself to his elder sister with the thickest of glue.

So much so that when news of Shalini's renal failure came, Amit rushed to Mhow (where her husband was then posted) without telling anyone and announced that he would donate a kidney to his sister. Unfortunately, due to chronic high blood pressure, he couldn't do so.

The Pundir household was a place of fun and happiness ever since the arrival of Shalini and subsequently, her younger siblings. All three grew together, tied in strong but invisible bonds of togetherness.

Each child brought a unique personality to the happy mix. While Atul was a bright student, Amit was a rebel. Shalini was a quiet child and the perfect foil to both her brothers.

During the days when they were studying in Mussoorie, both brothers eagerly awaited the arrival of their elder sister on the occasion of Rakshabandhan. They would keep waiting till the time they saw their father's car bringing her unfailingly, year after year. The memories of those long waits on Rakshabandhan are still cherished.

But both brothers, despite being very close to each other as siblings, would still choose their elder sister to convey anything they wanted to say to each other, especially if it pertains to matters of sibling rivalry! Thankfully, she was an excellent messenger who knew exactly what to say and when.

And, she was insanely injury prone!

She had the knack of getting injured / hurting herself even in the most unlikely of situations. Her mother narrates a few incidents with an amused smile.

Once, she recollects, Shalini came running to her, crying, with an eraser stuck in her nose! After a lot of attempts to dislodge it, her mother told her that they would now have to take her to a doctor who would need to operate upon her to remove the eraser from her nose. Upon hearing this, young Shalini started bawling even louder. While crying, she had a fit of sneezing and the eraser got dislodged from her nose!

Then there was an instance where she cut her hand quite seriously with a knife while attempting to peel a sugarcane. On another occasion, she burned her hand badly when she wrongly lit a firework during Diwali.

But perhaps the most serious injury that she suffered was in the form of a gash on her head when she was about six years old. It was bleeding quite badly and Shalini unassumingly came back to her room, used her mother's *dupatta* as a tourniquet and laid down on her bed. Her mother still isn't sure whether Shalini was sleeping or unconscious when she found her lying in the bed. Thankfully, medical intervention soon followed and her injury healed fully.

As mentioned before, she got injured a LOT!

At the same time, she had a tremendous capacity to endure pain. That head injury would have made any child of similar age panic. But then Shalini was no ordinary child.

Even the burn injury on her hand was only discovered when her father saw her hand clutched for a long time. Upon enquiring, she replied in the most *matter of fact* tone, *'Mera Haath Jal Gaya Hai.'*

Shalini bore insufferable pain for almost two decades towards the end. However, there was always a smile on her face. She could bear all the pain in the world, but she couldn't bear to worry her loved ones even to the tiniest bit. Often, this meant that she would choose to carry her pains without anyone getting even a hint of it.

She was indeed the darling of the entire family. She loved them all and in return, received immeasurable love from them too. In fact, at the time of her marriage, there were some issues between her father and his younger brother and it wasn't very sure that he would be there for the wedding.

But all acrimony was resolved when Shalini, in her quiet demeanour, asked her mother, *'Chachaji aayenge na meri shaadi mein?'* (Chachaji will come to my marriage *na*?)

THIS was Shalini – A *Lakshmi* to her family, beautiful daughter to her parents, a mother to her siblings, and the glue of happiness that kept them all together.

She was everything that a parent, a sibling, a friend, even an uncle/aunt could have asked for.

She brought with her fortune and bliss.

She was truly a blessing for them all.

03

YOU WANT ME TO MARRY THAT SERVANT??!!

It so happened that sometime in the early 80s, a cousin of (then) 2nd Lieutenant Ajai Kumar Singh, Mr KK Pundir who was a Magistrate, was posted in Dehradun. He knew Mr Yash Pal Pundir, a lawyer, by the virtue of being distantly related and being in the same town, both families too knew each other quite well and used to meet frequently.

KK's wife had a match in mind for the young cousin, Ajai. She had seen Shalini, the daughter of Mr Yash Pal and Mrs Suresh Pundir. A shy, convent educated girl with big eyes and a cheerful demeanour, her easy countenance and the shy smile was very endearing. She mused to herself to play cupid and in one of the social interactions said to Mr Yash Pal – *'Ye Ladki Aap Hamein de do.'* (Translation: Please give this daughter to us).

It was a pleasant surprise for Mr Yash Pal to hear this.

Taken aback by the unexpected marriage proposal for his young daughter, Advocate Yash Pal Pundir quickly regained his composure and replied with a gentle laughter, '*Ye toh aap hee ki hai. Aap hee le lo isko.*' (Translation: She is yours only. You may take her)

The most interesting part about this exchange between the two was that the young girl's father had no idea that it was actually a marriage proposal for his daughter to which he had committed! Instead, he thought that it was just another acquaintance who just wanted a daughter like his own!

But destiny had manifested itself and Shalini would soon meet her soulmate and ultimately embark on a lifetime of matrimonial bliss, though not without some dramatic moments before that!

Accordingly, when Ajai came home to Roorkee on his next leave, KK called him to Dehradun. Ajai gladly headed out with his father to meet his cousin at the Civil Court where his office was.

The plan was to spend a night at his place after catching up with him in office. However, it suddenly started raining heavily when it was time to leave and KK suggested that they take a lift in the car of Mr Yash Pal.

This was the first time Mr Yash Pal had a good look at his prospective son-in-law.

Then in the evening, Mr Yash Pal and his wife came over to the home of KK. Along with them were Shalini and his younger son, Amit. Normal conversation followed between the two, even as the kids got busy doing their own thing.

Realising that Mr Yash Pal hadn't quite understood his proposal, Mr KK said again, this time a bit more candidly that there was a young man in their family, 2nd Lieutenant Ajai Kumar Singh whom he was proposing as a match for Shalini. He further told him that Ajai was at that time at home on leave and that Mr Yash Pal should see him.

Even as the realization was setting in on Mr Yash Pal, in walked Ajai with a tray, carrying tea for everyone. As Lt Gen Ajai recalls fondly, it was quite a reversal of clichéd roles wherein it was the boy bringing tea for the girl and her family instead of the other way round!

Of course Shalini had no idea about what was transpiring. The same was to have been true for Ajai as well, but for his Bhabhi who sounded him out at the last moment and pushed him out with the tray for all guests!

To add to the scene was the fact that having had no warning whatsoever, Ajai was dressed in an old *Kurta-Pyjama.* In addition, having just returned from the physically gruelling Commando Course, he looked quite famished and under-fed; quite unlike the persona expected of an army officer.

However, thanks to his Bhabhi, Ajai knew that the young lady he was serving tea was a proposed match for him. Shalini, on the other hand, continued to be blissfully unaware!

Anyhow, his physical appearance notwithstanding, Ajai's future Father-in-Law took an instant liking to him.

Tea done, the guests started back homewards in their car. Enroute, Shalini's mother asked her, '*Wo ladka kaisa laga?*' (How did you find that boy?)

Confused, her daughter asked, '*Kaun sa ladka?*' (Which boy?)

Mother: '*Wo jo chai lekar aaya tha.*' (The one who brought the tea)

Shalini: '*Wo Naukar??*' (That servant??)

Yes, that was the first impression of her future husband that Shalini got. Not only that, it was reinforced by her brother, Amit as well!

For the time being, however, her parents decided to change the topic of conversation. Shalini *still* didn't know!

But regardless, the match was more or less finalized because not only her parents were happy with it, but even Ajai had agreed to the proposal and his father too had concurred. Upon returning back to Roorkee, Ajai's father told his mother and she too was alright with the proposed match for her son.

However, being the girl's parents, Mr and Mrs Pundir wanted the match to be formalized. So when Ajai came back on his next leave a few months later, both families decided to meet. The setting of this meeting too was the residence of KK who was now posted as the Munsif Magistrate in Rishikesh.

And Shalini STILL didn't have any idea of what was afoot!

KK had his residence in the same campus as the Court. It was a beautiful setting indeed, right next to the holy Ganga River. This was where both families were headed to, the prospective groom's family from Roorkee and the blissfully unsuspecting bride's family from Dehradun.

Unsurprisingly, Shalini was not very keen on making the trip. Her parents tried to convince her, saying it was a family picnic and that they would be going boating in the Ganga.

The young Shalini still wasn't keen.

Finally what clinched the deal was her favourite Chachi too being co-opted in the trip, resulting in Shalini too deciding to tag along!

So the families met.

This time Ajai had gone well-groomed and well-attired, lest he be mistaken for a servant once again!

Having already decided on the match, Ajai's mother blessed Shalini and gave her a ring that she had gotten prepared for her.

THIS was the moment Shalini realized what was afoot.

And she started crying!!

To be fair, she was still young, still in school.

She cried a lot that day, perhaps more out of the sudden enormity of the decision which she had to make and the suddenness of it all.

However, since she had been promised a picnic and a boat ride, the families went out boating in the Ganga, Shalini's eyes still swollen due to all that crying!

Once the boating was done, Ajai's bhabhi quietly arranged a moment alone for Shalini and him to talk to each other. And the setting could not have been more ironical since the only private space available for that was the court room of KK!

So the future couple got to have their first private conversation in a court room!

Thankfully, she was no longer crying.

All that Ajai asked her was whether she felt he was alright for her.

Still overwhelmed, Shalini didn't speak much, but managed to convey her acceptance of the *rishta* that would bind her with Ajai for the rest of their lives.

Before the families left for their respective home towns, Ajai also managed to tell Shalini that he would be in touch with her via letters, so that they both could get to know each other a bit more.

Thus ended what was possibly one of the most dramatic days in the life of Shalini till then.

Ajai too would have an equally dramatic day some months later when he would come to wed her. But that was still some time away!

After returning to Dehradun, Shalini's youngest brother, Amit, all of 10 years of age, refused the match point blank!

'इस आदमी से?', (WITH THIS MAN?) was all that young boy commented when he learnt of the proposed match for his sister!

Thankfully, no one paid much heed to him and waited for Shalini's response instead. All that she said was that she would accept whatever her mother decides for her.

A lot of factors were considered by Shalini's parents and found to be acceptable – Family background of the prospective match, old relationship between the two families and most importantly, a govt job.

But what finally clinched the deal for Shalini's parents was a quip by her father - जहाँ माँग के लड़की ले रहे हैं वहाँ इज्ज़त मिलेगी (Where they are asking for our girl, there she will get respect).

With this, the match was confirmed by the girl's parents.

And now began the most beautiful part of any relationship born out of an arranged marriage – The family sanctioned courtship!

In the case of Ajai and Shalini, it was to be a long distance courtship for most part, since Ajai's Battalion was then deployed in Akhnoor, near Jammu. Nathua Tibba was the exact location in the low hills that marked the India-Pakistan border in that part of the erstwhile State of Jammu and Kashmir.

Thus began an endless stream of letters in both directions between Dehradun and Nathua Tibba!

Both were writing a letter to each other every 2-3 days. At the same time, it just so happened that Ajai's Battalion had a lot of men hailing from Dehradun and thereabouts. So whenever he saw any soldier going home on leave to Dehradun, there would inevitably be a letter and a gift for Shalini that would be couriered via him.

Talking about gifts, it was quite a challenge for Ajai to find something suitable for her. This was due to two reasons. Firstly, having studied mostly in an all boys school and later, joining the National Defence Academy, his interactions with the opposite sex were practically nil. And secondly, sitting in Nathua Tibba, there were hardly any options for purchasing gifts!

Unsurprisingly, the first gift that Ajai sent to Shalini was a folding umbrella from the Battalion's CSD Canteen!

Ajai was still quite young and as he later realized, Shalini too was studying at that time. Hence, his plan was to get married after about 5-6 years. But then, destiny had a totally different plan for the young couple.

In between, he found himself appointed as the ADC to his Division Commander, Major General SC Gupta, Vir Chakra of Fifth Gorkha Rifles. Along with the new job came a well-appointed guest room for the first time in young Ajai's military career. It was nothing short of a cultural shock from the humble lodgings at the forward post of Nathua Tibba where he used a CGI sheet as a bed. Now it was almost as if he had been transported to a whole new world!

However, the most defining memory that Lt Gen Ajai holds of that short stint is the River Chenab flowing right next to his lodgings where he would sit listening to Pankaj Udhas gazals. This was the perfect, blissful setting for a young man in love.

Some time later, while training for a regimental mountaineering expedition to the Rathong Peak near the Kanchenjunga Massif,

Ajai finally found a bit more time at hand to increase the frequency of his letters to one per day.

Understandably, Shalini was soon flooded with those typical inland military letters which would mostly come in a bunch, thanks to the peculiarities of the postal services in the remote locations where Ajai used to be. It wouldn't be wrong to assume that even the local postman would soon be aware that the Pundirs had found a match for their daughter!

Incidentally, the couple had preserved all those letters, with the plans to go through them all over again once Ajai retires. This is one task that Lieutenant General Ajai Kumar Singh still plans to accomplish, though with Shalini only being there in spirit instead of flesh and bones.

After successfully climbing up Mt Rathong in May 1987, Ajai went home on a short leave before rejoining his Unit. The first thing that he heard as soon as he reported back was that the Unit had received orders for their anticipated move to a peace station.

It was nothing out of the ordinary .. not until Ajai heard the city where his Unit was headed – Dehradun!

His heart skipped a beat, as the implications dawned on him!

There would be no need for writing any more letters; not when he could see Shalini practically every single day!

Of course, there was a lot of leg-pulling of Ajai by his seniors in the Unit, who would fnever tire of remarking that even though he was just a youngster, he seemed to have enough clout to pull his entire Unit to Dehradun just so he could be closer to his fiancé!

Remaining days in Nathua Tibba went by in a breeze and Ajai's Battalion soon reached Dehradun. Ajai soon settled into a happy routine of peacetime soldiering, wherein come what may, he would dutifully present himself at 8, Old Survey Road, i.e. Shalini's residence every evening.

Those were happy days indeed for the young couple, but not so much for the father of the girl who followed a strict personal routine that included hitting the bed by 9pm. But now with his future son-in-law in his home every single evening, his nights just wouldn't end before 10:30pm. So much so, that he would end up dozing off even while sitting with Ajai on occasion. But then, he could hardly tell his future son-in-law to leave!

So Advocate Yash Pal Pundir continued to be sleep deprived for quite some time!

It wasn't that Ajai wasn't a devoted future son-in-law either! He too kept Shalini's family in good humour. Having been promoted to the rank of Captain shortly after the match was fixed, the sense in both households was that Shalini is lucky for Ajai. Needless to say, this was fully endorsed by young Ajai as well!

Even though said in a light-hearted manner nearly four decades ago, Mr Pundir still fondly remembers the sentiments of the young man who was shortly to be married to his only daughter. He also remembers his reply – 'ये है ही ऐसी भाग्य वाली', (she is indeed a blessed person) he had said.

Those days, not having a vehicle of his own, Ajai would borrow the brand new scooter that a fellow officer, Captain PS Rai, had purchased. The two were roommates and naturally, Ajai could commandeer his roomie's scooter whenever he wanted!

It was during this phase that one day he suggested to Shalini that she should learn driving. Not only that, his brilliant military mind went on to suggest Ghanghora as the place to learn due to limited traffic there. Of course, Ajai's Battalion being located in Ghanghora Cantt at that time was merely a 'happy coincidence'!

Life was blissful indeed .. set in a happy routine for the soon to be wedded young couple. At about this time, Ajai started realizing that his Battalion was in a peace station for the next couple of years at the max, after which they would move out to yet another field area. Unsurprisingly, he started veering towards the idea of getting married soon enough so that Shalini and he could get to spend some time together before the inevitable separation due to a field tenure.

Of course there were a couple of more triggers that led to an early marriage!

First was a New Year Eve Mess function one of the evenings wherein Ajai's CO suggested that Shalini too join in the festivities with the rest of the Battalion. However Shalini's parents declined to give permission for their daughter to be out at such late hours.

However, this prompted Shalini's parents to seek to formalize the *rishta* which had thus far just been a verbal agreement between the families, without any formal ceremony.

Thus the very next, Advocate and Mrs Pundir went out to Ajai's native place near Roorkee and proposed that the couple be formally engaged to each other.

The ceremony took place soon enough on a hot day in the month of May.

Pretty soon Ajai was back at the residence of his future Father-in-Law, once again seeking permission to take Shalini out for yet another evening function in his Battalion. Engagement done, he was much more confident of getting a positive response this time.

But alas, that was *still* not to be!

Shalini's parents were still reluctant to send her out with him at late hours.

Hence came the decision to get them married soon!

Now this is not to say that the two never got to meet each other in this duration. Shalini's *Mausi* and *Chachi* played a key role in setting up *secret* meetings for the couple before marriage. Of course, those being days when mobile telephony wasn't even thought of, on many an occasion, the two just couldn't locate each other despite both being in the same location. That only added to the *thrill* of stealing a few moments with each other!

Time kept on flying and pretty soon it was 19th Feb 1988, i.e. their wedding day.

It seemed that finally the wait for Shalini and Ajai to be bounded together in holy matrimony was over.

However, the marriage itself wasn't without its own fair share of *excitement* either!

Shalini's father had booked a Dharamshala for the groom's party to stay while in Dehradun. But just about a week before when he went to check out the place, he was told that the Dharamshala had no record of any such booking in his name.

He was horrified at this sudden and unexpected turn of events on the eve of his daughter's wedding.

But help from some other dimension was on its way even as he tried desperately to sort out the matter with the Dharamshala. That night, Yash Pal Pundir saw his late father in a dream. He wasn't very pleased with Yash Pal and admonished him! He said, *'Who is it that you are earning for? Go and book Hotel Drona for Shalini's wedding.'*

Shown the path by his late father, Yash Pal booked the said hotel the very next day instead of wasting time trying to convince the management of the Dharamshala that he had a booking with them.

Shalini's grandfather would again play a key role in yet another major event in her life just about two decades later, giving her a renewed lease of life.

With marriage and a lifetime of companionship looming, along with a lifetime of responsibilities as well, Ajai decided to take some *time-out* a day before he and his family was to go over to Dehradun for the marriage ceremonies.

Now it was right before marriage, and customarily, the groom was never let out of the house alone. So he took his younger brother, Sandeep, along on a scooter and the two just drove along the nearby Ganga Canal, finally halting some way ahead.

Here, the two brothers just sat quietly, with the waters of the holy river flowing by. Sandeep played his part well, by letting Ajai be alone with his thoughts, relishing his very last moments of bachelorhood!

About an hour later, Ajai was ready to get married!

On 19th Feb, the groom's family reached Dehradun and were promptly accommodated in Hotel Drona, along with another hotel close by.

The marriage ceremony next day was scheduled at Hotel White House, which was a fair bit of distance away from Hotel Drona. So it was decided that the Baraat would reach a designated spot in vehicles before commencing the ceremonial procession on foot.

But then it wouldn't be a memorable marriage ceremony if everything went as planned!

Unsurprisingly, being the army man that he was, the groom reached the designated spot right on time, decked up in his Sherwani and wearing a regal turban. The band was there too, as well as the *ghodi* that was to carry the groom to the wedding location.

However, there was one minor hitch – none of the Baraatis were there!

Ajai was getting worried that he would be late for his own wedding, but more than him, it was the band master who was sweating. Apparently, his band was booked for yet another wedding in a different part of the city right after this one!

Thankfully, the Baraatis gradually started arriving once they realized that if they delayed things any further, the groom might decide to reach the wedding venue all on his own, and once they had mustered decent numbers, the Baraat procession commenced!

Of course, with Ajai's Battalion located in Dehradun, all officers and ladies were there in full strength, led by the Commanding Officer himself – Colonel MS Samuel!

Dancing to their hearts' content, the Baraat procession slowly inched their way to Hotel White House, much to the worry of the band master. However, with the distance not being much, they ultimately arrived and the Band quickly rushed to their next wedding.

Once there, Ajai was escorted to the stage by two of Shalini's uncles.

As is true for all Indian weddings, this one too was quite a melee and the most definitive memory Ajai has of this part of the night is that of his turban somehow getting pulled and getting loose.

Rest of his evening would be spent worrying about his turban .. until an even graver problem would divert Ajai's focus, in just about a couple of hours!

Anyhow, moving on with the initial ceremonies of the *Welcome Aarti, Varmala* etc, Ajai realized that there was still a lot of time before the *pheras* since the auspicious muhurat was at 1am at night.

After some quick thinking, the groom decided that in the interim he will go back to his hotel and re-tie his turban that had come loose.

Accordingly, he commandeered Captain Sanath Gopinath of his Battalion, who happened to have a Willys Jeep. Together, the two went back to the hotel and straight to Ajai's *Tau Ji* Thakur Mahavir Singh who was still there and was the only one who could tie his turban.

One of Ajai's cousins also requested to came along with them. Not thinking much of it, Ajai and Sanath took him also along.

So leaving Sanath and his cousin outside the hotel, Ajai was soon in the room of his Uncle, and requested him to re-tie his turban. But the said Uncle was somehow not in a very happy mood. The reason for that soon became clear when he told Ajai that he had been looking for a glass of milk but wasn't able to find any hotel staff.

Unsurprisingly, a few moments later, Ajai, all decked up for the day of his marriage, was searching the hotel for someone to bring his Uncle a glass of milk!

The much awaited glass of milk was finally delivered to his Uncle and somewhat pacified, he re-tied Ajai's turban.

Finally at peace with respect to the turban *situation*, Ajai happily came out of the hotel, but only to be presented with a situation that was far worse than a loose turban – Captain Sanath was nowhere to be found!

It was already 40 minutes past midnight and with the *feraas* just 20 minutes away *Ajai* was at his wits' end, trying to think of a way out, standing outside the hotel about 3km away from the marriage venue!

At that moment, totally out of options, all he could do was to curse and repeatedly tell himself, '*इतनी मुश्किल से लड़की, मिली अब फ़ेरे भी नहीं होंगे*' (I got a girl with such difficulty, and now even the pheras might not happen).

It was almost as if some invisible power was testing the young couple and trying to bring in as many hurdles in the process of their Union as it could.

Somehow, as if by magic, a very rare sight presented itself to Ajai – He saw an autorickshaw driving down the road. It was something that was very rare such late at night in Dehradun of those days.

But it wouldn't be wrong to say that the autorickshaw driver saw something even rarer – that of a Bridegroom, decked up in a Sherwani, turban, kalgi and even wearing a varmaala, standing alone at the roadside and hailing him, that too at such a late hour.

It was a miracle indeed that the autorickshaw driver decided to stop, instead of speeding away thinking he had seen a ghost!

The bewildered face of the autorickshaw driver said it all!

It was as if he decided to stop just to see who this character was, standing like a bridegroom by the roadside in the middle of the night!

But regardless, he agreed to drive Ajai to his marriage venue. It was a short ride, but now Ajai had another problem at hand – he didn't have any money to pay the driver!

So here was the scene – the bridegroom reached his wedding venue all alone, in an autorickshaw and was desperately searching for someone, for anyone in fact, who could pay his autorickshaw fare!

As if he was waiting for this very cue, Captain Sanath suddenly appeared at the scene, in a far darker mood than what Ajai's Uncle had been in back at the hotel!

Fare paid, Ajai asked Sanath as to where had he vanished at the last moment.

Sanath just let lose at Ajai's query .. Apparently, he himself had had nothing short of a nightmare time during the short trip to sort out Ajai's loose turban!

Apparently, when Ajai went in the hotel to meet his Uncle, his cousin requested Sanath to drop him at another nearby hotel where he was staying, saying that he had some work. Since that hotel was pretty close by, Sanath thought nothing of it and drove that guy over to his hotel.

And then the guy just vanished!

After waiting for 15 minutes, Sanath realized that Ajai's turban would have been re-tied and he must be waiting for a ride to go back to his own wedding. Getting impatient and not knowing which room that guy was staying in, Sanath went inside the hotel and started knocking on all doors.

On his fifth or sixth knock, he found Ajai's cousin playing cards with six more young guys.

Sanath swore that if he hadn't been Ajai's brother, he might just have killed him then and there!

But somehow composing himself, Sanath asked whether he intends coming back with him, to which the young cousin dismissed Sanath as if he were a cab driver, saying that he wouldn't be coming and that Sanath may carry on!

It was only because Sanath was worried about Ajai getting delayed, that the young guy was spared major bodily harm that night!

Sanath rushed back to Ajai's location, just in time to see him getting into the autorickshaw. Thinking that stopping him midway would only delay him more, Sanath simply followed the autorickshaw to the marriage venue.

It seemed that this much was enough *excitement* for the wedding function, and rest of the ceremonies happened without a hitch and Ajai and Shalini were finally united in the unbreakable bonds of matrimony.

But then, it seemed that some power still wasn't done trying to put a spoke in the wheels of destiny.

Just before the time of *vidaai* came the sad news of the passing away of one of the uncles of Ajai, back home in Roorkee. He had attended the wedding and then rushed back home in order to milk the buffalos. It was while milking them that he suffered a heart-attack and passed away.

This news naturally created a commotion in the midst of the wedding festivities.

Ajai's family were reeling from the sudden demise of a loved one, while Shalini's family were worried about it tainting their daughter's married life even before it had commenced.

But thankfully, saner heads prevailed.

After a quick chat with his father, Ajai and he decided that Shalini would not come home to Roorkee during a period of mourning. Instead, with his Battalion located right there in Dehradun, Ajai would take his bride there after the *vidaai* and thereafter, spend a few days at Shalini's place before coming home to Roorkee.

Thus, the groom's family left for home without their newly married son and daughter-in-law. Meanwhile, Ajai requested his Father-in-Law to have someone drive him and Shalini down to his Battalion location in Ghanghora.

All things considered, it seemed a fair decision, given the circumstances. However, one key party in this hastily planned scheme of things had absolutely no idea.

It was the groom's Battalion, to which he was now headed!

The first inkling anyone in the Battalion got about Ajai and Shalini coming to them for a day was when Ajai took a detour and went to the Adjutant's office in a neighbouring Battalion in Birpur. From there, he called up his own Battalion from an Army line in order to apprise them of his situation and request for a guest room for himself and his bride.

He was wearing a fine three-piece suit while everyone else around him in that Battalion were in uniform, mind you! Similarly, Shalini too waited in the fully decked up car outside the Adjutant's office, in her bridal suit, while her husband made some frantic calls!

Ajai managed to reach Major TP Singh of his Battalion on phone, and quickly apprised him of the situation.

First words out of Major TP's mouth upon hearing the story were – *'Don't come to the Battalion.'*

Now Major TP Singh was a burly Sikh gentleman whom the rank and file feared. He was the Battalion Quartermaster at that time and had in fact, attended Ajai and Shalini's wedding the previous night.

Unsurprisingly, inside Ajai's head a whirlwind of thoughts and emotions had commenced the moment he heard those words out of Major TP Singh's mouth.

But that didn't matter to Major TP Singh as he carried on speaking further.

'Wait in the Adjutant's office. I will call you back.'

He called back after 10 minutes.

Those were the longest 10 minutes of Ajai's life. Here he was, dressed up in a fine three-piece suit, sitting in the office of the Adjutant of the neighbouring Battalion while his bride waited outside in a car, beautifully decked up in her own bridal attire.

On this call, the first words out of Major TP's mouth once again left Ajai scratching his head.

'Don't go to the Officers' Mess', were the instructions.

But this time Ajai decided to wait and let him speak a bit more.

'Come straight to my house', was the next order for Ajai and Shalini.

And thus came Shalini to Ajai's *other* family, i.e. The Regimental Abode, welcomed into the home of one of the most *dynamic* senior officers of the Battalion who had worked quite a bit of magic within the 30 minutes that it took from Ajai's first phone call to the couple reaching there.

Within those 30 minutes, Maj TP Singh had managed to deck up his house to the extent he could, in order to welcome the youngest bride of the Battalion. Not only that, he had managed to get all officers and ladies of the Battalion as well to his residence.

This was no simple feat, in the days when let alone smartphones, even landline telephones were a rarity!

Thus began Shalini's Regimental Life, with a mighty fine reception at the house of Major TP Singh. The Battalion observed an undeclared holiday that day, since all officers and their better halves were busy welcoming the young couple!

Not only had Major TP Singh managed to gather the entire flock of the Battalion officers and ladies, he had also arranged so that all ceremonies of a new bride entering her *sasural* were carried out as per prescribed rituals. The *Lakshmi* that Shalini was, her first steps into the house of Major TP Singh were after stepping into a *paraat* of colour, so that her first steps into the house stay imprinted on the floor.

Soon, Shalini's parents and some other family members too joined in. Then there was the traditional game of the newlyweds searching for a ring hidden in a *paraat* filled with coloured water and flower petals. Shalini defeated Ajai in that game quite resoundly, over and over again!

The atmosphere at Major TP Singh's place was lively and a good, sumptuous lunch soon materialized from the kitchen of the house, along with liberal supplies of chilled beer as well.

Thus began Shalini and Ajai's married life – On a high despite all the challenges that came their way in the run up to their nuptials.

After resting for a while during the afternoon, Major TP suggested that Ajai take Shalini out for a drive in the evening. Barely knowing how to drive, he took out the fully decorated blue coloured Maruti 800 and took Shalini to open grounds near Ghanghora where they spent an hour sitting by the Tons River which flowed in a soothing gurgle, before returning home to Maj TP Singh's place.

Almost three and a half decades since that day, as this book is being compiled, Lieutenant General Ajai Kumar Singh is in the process of constructing his retirement house next to the Tons River almost right across the same spot. This is also in sync with Shalini's dream of having a post retirement home by a stream of flowing water, close to a forest and with a good view of the Mussoorie Hills. Such is destiny, leading the couple, of whom only one is in physical form, to complete their journey of togetherness almost at the very place where they commenced it.

The young couple spent that day with their lovely hosts, Major and Mrs TP Singh who left no stone unturned to ensure that they don't miss their family. Next day Ajai and Shalini went back to her parents' place where they would stay for about ten days before heading home to Roorkee.

This is the story of how Shalini and Ajai got hitched into the sacred bonds of holy matrimony, despite the many challenges that came by in the process.

This is the story of how they commenced their journey of matrimonial bliss that lasted more than three decades, bringing with it further challenges, especially during her last days in this mortal realm. But the overriding memories that define their married life are of happiness and satisfaction of a well-lived togetherness, exploring the world together, bringing up two wonderful children, and meeting life head-on.

04

SETTING UP HOME

The newlywed couple wasn't able to go for their honeymoon due to the unfortunate demise in the family right after their marriage ceremony was over. Instead, after spending a day at the residence of Maj TP Singh, followed about ten more days at Shalini's parents' place, and with his leave rapidly finishing, Ajai thought it fine to go to Delhi to his elder sister's home in Janakpuri.

Accordingly, Ajai and Shalini landed up in Delhi and spent another blissful ten days there. In this duration, free from any liabilities / responsibilities, they made it a point to explore as much of the city as they could, visiting as many monuments, gardens and other places as possible.

Amongst them all, a visit to the famous Lotus Temple was perhaps the most cherished one wherein they both sat together in silence inside the magnificent structure. This might have been the first time that Shalini and Ajai indulged in silent communication with each other.

This was also the first time they meditated together, even if in the midst of hundreds of fellow visitors to the shrine.

Pretty soon, Ajai's leave was over and the blissful young couple reached back to Dehradun to be in their Battalion.

Shalini was finally home .. to her military family, that is!

Life seemed all set hereinafter, but then, with the twists and turns that life had thrown their way, it wasn't surprising that there was one more googly that awaited Shalini and Ajai as soon as they reached back to their Battalion in Dehradun.

They realized that they weren't authorized a government married accommodation because they were too young, atleast in the eyes of the archaic military rule that said that officers younger than 25 years of age cannot be allotted married accommodation!

But instead of fighting with the rules, they made the best with what they got in lieu – a small guest room right behind the Battalion Officers' Mess. The guest room complex comprised 4-5 such guest rooms which the Battalion maintained for the periodic visitors that came their way.

Being in the Officers' Mess, there were Squash and Tennis courts right next to it, but most importantly, it was in a beautiful part of the Ghanghora Cantonment of Dehradun and was a good area for long, leisurely walks. All in all, it was an ideal setup for a young couple that were just about commencing their marital life.

Their first 'home', if it can be called thusly, was a mere two room set. Even though it suited the young couple, but there was one fundamental issue which Shalini was faced with – there was no kitchen for the young bride to cook for her husband and herself!

But, undeterred, Shalini took a major decision to ameliorate this situation.

She decided to 'capture' part of the *Verandah* outside her guest room and convert it into her kitchen!

Once Shalini made up her mind to establish a kitchen in the *Verandah,* she was able to quickly get it covered and partitioned off from the rest of the guest room complex while Ajai got hold of a long table to place in their newly expanded lodgings!

Thus started the household of Shalini and Ajai!

But if you think that once her kitchen was established, Shalini started churning out mouth-watering dishes one after the other, you would be absolutely wrong!

Barely out of teens, the young lady had absolutely no idea about how to cook!

But then, as was typical of her, instead of using the lack of a kitchen as an excuse, she created a kitchen out of nothing and used that as an excuse to commence on a journey towards creating culinary magic.

Of course, being in her own hometown and close to her mother, helped a lot!

Shalini had been an absolute novice at cooking when she got married. But this fact never deterred her. Instead, it spurred her on to learning and mastering the art of cooking. Unsurprisingly, with her mother just a call away to guide and teach her, Shalini didn't take long to become an excellent cook.

And Ajai too was a willing *guinea pig* as she went about experimenting and learning!

Pretty soon, the young couple were ready to host their first guests. And they chose their first guests well – two coursemates of Ajai who too were posted in Dehradun!

A word about coursemates in the Indian Army. They are a bunch of officers who have trained together in various Training Academies of the Indian Army right from their first day in uniform. The bonds that bind coursemates in the Indian Army are unique and unbreakable indeed. Growing up in service, they remain each other's biggest pillars of strength, sounding-boards and even critics. In a hierarchical organization that the military is, coursemates are nothing short of a blessing, for they are the ones with whom no formalities or even protocols apply!

So Ajai invited two coursemates to a meal at Shalini's and his humble lodgings. They were Capt Rajiv Ahuja of 2 Guards Battalion and Capt BS Raju of 11 Jat Battalion. Rajiv left Army after serving for eight years and rose to international acclaim in the field of IT. Raju superannuated as General Officer Commanding-in-Chief of South Western Command after an illustrious career spanning over four decades.

Shalini and Ajai were thrilled at this wonderful occasion of playing hosts in their own home for the very first time, so what if their 'home' at that point in time was a mere two room set.

Shalini had done it up to the best of her ability, making it into a makeshift 'drawing room' with a sofa and a centre table on one side and a hard bed 'Takht' on the other side.

It was an amazing evening, with the young people spending a blissful time together. The two coursemates of Ajai that had come over that evening, had a *lot* of stories to tell Shalini, at times even at the cost of putting her husband in a tight spot. But then, such are coursemates!

And having met her for the first time, they too were in the process of initiating Shalini into their own fraternity of coursemates in their own way!

All in all, it was a joyous evening, filled with light banter and stories and anecdotes that kept Shalini enthralled. Of course, as Lieutenant General Ajai Kumar Singh recounts, Shalini had learnt cooking by then and the food was also 'reasonably' good!

So here was another *first* for the young couple – after having established their first home, they had also hosted their first guests. Pretty soon, Shalini would be known as one of the most gracious hostesses, willing and able to host any kind of and any number of guests even without any prior notice.

Thus passed the blissful days in Dehradun as Shalini rapidly adapted to home and regimental life. Despite being the youngest lady in the Battalion, Shalini proved herself to be a keen observer of military etiquette and was always correct in her approach as part of the military fraternity.

While her days were busy looking after her household, evenings were mostly full of social engagements due to the Battalion having found a good peace station after a long stint in field. Further, the newlyweds were invited by all officers of the Battalion one by one in order to personally welcome Shalini into the family and get to know her. Thus, she too was soon quite well-acquainted will all officers and ladies of the Battalion, making bonds that were to last throughout her lifetime.

One of the best things about Dehradun for the young couple was its proximity to Mussoorie, and to top it up, Shalini's parents owned a house in Mussoorie!

This, combined with a fact that Ajai was the proud owner of a Maruti 800 car in that era, made for an ideal situation wherein there were a *lot* of forays to Mussoorie.

In fact, any talk of that car – Bayer Blue Coloured Maruti UMS 5654 – still evokes a lot of nostalgic memories of the times Shalini and Ajai started their own journey of togetherness in this lifetime, through many different places geographically as well as emotionally.

Shalini herself had spent the best part of her childhood in Mussoorie and studied there as well. Thus she had many friends and other acquaintances there and also knew the small hill-town in great detail. Thus, trips to Mussoorie were eagerly awaited not just by Shalini and Ajai, but also by any others from the Battalion who could tag along with them!

In this duration, Ajai would occasionally have to go away from Dehradun for short durations on various official events / commitments that came his way. Such absences would vary from a couple of days to a couple of weeks. In this duration, Shalini would move out to her parents' place where she would work actively to further hone her culinary skills and look forward to welcoming Ajai with new dishes when he returned. Her transition to an accomplished cook within a few months was indeed surprising to those who had known her as a total novice in the kitchen before marriage.

All in all, destiny could not have given a better start to a life of matrimonial bliss for Shalini and Ajai who were starting out on their own, yet were still close enough to their family elders to be able to lean on them whenever required.

Time seemed to fly by, and one fine day Ajai's Battalion was presented with a unique requirement – that of sending an officer to their Brigade Headquarters as the Camp Commandant.

The job of a Camp Commandant was relatively less taxing and Ajai's Commanding Officer, in his wisdom, decided that this would be a good opportunity for Ajai to spend some more time with his wife. And thus changed the office route of Captain Ajai, wherein instead of his own Battalion Headquarters, he would now head out to the Brigade Headquarters.

As his CO had correctly assumed, this new job brought about a total change of environment for the young couple. Ajai's tasking in the Brigade Headquarters was predictable and his routine rarely varied. At the same time, it added immensely to his professional growth by acquainting him with the intricacies and various facets of commanding the brigade camp as also the staff-work in a higher headquarter.

But as mentioned earlier, the best part of this new assignment was the set routine. With life a lot more predictable now, Shalini and Ajai made it a high-priority mission to visit Mussoorie as also Ajai's hometown of Roorkee as many times as they could, and meet all relatives in and around their home in Dehradun.

It did immense good to the newlyweds, especially Shalini, who got to know and get well-acquainted with Ajai's relatives and establish herself as the *BahuRani* of the house.

It didn't take long for Shalini to win the hearts of her husband's family.

She did this mostly by being courteous and correct – basically just by being herself!

In any case, it was very difficult for anyone to NOT like Shalini once they got to know her!

However, in this case, Shalini was entering a totally new world when compared to the one she had grown up in – from being a 'City-Girl' to being the *BahuRani* of a rural household.

Her first visit to Ajai's village Thaska, near Roorkee, was full of trepidation, but for Ajai! As far as Shalini was concerned, she was eagerly looking forward to it!

Being a newly married *Bahu Rani* in a traditional Rajput household in the mid 1980s, Shalini had to cover her head in a *ghoonghat.* This was a first for her, but she took to it without any fuss and quickly got used to it. She also got used to the village ladies coming over to see her, which they did by lifting her ghoonghat and taking a critical look at her, including the clothes and ornaments that she wore.

It was a totally new experience for her, but she took to it with her characteristic cheerful nature and pretty soon, this young city-girl was totally at home in the small village that her army officer husband had grown up in.

Soon it was time for Shalini to meet Ajai's maternal grandparents who lived in village Salawa in Meerut district, near the town of Sardhana. Ajai had spent quite a major part of his childhood with them and was always given a royal treatment at their house because his mother was an only child! Naturally, he was keen to show them his life-partner and seek their blessings for her too.

Unsurprisingly, his Nana-Nani were absolutely delighted to meet Shalini who was once again expected to be in a *ghoonghat.* To be fair, Shalini wasn't physically very comfortable in a *ghoonghat* and possibly didn't even like it. But not once did she complain since it was tradition and she understood that this was expected of her as a young bride in the family.

To her credit, Shalini abided by all the customs at Ajai's parental villages. And she did it uncomplainingly, winning over everyone in the process. It was a key facet of Shalini's personality – she was quite willing to adhere to conventions in order to become part of a family, be it Ajai's military family or his parental family, even if she wasn't entirely comfortable doing so.

This was yet another defining trait of Shalini. For the sake of larger good as part of a family, she was willing to adhere expected social conventions even if she possibly didn't always agree with them.

In addition to being the youngest bride of the family and a natural object of curiosity for village based family members of Ajai, Shalini's big eyes too were a frequent topic of talks. Of course, she being fluent in English was yet another big thing in the villages where Ajai's family hailed from!

Thus passed the Dehradun tenure, slowly yet steadily. Those were exciting times for Shalini as it was where she and Ajai started their married life together. It was an excellent tenure and Dehradun was a beautiful place as well as her hometown. So, while she had her own space to grow and test her wings, yet maternal assistance too was just a call away whenever needed. This was how she settled down in her new role as a wife, a *bahu* as also a Regimental Lady in Ajai's Battalion.

Those months in Dehradun and with Ajai's family were nothing short of a *Foundation Course* for Shalini. Thanks to her innocence as well as innate intelligence, Shalini was quick to win hearts all around in her new family and adjusted remarkably well to all the varied roles with due diligence and more importantly, dexterity.

What also helped was the fact that she never wore a mask, and on the contrary, was always very spontaneous. Any kind of emotion showed in her face almost instantly. If she didn't like something or someone, it was absolutely apparent to anyone who cared to see!

As is natural for all married couples, Ajai too wasn't immune to a rebuke or a silent treatment from his bride once in a while.

One particular incident stands out in this context. It so happened that while on a visit to Roorkee, Ajai apparently overreacted to something that Shalini said or did, and she didn't quite like it. Yet, being in her in-laws' place, she didn't say anything while over there since it was a private matter between the two of them.

But on the way back to Dehradun, she was giving the silent treated to Ajai. He too was not very happy. There was absolutely no verbal communication between the two, more so since Shalini had turned the volume of the car stereo really high.

Ajai, lowered the volume to more tolerable levels, but Shalini wasn't one to back off and turned it back up.

This happened thrice before Ajai got fed up, pulled out the cassette out of the car stereo and threw it out of the car.

Not one moment later, Shalini fished out the cover of the cassette and threw *that* out of the car.

There was a momentary pause in their *fight* as both took in the sequence of events that had just transpired.

And then they both burst out laughing!

The fight was forgotten and the rest of the journey was much more enjoyable, though without any audio cassette to play in the stereo!

This was yet another amazing quality about Shalini – while she was quick to show her emotions, but at the same time she didn't let them rule over her. On the contrary, she was just as quick to reconcile and get on with life.

Pretty soon, sometime in April or May of 1988, came the happy realization that Shalini was pregnant. The due date was to be in Dec / Jan. This news of impending parenthood brought the young couple great joy.

In Oct 1988, Ajai's battalion got mobilized for a major exercise in Punjab near the town of Ferozepur. He was to be away for a few weeks. Resultantly, Shalini moved back to her parents' house. Her parents too were thrilled to have her back, as were the two little devils that her brothers were. Happy as she was, she still waited longingly for her husband to be back.

Meanwhile, Ajai too looked for the first available opportunity to get back to Dehradun. However, professional commitments kept him busy till the time the exercise got over as scheduled after about a month.

Not willing to wait any longer, especially for a slow-moving convoy that would take three days to reach Dehradun, Ajai took permission from his Commanding Officer and took off for Dehradun in a vintage Nissan 1-tonner carrying essential equipment and stores, with just the driver for company!

They drove non-stop throughout the day and the entire night, taking turns to sleep and drive, reaching Dehradun early the next morning.

As soon as he was in Dehradun, Ajai made a beeline for his in-laws' home where Shalini was, unaware of the nearly 20 hour non-stop drive by him in order to reach her as soon as he could.

A few weeks later Ajai got the message that he was detailed for the Mortar Course in the small town of Mhow, near Indore. He was forced to move at a very short notice, practically rushing to join the course without any preparation whatsoever.

He reached Mhow by train, but found no reception arrangements there as are normally done for officers arriving there for courses. So he found his way to the Infantry School and presented himself to the powers that be, only to be told that if he was there for the currently ongoing Mortar Course then he was very late, and if not, then he was very early for the next course!

Apparently, Captain Ajai Kumar Singh was 10 days late in reporting for the course due to a clerical error in the detailment letter.

There was no way he could be permitted to join the course since he would not be able to catch up with fellow trainees this late. So, the procedure to formally send him back to the Battalion was initiated by the Infantry School.

Meanwhile, unknown to Ajai, back home in Dehradun, Shalini went into labour.

On that fateful day, while Ajai was in the local market in Mhow to purchase a pair of shoes, someone just walked up to him and asked whether he was Capt AK Singh. When Ajai replied in affirmative, that officer extended his hand and congratulated Ajai for having become a father!

This was how Ajai came to know about the arrival of his son Abhinav, on 21 Jan 1989.

Ajai's fatherhood was soon the talk of the entire Mortar Wing of the Infantry School, and as the administrative personnel hastened his departure formalities, the rest of his coursemates were relentless in their demand for a befitting celebration to mark the occasion.

Thus, the first party for Abhinav was hosted by his dad in the Student Officers' Mess in the Infantry School in Mhow! Knowing the appetite of young officers for solid as well as liquid goodies, especially when they were gathered together for a course from varied parts of the Indian geography, the bill was unsurprisingly, quite hefty!

But then, it was worth each and every penny, given the arrival of Abhinav in the lives of Shalini and Ajai.

Ajai rushed back home. It was a few days since the birth of Abhinav, but Shalini was still in Coronation Hospital, having undergone a caesarian section during childbirth. This wasn't entirely unexpected, because a couple of months earlier, during a routine ultrasound, it was discovered that the child was in a breach position and the doctor wouldn't permit a normal delivery due to the inherent risks involved.

Shalini wasn't entirely happy at Ajai having been away during this time, but being an army wife, she knew it was something that was not under his control.

Anyhow, after getting discharged from the hospital, Shalini went on to spend some more time at her parents' place due to the regular checks that she required to go for, as she recovered from her surgery. Almost every time, it would be her parents who would end up taking her to the hospital since Ajai was tied up in work and was quite busy in office.

Interestingly, Shalini herself and her siblings too had been born in the same hospital, and her parents had made similar trips all those years ago! Unsurprisingly, they knew quite a few people in that hospital who still remembered them.

Thus passed Shalini's wonderful days in Dehradun as a newly wedded young wife, and later, a mother. Before long, as time passed by, Ajai received his posting orders to go to the Commando School, Belgaum as a Commando Instructor.

Pretty soon, the young couple was busy winding up their little nest in Dehradun. But far from being sad about leaving, they were looking forward to yet another wonderful opportunity to move out and commence a brand new life in a much different setup that the Commando Wing of The Infantry School, Belgaum promised to be.

While they sent their household stuff and the much loved blue Maruti 800 car to Belgaum in a truck, they themselves took a direct flight from Delhi to Goa, where they planned a brief layover before heading out to Belgaum.

Shalini had an uncle who lived in Goa, working for the Inland Transport Authority that looked after ferry operations in the state. He was there at the airport to receive his niece and her husband.

After a quick lunch at his home, the young parents decided to head straight to Belgaum in a bus. It was a four hour long journey, but with a small baby it was still three hours too much, especially since the bus was already full and there was no place to sit!

Thankfully, the people on board the bus that day were really nice and helpful and one gentleman gave his seat to them and they could finally sit and put Abhinav down. Unconcerned all these happenings around him, little Abhinav continued to sleep all the way to Belgaum.

As the bus entered Belgaum, the first signs of settlement were small thatched huts by the roadside. Shalini wasn't too impressed at the prospect of setting up house in a sleepy village that Belgaum looked to be, especially with a tiny kid to take care of.

What added to her sense of disappointment was the picture that Ajai had painted to her of Belgaum being a very good place. For a young lady born and brought up in Dehradun / Mussoorie, it was a big letdown, atleast at the first glance.

But it wasn't long before Ajai was proven right and Shalini developed a special love for the place where she set up her first house away from the shadows of her and Ajai's parents. This was where she finally got to test her wings as a home-maker for the first time.

Their initial lodgings were in a small, two-room guest room which didn't have a kitchen. This time, however, Shalini didn't have the luxury of *capturing* the verandah for a makeshift kitchen. So, their meals would come from the Officers' Mess.

A word about the Commando Wing. It was a training establishment where young officers and NCOs would come for their mandatory Commando Course. Being a training establishment with a single, highly structured course, life as an instructor too was equally structured. Moreover, it being a physically intensive course for as instructors, adequate rest time was built into their schedule, thus giving them more time to spend with their better halves.

Thus, it turned out to one of the most cherished tenures for Shalini and Ajai.

What added to the fun in those days was the fact that along with Ajai, 12 more of his coursemates were posted there at the same time, including quite a few who too were recently married. Thus Shalini got to make new friends and acquaintances.

It was her first exposure to setting out on her own, without any encumbrances of Regimental life in the Battalion or being in the proximity of her mother. Here, she could learn from the experiences of other ladies her own age and in a highly relaxed environment.

Pretty soon, they got allotted a house.

Technically speaking, it was their first proper house after marriage – a beautiful ground floor flat named Jessie Mansion in a civilian area about four kilometers from the Commando Wing. It was part of a triple storied building that had been requisitioned by the Army for the officers posted in Belgaum.

Shalini soon got busy converting that house into their first *home*. This was an entirely new endeavour for this young girl, and that too with a little baby to take care of. To top it up, the salary of an Indian Army Captain in the late 80s wasn't too great, yet Shalini managed to create a beautiful nest for her little family, one which pretty soon became the hub of social activities of their group.

Come to think of it, that house was nothing short of a phenomenal achievement for a young lady with a small child to take care of, especially given the limited resources available to her at that time.

It was a well-set and functional household that Shalini created, one that was much appreciated by anyone who dropped by. And pretty soon, almost every other day someone or the other would drop by, whether invited or otherwise!

Social life for the officers and ladies of the Commando School was highly active those days. Almost every evening, they would be either visiting someone, or hosting guests at home.

This active social circle helped a lot because, given the nature of the job, Ajai and other officers would be out of home a *lot*, and that too at odd hours. So Shalini also soon learnt to be on her own for a few days at a time, every so often. Wives of Ajai's colleagues who were her new friends were a great backup on such occasions, as all ladies were in the same boat, with husbands away for upto a few days at a stretch.

Thus, even though Ajai was busy training young officers to be commandos, Shalini too was herself undergoing a training of sorts at staying and managing things on her own!

And then life bowled a googly their way .. Ajai came down with Hepatitis A, and was admitted in the local Military Hospital for a long time. But not to be deterred, Shalini was right by his side, nursing him back to good health. Of course, she marshaled the help of her new friends and needless to say, her mother was also called over to Belgaum, especially to help take care of Abhinav.

This was also the beginning of a special bond between Abhinav and his maternal grandmother, who would end up taking care of him for quite a while in the years to come.

After a couple of weeks in hospital, Ajai was discharged, but with a sick leave of four weeks in order to help him recuperate. They flew down to Dehradun, and spent the sick leave equally between Roorkee and Dehradun, in care of family.

After four weeks, Captain Ajai reported back to the Commando Wing and was put as the Coordinating Officer (DS Coord) for running the many courses that carried on simultaneously and/or in quick succession. This was a desk job and physically much less demanding, and Ajai was entrusted with this both, due to his organizing abilities as well as to let him regain his health.

In the meanwhile, Shalini was once again on the family way. Yet she never once let her pregnancy become an excuse in discharging her responsibilities as a home-maker!

Almost everyone from the extended families of Ajai and Shalini made it a point to visit them while in Belgaum. And mind you, this was in *addition* to the steady stream of invited as well as impromptu visitors on practically a daily basis!

Through it all, Shalini was always the perfect daughter-in-law / hostess. In addition to hosting various members of family, she was also the one entrusted with actually planning their entire itineraries as well!

Of course, she was also looking after little Abhinav as also their little daughter Sanjana who was growing fast within her!

Before anyone knew, it was already their seventh month in Belgaum and Abhinav turned one year old on 21 Jan 1990.

Shalini, who was five months pregnant at that time, took it upon herself to plan for a grand celebration. The venue she chose was the Officers' Institute in Belgaum, the Meads Club.

They decided to invite the entire Commando Wing for the occasion, including the Commander of the Wing, Colonel Gonsalves as well as the Deputy Commander Lieutenant Colonel VK Singh, who later rose to become the Chief of Army Staff.

During the birthday party, Abhinav, who had just about started learning to walk, somehow reached the bar and managed to take a few sips from some unattended drinks before people noticed and pulled him away.

This adventure had an unanticipated impact on Abhinav – he started to walk confidently on his own!

So much so that he kept walking the entire night, refusing to sit down for even a moment. That night Shalini and Ajai didn't get to sleep much, thanks to their one year old toddler who continued to test his feet!

It was a beautiful time of togetherness for the young couple. Each and every moment together was cherished. Shalini too grew with the responsibilities of running and managing a household, soon becoming adept at managing the requirements of the house, finances, a young child, the never-ending stream of local visitors and relatives from near and far, and the nuances of life in a military cantonment.

Goa being close by, and with the availability of a car, trips to Goa were very frequent.

Ironically, Shalini was very scared of the water at that time. She would stay on the beach, looking after Abhinav, even as Ajai and other friends would enjoy in the waters. On the few occasions that Ajai could convince her to take a few steps in the water, she would run away shrieking, at the very first wave that came by. And on the rare occasion that she stayed on, the receding waters that would shift the sand under her feet, would scare her even more!

Thankfully, she grew out of those fears as time passed!

As mentioned earlier, it was a tenure of sheer bliss, though not without the occasional *interesting* incidents. One such incident happened one fine evening when Ajai, after having come back from office and having lunch and just sitting idly at home suddenly remembered in the evening that he had called some officers for dinner that very night.

Shalini was *NOT* amused!

Understandably, Ajai was too embarrassed to say anything as Shalini glowered at him.

But then, she quickly composed herself. There was, after all, guests to be hosted. So she quickly took charge of the situation instead of getting overwhelmed, and ordered Ajai to rush to the market on his Kinetic Honda scooter, since parking a car would consume valuable minutes!

Unsurprisingly, a fabulous dinner in her signature style was ready by the time the guests arrived!

Mind you, this, from someone who was a complete novice in the kitchen less than two years ago!

Lieutenant General Ajai Kumar Singh still fondly remembers that evening, calling it his own way of training her in quickly organizing a social get-together!

But jokes apart, this skill of quick thinking and even quicker execution came in very handy as Shalini and Ajai put more years behind them as a couple.

In the midst of all this, in April 1990 their daughter Sanjana too came into their lives, thus completing the happy family. Shalini had gone to her maternal house Dehradun for the delivery that happened in the Vaish Nursing Home.

As the two-year tenure came to a closure, Ajai received an interview call for a position in the Indian Embassy in Nepal.

The Indian Army employs a large number of Gorkha soldiers hailing from Nepal. While in service as well as after retirement, the Indian Army looks after the welfare of these troops and consequently, the Indian Embassy in Nepal has a fairly large military component.

Ajai had been interviewed for the post of the Assistant Military Attache (Pensions) in Nepal. The interview had gone well and Ajai was hopeful of being shortlisted for this diplomatic assignment.

However, one fine day not very long after the interview, he received his posting order to a 2/11 Gorkha Rifles, which was a sister battalion from the same regiment.

At that point in time, in 1991, the battalion was deployed in really intense counter-insurgency operations in the Kashmir Valley in the notorious areas of Uri, Baramula and thereabouts. So there was no way that Shalini and the kids could accompany him there.

Thus came their first separation as a military family.

While Ajai moved on to Baramula, Shalini shifted to Roorkee. Their household stuff too was packed and stored in the large house that the family owned there.

Despite the occasional trips to her own parents in Dehradun, Shalini spent bulk of those days in Roorkee at her in-laws' home. This was the first time that she was actually staying with them, not counting the short trips immediately after marriage.

But once again, this city girl, in her unique way, soon became one of them, through nothing else but just being the efficient young lady that she always had been.

Ajai's was a joint family and a fairly large one at that. This was Shalini's first time in such a large household, but soon she found her own place in the family and started to play a key role in the household affairs, despite her young age.

Shalini's 86 year old Mother-in-Law still remembers those days from more than three decades ago. She remembers her as being really quick in finishing her assigned work and then moving on to the kitchen to help her sister-in-law prepare meal after meal for the large family!

Meanwhile, the exchange of letters between Shalini and Ajai had recommenced with renewed vigour, with both of them writing one letter every single day to each other!

At Ajai's end, connectivity was really bad due to the lack of infrastructure as well as the disturbed situation in that part of the Kashmir Valley at that time. Add to this the fact that his battalion was part of a formation that would move very often, there were times when no mail would arrive for days together and then suddenly, Ajai would get 8-9 letters from Shalini in one go!

However, through all this, Shalini continuously prayed for her husband's safety since news coming out of Kashmir those days was almost invariably always negative.

This phase of separation continued for almost a year before 2/11 Gorkha Rifles got re-deployed in a peace profile at a place called Miran Saheb near Jammu.

This was yet another opportunity to set up another home together, and Ajai coordinated things in a manner that Shalini would reach the location just before the Battalion too arrived. Ajai's younger brother Sanjay was entrusted with the task of accompanying Shalini during the journey to Miran Saheb.

The Battalion reached Miran Saheb at night and after the routine fall-in etc, it was nearly 10:30pm before Ajai could reach home.

Yes, they had a home pre-allotted at Miran Saheb!

What happens in the Indian Army is that any Battalion coming to a peace station is pre-allotted four or five houses from the *Station*

Pool, so that atleast the Commanding Officer and a few more officers can setup home straight away.

In this particular instance, one such house was pre-allotted to Captain Atulya Sokankey of 2/11 Gorkha Rifles, who happened to be a coursemate of Ajai's. Interestingly, Captain Atulya didn't intend to get his wife to that location for some time, so he gladly offered that house to Ajai instead.

In her usual style, Shalini got busy doing up the house and pretty soon, transformed it into yet another welcoming abode for family and friends.

It was a new location, new Battalion, and new people for Shalini as she went about creating a new life for her little family. But then, it was still the same Army as also the same Regiment, so despite the *newness* of the situation, she was soon thriving there as well.

What someone might have seen as challenge, Shalini saw as an opportunity instead .. an opportunity to make new acquaintances, new friends and a whole new family amongst folks from 2/11 Gorkha Rifles and other Battalions etc in Miran Saheb.

This is the beauty of life in the Indian Army. It takes you places, literally! You get to see small and big towns and cities that you may never had travelled to otherwise. But more than the physical mobility, it gives immense mental and emotional power, especially to the ladies, who have to work hard to create new nests and establish new roots, only to leave them behind every two or three years and restart the same process all over again in new surroundings and often, new circumstances as well. This part of military life played a very important part in Shalini's life as she matured into a quintessential Indian Army Wife, one with compassion, empathy, ability to see the larger picture, and most of all, a huge circle of friends spread out all over the country.

Shalini was very fond of eating non-veg food, and the town of Jammu being literally a stone's throw away from her new home, was the ideal place to pamper her palate!

Every other day, Shalini, Ajai and their two little ones would be in Jammu, patronizing one or the other from the hundreds of outlets known for mouth watering non-veg dishes.

In this duration, Shalini and other ladies of the Battalion were also taken to see the forward areas along the India-Pakistan border where their husbands showed them the bunkers etc from where they would be entrusted to fight in case of war. Shalini showed a keen interest in absorbing all this new information because it wasn't very often that one could get such an opportunity.

This way Shalini also got to know what is a typical operational deployment and routine in forward areas.

After a few weeks in Miran Saheb, Shalini was ready to host a housewarming party for the officers and ladies of 2/11 Gorkha Rifles, and invites were duly sent out.

Interestingly, on the day of the housewarming, Ajai received orders posting him back to his parent battalion, 7/11 Gorkha Rifles.

It was time to uproot a newly built nest and build a new one, this time in the quaint little town of Tibri, near Gurdaspur in Punjab where the Battalion was then located.

Unperturbed, and after hosting a great housewarming, Shalini got busy packing up the boxes that she had opened hardly a few weeks back!

On the appointed day, the young family bid an emotional farewell to their current family at Miran Saheb and drove *homewards* to Ajai's parent battalion, thus ending yet another chapter in Shalini's life and at the same time, heralding a new, equally interesting one.

05

GROWING ROOTS

As they drove down from Miran saheh towards Tibri, Shalini and Ajai were leaving behind a tenure and place that had given them many beautiful memories and made them that much more mature, both individually as well as a couple.

For Ajai, it was his first experience of intense counter insurgency / counter terrorism operations in the Kashmir Valley and taught him many valuable lessons in all aspects related to soldiering in such a challenging environment.

These would stand him in good stead over the next couple of decades as he came back to the Kashmir Valley again, first while commanding his battalion and later as the General Officer Commanding of a formation deployed in the thick of operations in the hinterland.

On the other hand, Shalini too learnt how life is for a typical army wife when her husband is not only physically far away, but that too in a place that *demands* that he put his safety on the line for sake of duty.

This was their first separation as a military couple post marriage. To be fair, initial part of their courtship period too had seen similar circumstances, but now things were much different. Not only had they been married for nearly five years, but also were parents to two young and very energetic kids!

But life went on, and as is true of any army wife, Shalini too got busy with the business of bringing up Abhinav and Sanjana, while establishing herself as an ideal *bahu* in her husband's family in Roorkee.

Looking back, those days spent living in a joint family in a rural setup were greatly instrumental in Shalini cementing the nascent bonds with her husband's family and vice versa. They also were live and practical lessons in living in harmony, overcoming differences and continuing to function as part of a large family where everyone had their own place and responsibilities.

Unsurprisingly, Shalini soon endeared herself to the entire family. She was always very quick and very methodical in completing her share of household chores. Despite her young age, she held her counsel instead of getting into unnecessary arguments with anybody. But at the same time, she was very righteous and was known for making her opinions known without any hesitation.

In fact, amongst the many beautiful qualities that defined Shalini was also the one about she never being a diplomat! She just couldn't hide her feelings. She was such a pure soul that if she had anything good to tell, she would definitely say it out, while on the other hand, in case she wasn't happy with something she would hold it back but it would still be very apparent on her face and in her demeanour!

As they say, life has a way of ensuring that valuable lessons are learnt at appropriate times, for guiding you whenever need arises subsequently. The lessons that Shalini and Ajai learnt in those days came in handy as they both grew in age as well as stature over the months and the years that followed.

They reached their Battalion in Tibri sometime in late afternoon and went straight to the Officers' Mess where a bachelor officers' accommodation was earmarked for them till such time Ajai got allotted a suitable married accommodation.

Shalini once again got busy, turning that temporary two-room set into her own nest. Meanwhile, Ajai too got on with the nitty-gritties of the typical battalion routine in a peace station. He knew all officers except for a few who had gotten commissioned while Ajai was away to Belgaum and later, to 2/11 Gorkha Rifles.

Beside those youngsters (as they are referred to in the Army), the then Commanding Officer of the Unit, Col Madan Gopal too was someone whom Ajai didn't know very well. Col Madan Gopal had come over from 5/11 Gorkha Rifles to command 7/11. Ajai had met him very briefly about eight years ago when he had gone to the Regimental Centre as a newly commissioned officer for two weeks of orientation. (Then) Major Madan Gopal was also posted there at that time.

Anyhow, Shalini and Ajai soon became part of the Battalion life as if they had never left in the first place! This was also the time for Shalini to re-acquaint herself with Unit life, now as a well-established Unit Lady, instead of the young bride that she was when she first came to the Unit in Dehradun.

She was a quick learner indeed and pretty soon got well-acquainted with other officers' wives who were there in Tibri. Old bonds were reaffirmed while new bonds were created.

At the same time, she also reached out to, and got to know the wives of the men of the battalion. It was typically expected that all officers' wives would know the wives of all men of their companies in order to help / guide / counsel them whenever needed. Shalini too was no exception and came to know about most of the wives of the men from Ajai's company.

This was a unique experience by itself, for two reasons. Firstly, men of the Battalion hailed mostly from Nepal, Darjeeling and thereabouts. So setting up home in rural Punjab was a unique experience for them all. But then, as is typical of Gorkhas, they took to life in the Land of Five Rivers with full gusto!

Secondly, in addition to being a company commander, Ajai was also the Battalion Adjutant. Along with that appointment also came an added responsibility towards more ladies for Shalini. But the ever-smiling person that she was, she was only too happy to make more friends amongst the wives of Unit men!

In fact, Shalini also went beyond what is normally expected of an army officer's wife, and soon acquainted herself with the daily routine of the entire battalion as well as making an effort to know not just about the young ladies of her husband's company, but also about the men that formed part of the company.

In the middle of all this, Ajai got allotted a suitable married accommodation in the Tibri Military Station. This led to yet another spurt in Shalini's routine since the kids (who were being looked after by Shalini's mother) could now join them as well. However, as it transpired, only Sanjana joined her parents in Tibri, while Abhinav continued to stay with his *nani*, having become very attached to her. Of course, he would come over every once in a while to stay with his parents as well, but that was only during school breaks!

Abhinav continued to stay with his maternal grandparents in Dehradun for another few years.

Setting up the house in Tibri was yet another adventure on which Shalini embarked, practically on her own since Ajai, being the Battalion Adjutant, had very little time to spare. But this time, with the benefit of the recently set-up and equally quickly packed-up house in Miran Saheb, Ajai wasn't surprised when Shalini set-up their newest house in a very short time.

Little did he know that the girl that he had married, would make it a habit of quickly setting up and packing up houses that they would get allotted in the years to come, in practically every corner of the Motherland, thanks to the nature of his job!

Shalini was very methodical in her approach and there always was a method to the madness that comes with any such move. She was an excellent planner, something which reflected in the way she would orchestrate the frequent moves. She never needed to make any lists, because she would just remember what item was packed in which box. In fact, all that Ajai contributed in was the packing of his books, his uniforms and his shoes!

So it was hardly a surprise when she announced that their house in Tibri was ready to receive their first formal guests! She had done a marvellous job of creating a cozy and welcoming abode in Tibri, and anyone that came visiting was suitable awed.

Add to that the fact that Ajai was very fond of unwinding with friends and colleagues at the end of busy days in office that he had to spend as the Adjutant, and pretty soon, their house was the hub of a large number of get-togethers.

The guest list too was varied, with a steady mix of seniors, juniors, coursemates and their families from within the Units and the Headquarters located in Tibri Military Station.

But the most cherished and at the same time, the most relentless guests were the young bachelor officers of the battalion who didn't even need an invite to just come over for a drink and a meal! To be fair, even the best of the cooks in the Officers' Mess couldn't better a home-cooked meal, and when it came to Shalini, her culinary skills were in any case, legendary!

In fact, this pretty much sums up the oft repeated phrase that 'Army is a way of Life'. This was how folks in the Army make the most of being located in the middle of practically nowhere and left to create their own little oases of companionship and camaraderie. This is also precisely the reason why the Indian Army is one of the best fighting forces in the world – these bonds that are formed in field and peace times.

Soon she was hosting a get-together at her home pretty much every other day. But where someone else might have just given up and started complaining, Shalini, on the other hand, loved playing hostess to any and every one who walked into her house!

She, in any case, was quite adept at organizing get-togethers at very short notice, Of course, the experience of her days in Belgaum did come in handy for this as also for becoming a good judge of just how much a young officer of the Indian Army could eat in a single sitting, to which the simple answer is – A LOT!

The wonderful hostess that she was, Shalini wouldn't just end up spending a get-together cooped up in her kitchen throughout. Instead, she would plan it out in a way that she had enough time to interact with her guests.

Unsurprisingly, Shalini soon became a hit, especially amongst the young officers' crowd who were assured heavenly meals and a patient hearing for any issues that they might have been facing, because she would not only patiently listen to them, but also offer valuable advice. So much so, that her home became a de-facto second home for all youngsters of the Battalion!

In fact, one is tempted to opine that having grown up with two younger brothers, Shalini pretty naturally assumed the role of an elder sister to the young officers of her husband's battalion as well.

Then there were the 800-odd jawans of the battalion and the wives of about two hundred of them who had chosen to join their husbands in Tibri as well. In order to keep them engaged, as well as to teach them new skills, the Army Wives' Welfare Association (AWWA) used to organize various activities for them.

Shalini became a willing and smiling contributor to all AWWA related and other activities that fell under the collective ambit of what is referred to in the Indian Army as *Family Welfare*.

She not only got to know the men of the Battalion and their wives a bit better by doing so, but also picked up their language, Gorkhali, in the process. She was always be concerned about the well-being of the soldiers of the Battalion as well as their families. In fact, such was her connect with them that she was soon able to recognize most of the 200-odd wives of soldiers of the battalion by face and name, as also remember any issues that they were facing.

Needles to say, Shalini, all 23 years of age, was soon the favourite of the soldiers' wives in the battalion. Mind you, her own age wasn't very much either and in many cases, she was actually younger in age to the soldiers' wives. But then, she had that magical charisma as part of her personality which made her the natural go-to person for wives of soldiers from other companies as well!

Of course, about 27 years after that Tibri tenure, as this book is being written, Lt Gen Ajai Kumar Singh reminisces about those days with great nostalgia. He explains this aspect of his late wife's personality with a simple, yet profound remark – 'Once responsibilities come, maturity follows!'

But even in her maturity, Shalini always retained a childlike curiosity and that childlike charm. That never left her. In her heart, she was always a young, teenage girl, right till her very last breath.

Yet, she discharged her responsibilities as one of the senior ladies of the Battalion with great maturity. It was no wonder then that she was soon very well adjusted with the nuances of Unit life in a peace station.

But it would be wrong to say that it was always very smooth sailing for her. Given that there are many different personalities even amongst the wives of the dozen or so officers in a peace station, there was bound to be some friction once in a while. However, through it all, Shalini never took any sides and remained steadfastly neutral and thus, was on good terms with practically every lady of the Battalion.

At the same time, she was also someone who didn't quite hesitate in speaking her mind. In that respect, she was very candid and very direct; a true Adjutant's Wife!

The above aspect of young Shalini's personality was highlighted for all, thanks to an incident related to a meeting of Unit ladies chaired by the CO's wife. Agenda of the meeting was to plan the organizing of a major AWWA event that had been entrusted to the Unit.

Somehow, in the course of the meeting, the CO's wife ended up admonishing Shalini for something which wasn't her fault. Shalini told this clearly to her but it had no impact on the admonishment being unfairly administered to her.

So Shalini just walked out of the meeting, her dignity intact.

Now this was a very major thing to happen in a Unit – a lady walking out during a meeting chaired by the CO's wife. But then, that is just the way Shalini was – if anyone could do the unthinkable, it was she!

Instead of getting in an arguing match with a senior lady, she put forth her point of view, and when it was disregarded, she just walked out. It was a point well made.

Shalini was always forthright, always spontaneous, always correct in her approach and most importantly, always direct.

Unsurprisingly, the relationship between Shalini and the CO's wife became a little challenging due to this, but thanks to her childlike enthusiasm, ultimately no one could remain frosty with her, not even the CO's wife!

Interestingly, despite everything, Mrs Gopal, the then CO's wife always had a soft corner for Shalini, in a way looking at her as her own daughter. She ended up being quite close to Shalini as the years progressed. Of course, the incident of Shalini getting admonished was ultimately found out to have been due to the stress that Mrs Gopal herself was under, due to the huge task at hand that day and indirectly meant for someone else sitting there. However, Shalini was too simple a soul to take an unwarranted admonishment and hence her reaction!

It was an enduring quality about Shalini – her candid, no-nonsense nature coupled with her spontaneity always endeared her to one and all.

In fact, as her sister-in-law, Priti reminisces, she says that she used to think she was Shalini's favourite .. until one day towards the very end she realized that practically *everyone* who had come across Shalini would think the same way about themselves! Priti herself explains it by saying that indeed *everyone* was Shalini's favourite!

And the blissful days in Tibri continued ..

Since it wasn't very far from Dehradun and Roorkee, whenever time permitted, the family would just pack up and drive homewards, thus creating further memories with their much fondly remembered Maruti 800 car, UMS 5654 while at the same time, maintaining intimate contact with both sets of in-laws.

Thanks to the freedom offered by the virtue of owning a car, Shalini and Ajai never wasted any opportunity to explore the world around them. Shalini was always game when it came to exploring new places, a small child notwithstanding. And to complement this wanderlust within, her skills at quickly packing up for trips of any duration were legendary as well!

As their relationship matured, this young couple too had their fair share of issues once in a while, with it being a young marriage and both coming from different backgrounds. Maintaining a healthy balance between own priorities and those of two different sets of parents too was a challenge at times, though not very often.

But looking back, Lieutenant General Ajai Kumar Singh says with firm conviction that it is the husband who has a very important and pivotal role to play in such situations, for the simple reason that the wife has chosen to leave her own maternal home in order to create an entirely new life with him. Thus, it is the unsaid responsibility of the husband to ensure that she lives happily.

It is the husband who has to play the major balancing role, with the wife too having an important role along with him. She too needs to adjust to the new realities in her life, though without losing what she learnt during her own upbringing. This assumes an even greater importance wherein cultures are very different. What is unsaid is also the fact that every family has a different set of dynamics within, which cannot be adjudged between right and wrong. Instead, it is just 'different'.

So getting married into, and creating her own space in her husband's family is a major challenge for any girl, especially someone as young as Shalini was. But then, she just moved in as part of Ajai's extended family as if she had always been a part of them! Ajai too played his role as a good balancer, and the faith that her husband would always be by her side helped her settle down that much more confidently. Of course, with the benefit of hindsight, there were some occasions when Ajai feels he couldn't play a good balancer, but Shalini could easily take such aberrations by her stride.

Both Shalini and Ajai being strong-headed individuals meant that they weren't immune from the occasional husband-wife fights either! So yes, they too had their fair share of arguments, just like any normal couple would.

But it is here that yet another trait of Shalini would come to the fore.

You see, Ajai had a tendency to stop talking to his wife after an argument. But here too, he just couldn't win!

'Silent Treatment' from her husband was just not acceptable to Shalini. Even when angry with him, she just wouldn't accept that. Instead, even while in the middle of a fight, she would still take time out to counsel her husband and tell him that whatever be the reason, they should never stop talking with each other. Communication between a couple should *never* cease; it should carry on regardless.

Those were profound life lessons from a young lady to her husband who was many years older than her!

Typically, arguments between Shalini and Ajai would never last long. Here too, it was she who deserves all credit because she was such a spontaneous girl that within no time she would be back to being her normal self, getting over whatever be the issues between them.

All in all, life in Tibri was quite *happening* and the days just rushed by. Shalini extracted the most out of this new set of experiences and circumstances by fully immersing herself in it.

Dussehra, or as the Nepalese call it – Dassain, is the single most important festival of the Gorkhas. Being in a peace station, it was a given that the festival would be celebrated with great vigour by the Battalion. Here too, she was in the thick of the things and used this opportunity to learn more about the culture of the troops of the Battalion.

But celebratory times were not just limited to festivals! With the Battalion officers often away with most of the Battalion for various training exercises every once in a while, Shalini and the other ladies would mostly be on their own. These times were very aptly utilized by them all to not just re-affirm their bonds, but also to have a gala time amongst themselves!

Meanwhile, little Sanjana too was growing up fast. Abhinav had been staying with her mother and only came over to his parents' place during holiday seasons. So Sanjana was in for a lot of pampering as well as grooming by her mother.

All of five-years old, she was not just the best dressed, but also the best behaved child in the Battalion. Shalini was an excellent mother, and it reflected in her daughter. Sanjana was growing up fast to become a bubbly child who had inherited much of her mother's spontaneous nature.

Shalini would not hesitate to discipline her child whenever required either. Sanjana, who now runs a Production House of her own, still remembers how she was pampered, yet was also kept in discipline.

Of course, such disciplining only happened when absolutely warranted, wherein Shalini wouldn't hesitate one bit in correcting her kid. On all other times, she would be a playmate to Sanjana as well as a teacher, answering all questions typical of a young and naturally curious child that Sanjana was!

A word about their immediate neighbourhood wouldn't be out of place here.

Ajai had been allotted a ground floor flat as part of a block of houses that had four such flats – two on ground floor and two above them. Their immediate neighbor on the ground floor was an officer from the Armoured Corps while the neighbour occupying the house above theirs was a Signal Corps officer. The third neighbour too was an officer posted in another battalion in the station.

It was a lively block, just like many such blocks in most military stations. Once the husbands were off to their respective offices, and the morning household chores done, the ladies would often get together in one of the houses for a cup of tea.

There was an incident during a particularly heavy monsoon season when a small stream nearby overflowed, causing flooding in parts of the Tibri Military Station. The first houses to be affected were those of the two Brigade Commanders. Ajai still very distinctly remembers the evacuation of both Brigade Commanders in a 3-Tonner!

Unsurprisingly, given the way life continued throwing challenges their way, the block housing Shalini and Ajai was right next to the Commanders' residences. What made an already bad situation even worse was that the flooding happened overnight and caught everyone by surprise when they woke up in the morning in ankle deep water.

The water was extremely dirty too, since even the sewage lines had flooded and overflowed. They got round to salvaging things right away, first placing things on the bed and subsequently putting them in the home of their upstairs neighbours.

The water receded after a few days, but a lot of damage had already been done by then. Amongst the losses were most of sarees that Shalini owned, as also the *Achkan* that Ajai had worn on the day of their wedding.

In a way it was an immensely challenging situation, yet Shalini still managed to give it a different perspective, thanks to she being herself throughout those days!

New sarees gradually kept coming Shalini's way as she shopped hard to replace her hugely dwindled wardrobe, as time in Tibri moved on.

Life was blissful indeed, until the day Shalini received a shock, literally.

Sometime in this duration, Ajai was out in a *Telebattle Exercise* with officers of the entire Brigade in the Ops Room when he received a message that Shalini had received an electric shock and was unconscious.

Naturally, he rushed home and saw her lying on the bed, her mouth frothing.

Those were the days of no mobile phones and even the landline telephones weren't very common. But Major Charanjit, the Signal Corps officer living upstairs had a landline on which Shalini and Ajai's family would call at times. In order to tie up a signal to indicate a phone call, an electric bell was installed in Ajai's home, with the switch being at Major Charanjit's residence.

Over time, the electric wire connecting to the bell had worn out, unnoticed. That day, as Shalini was hanging freshly washed clothes to dry on a rope near that electric wire, the exposed part of the wire touched her just behind her neck. With wet clothes in her hands, and she standing on top of a metallic box in order to hang them, the conditions sadly made a perfect blueprint for disaster.

During this time, Abhinav was with his parents on a break and Sanjana was I at school, the child ran out and called the first person he saw. Such was the severity of the shock that she was violently thrown off the box and fell on the ground. The person who Abhinav called was a domestic help who passed a message to Ajai via the official army line at his home.

Shalini was immediately taken to the Military Hospital where the wound on the back of her neck was treated whereafter the doctor said that she was fine and discharged her.

However, this was the beginning of a myriad of medical issues that Shalini started suffering from.

Even though no medical / scientific explanation is able to attribute that to it, Ajai still feels to this day that the electric shock changed something within her body wherein a perfectly healthy young lady began suffering from periodic episodes of illness, leading ultimately to a kidney transplant less than a decade-and-a-half later, and her passing another 11 years thereafter.

But then, the human body being the amazingly complex machine that it is, such issues might just not be related to that electric shock after all. Yet, fact remains that Shalini started suffering from episodes of extremely high blood pressure and other such issues *after* that contact with the naked wire.

The young couple that they were, Ajai and Shalini soldiered on, while still trying to come to terms with bouts of ill-health that would afflict Shalini every once in a while.

In the meantime, they got a break from the Unit routine when Ajai got his orders to attend the mandatory Junior Command Course at the College of Combat in the quaint little town called Mhow, about 20 km from Indore.

Despite a passionate case taken up by Ajai's CO for cancellation of the course, he ultimately had to let him go attend that 12-

week long course. However, due to the short notice of move, no confirmed rail reservations were available.

So the natural course of action was to drive all the way from Tibri to Mhow in their trusty old Maruti 800! Not only was this Ajai's first time travelling that far by road, but to add to the challenge, he had no idea of what route to take.

Hence he did the most logical thing that came to his mind – He took out a copy of the Eicher Road Map of India that he always kept with him, and drew a straight line from Tibri to Mhow!

That done, he looked at the nearest road network and pretty soon he knew the shortest route to his destination that was almost 1,500km from home.

Incidentally, that worn out Eicher Road Map is still one of the old, nostalgic possessions of Lt Gen Ajai Kumar Singh!

Shalini packed furiously as well as intelligently for the nearly three-month long outing. Since they would be staying in a temporary accommodation during the course, she also carried a small set of essential items for establishing a kitchen there as well, right from the smallest pots and pans to her gas-chulha!

Of course, an LPG cylinder too had to be carried along with all that other kitchen stuff. The poor old Maruti car was soon filled to its fullest capacity, but everything was arranged so beautifully by Shalini that the rear seat was only half full, so that Sanjana could comfortably snooze as well!

This was yet another quality of Shalini - Whenever the situation permitted, she would gladly uproot herself from her comfort zone in order to be with her husband, even if he was going out for just a couple of days, unlike the three months that he would be away from the Battalion in this case.

Their first halt, thanks to that road map, was the dusty little town of Sardar Shahar in Rajasthan. Enroute, they halted for lunch at the Ferozepur Military Station, before entering Rajasthan.

The first sight that welcomed Shalini and Ajai in Rajasthan was not just the deserts, but also a sandstorm that seemed to have timed itself perfectly so that it could deposit fine particles of dust inside their car! Pretty soon they were practically breathing dust! It was quite an eventful first experience of deserts for Shalini and Sanjana.

They reached Sardar Shahar in the evening and Ajai started asking around for a hotel so that they could stay for the night.

He still remembers one of the locals looking at him from top to bottom, as if trying to size up the young visitor who didn't know that Sardar Shahar didn't have any hotels!

Ultimately someone told him that they could find some place to stay the night near the bus-stand. Thankfully, they were able to rent a room there. The facilities were very basic, but they were just thankful to have a roof over their heads for the night.

So basic was the set-up that they didn't even serve food. So Ajai went back to the bus-stand and brought some local food from there. It was typically Rajasthani fare, full of chillies as well as sand! But then, Shalini was still able to *fix* it and make a meal out of it.

The family started off early next day towards Chittorgarh which was to be their next halt, finally reaching Mhow on the third evening. Thankfully, theirs was a well-maintained and reliable car and Ajai himself was quite fond of driving. So the three-day journey was quite a pleasurable family time for them all.

Ajai's Junior Command course commenced on the appointed day. The next three months were a different experience altogether for Shalini as she came to terms with the academic environment that kept her husband and all his colleagues insanely busy.

While the husbands were busy studying for most part of their days, the ladies gradually got together and were soon well on their way to making the most of those three months of bliss, away from Unit commitments while at the same time, making the most of the time they got together with their husbands.

But when the husbands were away for classes, exercises or just studying for their exams while at home, the ladies were busy establishing lifelong bonds of friendship amongst themselves.

Those three months gave Shalini an opportunity to get in touch with Army life beyond the regiment. To be fair, she did get a glimpse when Ajai was posted at the Commando School not very long ago, but this time it was very different. This time, Ajai was himself a student, instead of an instructor that he was then.

She also got to know ladies whose husbands were from arms and services of the military other than infantry and what life was like in those arms and services. There was so much peer-learning to be done that Shalini soon got even busier than Ajai!

After placing Sanjana in a playschool, Shalini herself joined many courses in order to make up for her interrupted education, thanks to an early marriage when she was barely out of school.

She learnt (and at times, re-learnt) cooking and baking. Personal grooming was another course that she joined. Being organized by the College of Combat itself, this further added to her knowledge of how to be a senior lady in the armed forces family.

Overall, it was an excellent experience for her, being away from any responsibilities of home or Battalion, just concentrating on squeezing the most out of life in Mhow.

At the same time she also realized the importance of professional courses that her husband and his peers would need to undergo from time to time. This came in handy especially when Ajai told her about that he would be preparing for the entrance examination for the prestigious Defence Services Staff College (DSSC) course the next year.

The Staff Course is a major milestone in an army officer's career. Unlike the other mandatory courses which all officers undergo while in service, the Staff Course has limited vacancies and each year, a competitive entrance examination is conducted in order to fill up those limited vacancies. The competition is tough due to two reasons – Firstly, the vacancies are extremely limited, and Secondly, because the exam itself is a series of six papers over six days straight with no breaks in-between. The syllabus itself being vast, officers typically start preparing atleast six to eight months in advance.

Ajai explained all of this to Shalini as they drove back to Tibri after the course, this time much better prepared with respect to halts enroute!

Upon reporting back to his Battalion, one of the first things that Ajai did was to walk up to his CO and request him to spare him hereinafter so that he could now study.

The CO too was understanding, especially with the new Adjutant now in chair for three months, and he told Ajai to take command of the company located in Batala, which was about 40 minutes' drive away from Tibri. He also gave Ajai a young company 2iC to whom he could delegate the day-to-day administration of the company.

Ajai was quite happy at this, for about 24 hours, before life threw another googly at him!

It so happened that the next day when he reached office, the Battalion Second-in-Command, Lt Col Inder Narayan congratulated him on his posting. Apparently, the 'powers that be' in the highest headquarters of the Indian Army had decided that time was ripe for him to be posted out to a staff appointment. Accordingly, just a day after rejoining the Battalion, his posting order had come.

Major Ajai Kumar Singh stood posted to HQ 16 Sector in a place called Naugam in the State of Jammu and Kashmir.

In one last ditch effort to get his posting order cancelled, Ajai himself drove down to New Delhi and met the officer concerned, only to be told that the posting order couldn't be changed. He was further told that even before doing his Staff Course, he was being sent on a staff appointment, which showed that he was doing well professionally.

Having reconciled to reality, Ajai returned back and Shalini got busy packing up the household for their second bout of separation that was to commence soon.

Strange as the ways of destiny are, this unexpected and unwelcome tenure would soon turn into a boon for Ajai.

As she contemplated where to set-up home once Ajai left for his new place of posting, Shalini weighed the pros and cons and decided to move to Mussoorie now. She wanted to re-live her childhood days of bliss in that little hill-station in the lower Himalayas with both her kids as well as her grandmother who she was quite fond of. Also, this way, no set of in-laws of the couple would have reason to feel unhappy since she would be staying independently, away from both.

Thus it happened and as Ajai moved out to Naugam in March 1995, Shalini and Sanjana moved to Mussoorie, with Abhinav too joining them there.

This was the end of yet another blissful chapter in the life of Shalini, as also the beginning of yet another, equally blissful one!

06

THE SECOND PARTING

The Sector Headquarters where Ajai stood posted, was located near Kupwara in the State of Jammu and Kashmir, just North of Uri. The area, as he found out, was really challenging and the headquarter itself was under-staffed at that time, being an adhoc establishment.

So under-staffed was it that two key appointments – the Deputy Commander and the Deputy Assistant Adjutant & Quarter Master General, were not posted. However, it being a challenging area, need was felt for a staff officer dedicatedly looking after logistics. With Ajai having done the Quartermasters Course some years ago and performed well, he was selected for this appointment.

Since Ajai had just commenced preparing for the challenging Defence Service Staff College Entrance Examination, an attempt was made to continue serving with the Unit. However, since those efforts did not bear fruit, Shalini and Ajai made their peace with what fate had ordained for them, and started planning for the immediate future.

She didn't take long to decide to send the bulk of her household stuff to her parents' house in Dehradun, and herself move to Mussoorie with both her kids. Accordingly, when Ajai moved out of Tibri for Naugam in March 1995, she too moved back to Mussoorie.

It was nothing short of a homecoming for Shalini, having spent a substantial part of her childhood days in that quaint little hill-station. Abhinav too joining them there was an added bonus.

The family was nearly complete .. *nearly,* because of the fact that Ajai was far away, tasked with playing a crucial role in his new headquarters – that of keeping troops on the Line of Control supplied with not just their day-to-day needs, but also stocked for the severe winter season that was hardly a few months away.

The place Ajai had landed up in, was nestled in a beautiful part of the Himalayas on the Line of Control, far from any habitation except for military personnel.

Unsurprisingly, the old routine of one letter per day between Shalini and Ajai recommenced pretty soon.

For a change, since Ajai was tenanting a staff appointment, his routine was fairly well-set, even though quite busy. Yet, being in a headquarters, he had access to a military telephone line and through that, to a PCO Booth in the Divisional Headquarters in Baramula, which would in turn, patch him through to Shalini in Mussoorie.

It was quite a long and tedious chain of links that would take a long time for a phone call to materialize, but then those days of mid-1990s weren't even a fraction as fast-paced as life in current times is, and such waits were just taken in stride.

In fact, at times he would even get connected to the home in Mussoorie after a couple of hours, only to find out that Shalini was away on some errand!

All of this was taken in stride by Ajai and Shalini, because they both knew that this separation was a mere temporary blip in their togetherness that had lasted across lifetimes, and would continue thusly.

At the same time, Ajai was also clear about his priority in the immediate future. He had already applied for the Staff Course Entrance Examination which was to happen in September that year. Thus, besides focusing on his professional responsibilities as a Staff Officer, passing this highly competitive examination was also a key priority and he was already working hard towards that.

The one year long Staff Course is a major career milestone for an officer in the Indian Army because it opens up vistas for postings in key appointments, with commensurate increase in opportunities for promotion to higher ranks

Ajai was convinced that with the benefit of having seen him in the recent Junior Command Course, Shalini too was somewhat aware of the importance of this examination, though there wasn't much that she could do to support him in this endeavour, considering that she was currently living far away in Mussoorie.

Little did he know how wrong he was .. and that Shalini had already ensured that he got the perfect set-up in the last few days as he geared up for what literally was the examination of his life! We shall come to that in a while during this chapter.

Anyhow, being sure of what he wanted, Ajai walked up to his Brigade Commander soon after he settled down in his new appointment and requested him to be given time to prepare for the examination.

But the hands of the Brigade Commander too were tied. They were in the middle of the short spell of summer season during which all his forwards battalions needed to be stocked up for the long and unforgiving winter season that would soon descend upon them.

In fact, this was the very task that his DAA & QMG, Major Ajai Kumar Singh, was mandated to execute. Moreover, the job had to be extremely thorough because once the snows came back again, there would not be many opportunities to make up any shortfalls.

So the Brigade Commander made what was the best offer under these circumstances. He told Ajai that he would grant him the full 60 days annual leave that he was authorized that year. But that came with a few conditions.

Firstly, he told Ajai not to expect any more leave by the way of furlough or any other means because circumstances just didn't permit that.

Secondly, Ajai would need to ensure that winter stocking was done in the desired manner.

And thirdly, Ajai's being a key appointment, the Brigade Commander wanted him to find an officer to temporarily man it in his absence. For this Ajai would need to reach out to the Commanding Officers of the affiliated Battalions of the Brigade and find a suitable reliever on his own and train him in the intricacies of the job before leaving.

To be fair, this was indeed the maximum that the Brigade Commander could offer under the circumstances.

Where someone else might have given up under such daunting conditions, Ajai took it as a challenge and got right down to the job of planning and executing the winter stocking for the forward areas.

Meanwhile Shalini too had set-up her little nest in Mussoorie. Both kids were quickly enrolled in Hampton Court School, which was amongst the most renowned ones there. Not only would this ensure good education for them, but also allow some time for Shalini to catch up with the household chores and the daily letter that she would send across to her husband!

She had soon settled into a quiet and happy routine in a place that is often referred to as *Queen of the Hills*. Having spent a considerable part of her childhood there, not only was she back amongst the memories of those innocent days but also with the lifelong friends from those young years.

In addition, she was also back to being the favourite grand-daughter of her grandmother who was staying in the same house as well. Moreover, her grandmother was also a well-respected elder in Mussoorie since Shalini's late grandfather had been a highly respected SHO in Mussoorie in his days.

Of course, she continued to be an excellent mother to her kids – Loving and caring and at the same time, not brooking any truancy beyond the usual kiddie naughtiness!

While smothering her kids with love, Shalini was absolutely clear about their discipline and never failed to mete out punishment whenever warranted.

One such instance is deeply etched in Sanjana's mind. Once Shalini caught her using a bad word for Abhinav. The very next instance she took Sanjana to the kitchen and pretty soon her mouth was filled with one tablespoon worth of red chilli. She did the same with Abhinav when he repeated this grave mistake. Always correct and unbiased in her approach.

In those cold climes of Mussoorie, not only was red chilly good for kids, but in this case, it also helped clean up the little childrens vocabulary as well!

Then there was the incident of the kids getting caught in the kitchen without their footwear. This too was a strict taboo in the household, due to the cold weather and colder floors. What happened next is also something that both Sanjana and Abhinav still remember, especially since it forever cured them of the tendency to roam around in the house without footwear! Their footwear was locked in a cupboard, out of their reach.

At the same time, far away in an even colder Naugam, Ajai too was studying hard as well in whatever little time he had on hand after office hours. Sixty days weren't sufficient for such a competitive examination that had a success rate of less than 25%

and when his counterparts had upto four months of clear leave and furlough to prepare!

Finally when time came to proceed on his promised 60 days' leave, not only had Ajai already planned the entire winter stocking and started executing it, but he had also been able to arrange for Lt Col Rao, an officer from 17 Punjab, to relieve him, thanks to the magnanimity of Col Narula, CO of the Battalion.

To this day, Lt Gen Ajai Kumar Singh chuckles when recalls the surprised face of his Commander when he was told that all his conditions were met and that Maj Ajai was ready to proceed on leave!

The Commander gladly agreed to keep his end of the bargain and consequently Ajai reached Mussoorie some time in the month of July 1995, with all his books and notes for the upcoming examination.

It was here that Shalini's decision to move to Mussoorie instead of Roorkee or Dehradun proved to be worth its weight in gold. It was almost as if she knew that her husband would not be able to study properly in the midst of his or her extended family and that the quietude of Mussoorie was the perfect place for him to prepare.

But even though Ajai reached Mussoorie soon enough, that quietude was still some time away!

What happened was that he reached Mussoorie in the morning and quickly got busy setting up his study-room, opening up his books and notes and generally organizing his small study-room.

He was quick and soon had his study space well set. He *had* to be quick, since time was short and the exam dates were fast approaching.

But just about the time that he was done, the kids returned home from school.

In Ajai's words, '*It was chaos!*'

Having seen their father after nearly four months, the six year old Abhinav and five year old Sanjana were besides themselves with joy. Ajai had no choice in the matter, and ended up catching up with the little ones all through that afternoon.

And to top it up, there were two more young kids in the house. Unsurprisingly, any hopes of studying in presence of the kids were dashed, and Shalini suggested that he shift to a hotel instead. His Father-in-Law found him a good hotel near the Clock Tower, thanks to his good contacts in Mussoorie.

Ajai shifted there the very next day and set up his books and notes again, and recommenced his studies in earnest.

Thus commenced yet another chapter in Shalini's married life, one where every day she would carry lunch and dinner to her husband who was busy studying in the hotel room. It was not a short walk either, but she did it with great joy at being able to spend some time with him while he ate.

But, there still wasn't that quietude that Ajai was longing for!

It was peak tourist season, and predictably, Mussoorie too was flooded with tourists. The hotel where Ajai had rented a room was located in the midst of a popular site for tourists and there was a lot of ambient noise throughout the day.

And hopes of any quiet times in off-peak hours were dashed by the other guests in the hotel, many of whom would play music at great volume in their rooms.

Thus it was time to move again.

Another factor that played a part in this decision was the fact that Ajai didn't want Shalini to make the long trek to his hotel twice a day, carrying lunch and dinner for him.

So this time, Shalini's father found a hotel close to her Mussoorie home. It was a two-room set that was rented and Ajai finally got the quietude that he needed to study.

By the time he settled down in his new lodgings, the exam was barely 50 days away!

In order to ensure that her husband is able to fully concentrate on his studies, Shalini continued to bring him lunch and dinner, this time walking a lot lesser than in case of the previous hotel. At times the kids too would accompany their mother for a short family meal in their father's room.

It also helped Ajai take much-needed breaks from his studies and stay refreshed for the long haul that he was in for.

Shalini was extremely supportive throughout those days and never complained once, even though she was still looking after her own household and the two kids as well as her grandmother.

But Ajai too would ensure that every evening he would take time out to go on a long walk with Shalini, taking time out to enjoy the beautiful Mussoorie.

Of course, he also knew that once this leave and the examination was over, he wouldn't be left with much opportunities to visit home for the rest of the year. So together, Shalini and he decided that evenings were a time of togetherness.

Accordingly, every evening he would be at the doorstep of the house of his beloved, calling out for her, taking care not to be too loud about it. In turn, she too would quietly sneak out of the home to be with him.

Even though it looks like a typical romantic set-up of a Bollywood film, those who have little kids will understand the reason why Shalini and Ajai needed to be quiet about this whole affair!

Those long walks along the Camel's Back Road in Mussoorie every evening were eagerly awaited by both, for it would be their own time of togetherness and privacy, even if on one of the busiest roads in Mussoorie.

These walks would easily last upto an hour, giving Shalini freedom from the day-to-day responsibilities of running a household with young kids, and in case of Ajai, a much needed break from the 18 hours-a-day study routine that he was in the midst of, and rejuvenating him to carry on with his nightly revisions.

They would talk with each other, sit on benches by the roadside enjoying the views of the hills and the valleys .. basically enjoying each other's company.

The talks would be about kids, about Ajai's future and about life in general. The topic didn't matter. The companionship did.

In a way those days in Mussoorie were days of both, separation as well as proximity!

Those two months that Ajai was in Mussoorie just flew by and soon it was time to appear for the Staff College Entrance Examination.

Maj Ajai Kumar Singh had chosen Dehradun as the venue from where he would appear for the exam. Being in field, he had the luxury of choosing a venue anywhere in the country and Dehradun was the obvious choice.

Thus two days before the six-day battery of exams commenced, Ajai bid a temporary farewell to Shalini and the kids and came down to Dehradun. Here again, his Father-in-Law had arranged for a detached accommodation right across the road from his own house so that he could study without any distractions.

Ajai's next six days went by in a blur, with an exam each morning followed by a bit of rest and then back to studying for the next exam. At the end of the last exam on the Saturday, there was a huge sense of relief at just being over with it, but at the same time came the saddening realization that all his leave for that year was over and that the next bout of separation will last till atleast the next year, not that this particular leave could be counted towards *togetherness*, with he busy studying.

Thankfully, Shalini too had realized this and landed up in Dehradun with the kids for a couple of days of family time before Ajai departed for Srinagar and onwards to Naugam.

The results of the examination came sometime in the month of November. Not only had Ajai passed the exam, but he had made it in the *Competitive List*, i.e. he was amongst the Twenty top-scorers amongst all that had appeared.

Shalini's unstinting support and sacrifice had a huge role to play in this success that Ajai had earned. She had not only endured a separation even when her husband was merely a stone's throw away from her in Mussoorie, but she had also ensured that all his needs were met and he could stay focused on his studies.

In fact this was what spurred on Ajai as well, knowing that he was in a non-family station and spending his entire leave period just studying from morning till night. He knew that he just *had* to pass the exam in the first attempt itself (the army gives three attempts to eligible officers). Else the next year's leave too would go just like this one. For him, this was not the first attempt, but instead, his *only* attempt at clearing this exam, despite the break in his plans due to the unanticipated posting to Naugam and the consequent loss of time that would otherwise have been spend studying.

But as they say, proof of the pudding is in the eating!

Thus unsurprisingly, more than a thousand kilometres away from Mussoorie where Shalini was, on the day the result came, Ajai was one of the guests in the Jubilee celebrations of a Light Artillery Regiment in the location. Upon hearing of his success, the Second-in-Command of the Regiment announced to the entire gathering that the DAA & QMG had cleared the examination in a competitive vacancy and that the drinks were on him!

Then the first bottle of champagne was popped opened by the 2iC, and pretty soon everyone had a glass of their preferred liquor in hands and a lot of congratulations and friendly back-slaps started pouring his way.

To this day, nearly three decades later, Lt Gen Ajai Kumar Singh still remembers that the bill for all that celebratory liquor consumption that came his way, was pretty hefty!

But then, it was a small price to pay for yet another bout of togetherness with Shalini and the kids, possibly in a foreign country.

A *Competitive Vacancy* meant that he stood a good chance for getting nominated to one of the coveted vacancies for a Staff Course abroad, in one of the friendly foreign countries that offered such vacancies on a reciprocal basis.

However, the number of vacancies available for foreign staff course that year were low and resultantly, in June 1996, Shalini and the kids found themselves headed to the quaint little town called Wellington that was nestled in the beautiful Nilgiri Hills near Conoor.

With the bulk of her household stuff still unopened, Shalini quickly packed up the few belongings that were opened up for use in Mussoorie, bid farewell to her uncle and grandmother, and came down to Dehradun ahead of the impending move to the Nilgiris.

All household stuff was duly accounted for by the meticulous young lady and with active labour from both her brothers, loaded in a truck along with Ajai's car, and despatched to Wellington. She timed the move in a way that the truck would reach just ahead of them, so that no time was wasted in setting up the new house.

The family flew down to Coimbatore on the appointed day.

From Coimbatore, a taxi was hired to take them to Wellington. It is an immensely scenic route to drive on, despite it being a nightmare for those with motion sickness, given the insane climb up the hills on a road with more than two-dozen hairpin bends.

Seeing that part of the country for the first time, Shalini was truly mesmerized and thoroughly enjoyed it.

It was also the first time that Shalini and Ajai saw a jackfruit growing in the wild! From here on, jackfruit would taste just a bit more tastier for the foodie couple!

It being a course of instruction with fixed numbers of officers attending, appropriate accommodation was already earmarked for each and everyone even before they reached there. Theirs was at the famous 'Gorkha Hill'.

As usual, Shalini had that house transformed into a welcoming *home* in absolutely no time at all. The kids too were enrolled in the Holy Innocents' School, which was amongst the best schools in Coonoor at that time.

The one year spent in Wellington was truly blissful, especially with the benefit of a long separation just prior to that.

It was a period of togetherness that they were eagerly looking forward to and waiting for, especially since it was about seven months after the announcement of the result that the course commenced. And Abhinav too was back in the family after a prolonged stay in his maternal grandmother's care

The family was complete, with Ajai no longer in the field and both kids together.

Moreover, there were a large number of coursemates and other previously known officers and ladies who too had made their way to Wellington, and with all staying within a 10-minute walk from each other, the sheer amount of socialization during that year-long course was mind-boggling!

This was more so in case of the ladies since early every morning their husbands would leave for their classes and kids would be packed off to school. With the household chores done by about 10am, Shalini and other ladies would spend much of the day in the company of each other, often enjoying the late morning Sun while exchanging notes and just chatting!

So much so, that husbands coming back from college was often met with exasperated glares, since that would mean an end to the ladies' time together!

Beautiful, life-long bonds were formed between Shalini and many other ladies from that shared experience of Wellington. Bonds that withstood the test of times and carried on regardless.

But it was not all talk and no substance for Shalini. While Ajai remained busy with his academics, she too immersed herself into her ever continuing endeavour at self-improvement.

Despite being a well-rounded personality already by now, Shalini was always on the lookout to squeeze just that much more from life and from those around her. Thus it didn't come as a surprise when she announced that she had decided to make good use of the ITOW programme being run by the Defence Services Staff College for the ladies of the officers attending the course.

ITOW stood for *Institutionalized Training for Officers' Wives.* It aimed at offering grooming classes for the ladies and teaching them various skills of their choice. The aim was two-fold: Firstly, to ensure that they were well adapted for the future roles that they would need to play as wives of senior officers and secondly, to give them an opportunity to gainfully utilize their time at Wellington.

True to her nature, Shalini soaked it all in, with her trademark diligence. So much so that she was perhaps the only one that prepared copious amounts of notes on all topics. Her personal favourite amongst those was *Financial Planning.*

At that time Ajai used to joke with her about her new interest in Financial Planning, given the relatively modest salaries that Armed Forces offered at that time. But little did he know that this knowledge of her would come in so handy almost immediately after the Staff Course when he would find himself in a diplomatic assignment, making much more money.

As always, Shalini continued to be one step ahead of him, knowingly or unknowingly!

In addition to that institutionalized training, Shalini also got to learn a lot by the way of peer-learning by the way of her interactions with other ladies, including for the first time, ladies of officers from the Air Force and Navy as well.

Apart from this, the family travelled. A Lot!

Wellington was nestled amongst the beautiful Nilgiri hills, not very far from Ooty and many more, relatively unknown spots in the lap of Mother Nature. Thanks to the faithful little car of theirs, they hit almost every such place, near and far.

The very mention of those places still brings a nostalgic smile on Lt Gen Ajai's face. Places like Dolphin's Nose, Botanical Gardens, Coonoor, the local marketplaces and restaurants in and around Wellington, Coonoor and Ooty left indelible marks in their journey of togetherness.

Then there was a famous clothing shop in Coonoor. Famous, as it survived and even thrived on purely Armed Forces clientele! One specialty of the shop was that it had a huge collection of sarees of all styles and vintages. Shalini having lost almost all her sarees in that unfortunate flood in Tibri, she ended up making a large contribution to the financial well-being of the shop owner there!

As always, a large contingent from both their extended families kept visiting them from time to time, leading to a steady stream of visitors to their abode on the Gorkha Hill.

One interesting turn of events with respect to the visitors happened when both sets of parents – Shalini's and Ajai's landed up together. This led to unexpected logistical challenges which hadn't been fully appreciated by the couple, in the excitement of having their parents come visit them!

Suffice to say, a *lot* of lessons were learnt in that little duration when the parents stayed with them!

Of course, Shalini and Ajai managed the challenge successfully, with full support of their parents as well.

Fortunately, their visit was timed with the short break that comes by for the course in the month of December. This is a time when the Student Officers generally form groups and go exploring South India for about a week or so. But Shalini and Ajai didn't do so due to their parents' visit. Instead, they stayed on in Wellington and took their parents exploring nearby places of interest in Ooty and Coonoor.

The Wellington tenure saw Shalini in her elements, making a tonne of new friends all around. Life was good indeed, more so with the relative proximity to Tirrupur, a town famous for cotton clothing.

Naturally, Shalini went all out, shopping to her heart's content!

But then, bulk of the shopping was not for her, but instead for all family members. In fact, everyone in the extended family got some souvenir or other from that part of the country, thanks to Shalini.

Thus passed the days of bliss in Wellington and pretty soon it was time to bid farewell to the beautiful little town. Ajai stood posted back to his Unit which was in South Manipur at that time.

But then again, knowing their story so far, I don't think anyone would be surprised at the fact that this parting too didn't happen without a bit of *excitement!*

On the day of their departure, with all formalities done and movement order in hand, Shalini, Ajai and the kids were sitting in the military bus for their journey to Coimbatore, he got a message to rush to the office of the Colonel A (Col 'A').

Col 'A' is the staff officer who deals with routine administrative and personnel related issues as well as disciplinary issues.

Perplexed, and mentally going over his last few days to see if he might have done something wrong enough to warrant a summon from Col 'A', Ajai reached the Administrative Block.

Thankfully, the call was not for a disciplinary issue but instead to inform Ajai that he had been shortlisted for an interview for the post of the Pension Paying Officer at the PPO (Pension Paying Office) at Dharan in Eastern Nepal.

Procedure required that Ajai send a formal *Willingness Certificate* to the MS Branch in the Army HQ for further processing of the interview process. This was duly done and Ajai took a copy of the Signal detailing him for the interview as well one of his *Willingness Certificate* and headed back to his impatiently waiting family, as well as others in the now delayed bus!

Upon reaching back, Shalini naturally queried what was that about and Ajai told her that there is likely to be a change in plans for the next few days. Seeing her get further confused, he finally filled her in and told her about the interview call-up.

The interview was scheduled in Delhi less than a week hence. Thankfully, Ajai had taken some leave and the interview date fell within this period.

Fate had denied him a chance at joining the Indian Embassy in Nepal about six years ago. Now, it seemed that Fate was keen to make up for that lost opportunity earmarked for Ajai. But then, there was to be a bit more of the usual 'excitement' before that happened!

It so happened that on the appointed day, as he reached the Army Headquarters, Ajai was told to his horror that his name wasn't there in the panel!

Upon further probing, he was told that he had sent an *Unwilling Certificate* and hence his name had been removed from the panel of shortlisted officers.

But thankfully, he was in possession of a copy of his *Willingness Certificate* and duly produced that. Now it was the turn of the people in the MS Branch to go into a tizzy at this goof-up!

To cut a long story short, not only was Ajai accepted back in the panel and permitted to appear in the interview, but he also ended up acing it and getting selected for the coveted posting in Nepal!

Meanwhile, Gods of Destiny must have been having a good laugh at this turn of events!

Looking back, Lt Gen Ajai surmises that the unexpected tenure as DQ in Naugam helped him get shortlisted for the interview, since it counted as a Grade-1 Tenure in his profile. Thus, where other colleagues were now going for their Grade-1 Tenures post Staff College, he was already available for this foreign posting, having already done his own staff tenure.

The pre-induction formalities would take a couple of months before Ajai could join his new team in Nepal.

With some leave still in balance, the trusty old car took the family back to Roorkee and Dehradun to be with their loved ones before it was time again for Ajai to bid farewell to Shalini and the kids and rejoin his Battalion.

The Battalion at that time was located in a place called Sita in Tegnoupal District in South Manipur, fighting insurgency in that part of the country. Col Inder Narayan was commanding the Battalion at that time and having Ajai back in the Unit after his Staff Course, he promptly appointed him as the Adjutant!

Thus Ajai was back not only in the Unit but also in the same chair that he had left just about two years ago. Life had come full circle indeed!

But thankfully, being in the Battalion Headquarters, the CO permitted Ajai to get Shalini over to stay with him and quite soon, the couple were back together.

She took a flight from New Delhi to Imphal. From there, she took a day trip by road to Sita, escorted by a QRT (Quick Reaction Team) from the Battalion.

This was the first time she was seeing men of her Battalion in such circumstances, wielding weapons and ever vigilant. But that still didn't deter her from venturing out to the markets in Imphal to pick up a few things she knew would be needed for her upcoming stay!

Shalini's aim was simple – stay together with Ajai as much as possible. It was this pledge to spend as much time with Ajai that saw her travel all the way to a very remote part of the country just to be with him, despite knowing that this separation wouldn't last very long.

It was a very rudimentary setup in Sita, with wives of four officers staying there with their husbands. It wouldn't be wrong to call it a 'community living', with all families in a single, huge tin structure with makeshift partitions in-between to give some privacy.

All conversations could be overheard and participated in by everyone living there, and those few months were enjoyed to the maximum by all that were staying under that single roof, having made their peace with the circumstances just for the sake of being together!

It was a unique experience for the city born girl that Shalini was. If the rural setup of Ajai's household in Roorkee was a novel experience for her, then life in Manipur was something she hadn't even imagined, ever!

It was the first time she had stayed in such a remote and undeveloped area full of thick jungles all around. Snakes and scorpions were a common sight.

In addition, bright sunlight at 4am too took a while for her to get used to!

This was also the first time she was staying with Ajai in field conditions in an active insurgency area. It was also the first time she travelled to the North-East. There was a lot to soak in, including the sight of her own husband leading troops for operations every once in a while, despite him being the Adjutant of the Battalion. For most other part he would be monitoring the frequent operations by the companies (which were deployed at various locations) on his radio set.

Shalini's life in Manipur was simple, frugal and yet, extremely enjoyable.

With the Officers' Mess being close by, she didn't really need to cook but every once in a while she and the other ladies would find their way to the kitchen and dish out a welcome change in fare for their husbands.

Many a times, the officers and ladies staying there would have *Momo Parties*. With Gorkha troops being experts at making mouth-watering steamed momos, at times the crowd would have nothing but momos for dinner, chatting away amongst themselves!

These chats would not just get over with the dinner, but instead also continue through the thin partition walls in the tin structure they called home!

Shalini spent close to three months with Ajai in this setup, loving each and every moment of it.

Another good thing about being in Sita was the proximity to the town of Moreh on the India-Myanmar border.

Being on the border, Moreh was an important trading outpost and the best of the electronics, clothes and cosmetics were available there, thanks to the local trade with Myanmar.

In fact, not just for themselves but Ajai's Battalion would keep getting requests from officers posted at various places in Manipur and even Nagaland for procurement of television sets, refrigerators and such likes. So much so that they maintained a *Demand Register* and once a month a trip was made to Moreh to purchase the goods.

It was on one such trip that Shalini got an opportunity to accompany Ajai to Moreh on one such trip. There was so much shopping to be done, mostly for other people, that they had to stay there for the night!

Never before had she shopped so much, even if from the money of others'!

But that too was about to change, with the diplomatic assignment and along with it, a hefty jump in household income on its way!

07

A DIPLOMAT AMONGST THE FRIENDLY HILLS AND EVEN FRIENDLIER HILL PEOPLE

Shalini spent nearly three blissful months with her husband in South Manipur in the lap of nature, creating yet more memories in their journey of togetherness. Busy as he was, being the Adjutant of the Battalion and involved in active operations too, Ajai was also waiting to hear back from the Army Headquarters regarding his impending move to Nepal.

The pre-induction documentation took its time and finally in the month of August 1997, Shalini, Ajai and both kids found themselves on a New Delhi – Kathmandu flight.

Yet again, there was much *excitement* to be had at the airport. Not having realized the sheer time it would take to get through the immigration and other formalities at the airport, they barely managed to board the flight in the nick of time!

Destiny seemed to be quite persistent in making them sweat every once in a while, though without any malice!

The family soon landed in Kathmandu and now began an entirely new chapter in the life of Shalini – that of a diplomat's wife in a foreign land that was home to so many dear friends from the Army family back in India.

Ajai's duty station was Dharan in the eastern part of Nepal. But he was retained in the Indian Embassy in Kathmandu for some time initially, for initial orientation and briefings pertaining to his new role out there.

Billeted in Bharatiya Gorkha Sainik Niwas (BGSN in short), they were literally a stone's throw away from Thamel, the popular shopping district in Kathmandu. Needless to say, Shalini spent long hours getting acquainted with her new country via the shopkeepers of Thamel!

Of course, a visit to the revered Pashupatinath Mandir to seek *His* blessings as they embarked on this new journey was mandatory as well.

It took about a week for Ajai to relieve his predecessor, Col Chaturvedi, before he was cleared to assume charge as the Pension Paying Officer at Dharan.

They flew to the nearest airport of Biratnagar in Eastern part of Nepal on the appointed day.

This was the day when the true reality of how their next few years would go, dawned upon Shalini and Ajai.

While in Kathmandu, Ajai had been one of the hundreds of diplomats in town, here in the eastern past of Nepal, he was the only diplomat from any country that was to be permanently based here.

From Biratnagar, they drove down to Dharan. The drive was yet another beautiful one, passing through a lot of primary forests. It reminded them of the final leg of the road journey from Delhi to Dehradun when the road enters the thickly forested hills of Mohand Pass. So the drive didn't seem entirely new to them.

With the benefit of hindsight, it wouldn't be wrong to say that it was yet another homecoming for Shalini and Ajai, for Dharan would create such beautiful memories of them that it would find a permanent place in their hearts.

The quaint little town, nestled in the lap of the mighty Himalayas was (and continues to be) an amazing place.

Unlike previous postings, this time there already was a beautiful house waiting for Shalini to do her magic and create it into yet another nest for her family. Thanks to the small complement of staff at the PPO Dharan, it was already ready to move in. It was akin to a *Type-V* Bungalow, with a large lawn on which Shalini would soon cast her magic touch!

The work on creating the campus of PPO Dharan had just been completed and Ajai's predecessor, Major Arvind Chaturvedi and his team had worked hard and the campus looked really beautiful.

In fact, the house was so new that Major and Mrs Chaturvedi had barely stayed there for the last two months of their tenure.

Shalini and her brood spent the first two days in a guest room as protocol required a few days overlap between the outgoing PPO and the new incumbent. And as it turned out, the outgoing couple utilized those two days acquainting Shalini and Ajai with all the prominent locals of Dharan, apart from Major Chaturvedi teaching Ajai the nitty-gritties of the professional tasks that he was mandated to execute.

As it would turn out, these local acquaintances would be a godsend for the naturally outgoing person that Shalini was, as she built her own nest in Dharan, especially with Ajai spending at least ten days a month travelling to various parts of East Nepal for 'Pension Disbursement Camps'.

The Dharan tenure gave great independence to Shalini to spread her own wings, since even though he was only a Major, Ajai's was an independent and reasonably detached appointment with no immediate superiors in location. Needless to say, she made full use of it and blossomed into her own as the days in Dharan passed by!

Ajai's new job made him responsible for all Indian Armed Forces' Ex-Servicemen in all of Eastern Nepal. This was a huge responsibility indeed, for it involved not just disbursement of pensions (which in the late 90s was still disbursed in cash during Pension Camps on designated days), but also, as is the ethos of the Indian Army, about their well-being in all respects.

This latter part of his *unofficial* responsibilities could entail anything from rectifying errors in official documentation to even helping tide over domestic disputes or children's education / careers.

It was here that Shalini would soon become a respected 'elder' in the local community, regardless of her age, for her uncanny ability to connect with the ladies and veterans of the local community and help ameliorate their issues, with or without the help of the official setup under Ajai.

What awed even her husband was the fact that Shalini, at such a young age, was able to become not just one with the local Nepali community, but also create her own space as a trusted advisor.

But as far as Shalini was concerned, she was merely doing what came so naturally to her, thanks to the blessing of empathy that the Almighty had bestowed upon her as His favourite child.

Of course, she also made sincere and often laborious efforts on her own part to get to know the community. These came in the form of her accompanying Ajai to many of the Pension Camps that he would embark upon, whenever possible.

The first such camp that she accompanied Ajai to was in the small town of Tehrathum. The site for the camp entailed a 2.5km walk from the Tehrathum Bazar, which she gladly undertook in the company of Ajai.

The routine in such camps was such that Ajai would invariably get quite some free time. Whenever Shalini accompanied, the two would end up spending the evenings playing cards while relishing the staple Nepali dishes of momos and other such non-veg dishes.

Such journeys that Shalini made with Ajai, helped her know the Indian Ex-servicemen community as well as the rest of the local community in much of the Eastern part of Nepal.

She got a good glimpse into the factors that go into the making of a typical Gorkha soldier who is renowned for his cheerful nature as well as deadly soldierly instincts. She saw for herself the circumstances that they lived in and the hardships they faced, as also the way they continued to retain their typical cheerful nature despite everything.

The camps were invariably in remote areas and without many amenities. Yet Shalini would make it a point to accompany her husband on every opportunity that she got. This, when she could have just as easily stayed home with the kids and lived in the lap of relative luxury at the PPO Campus itself.

But then, her curiosity and wanderlust ensured that she ended up exploring just about as much of rural Nepal as her husband, despite the very basic road, health and other infrastructure there at that time.

It wouldn't be wrong to say that this city-born girl matured much beyond her years by getting to know the humble circumstances which still produced some of the best soldiers in the world and in fact, an excellent stock of human beings – full of life and empathy. Just like Shalini.

No wonder she fitted so well into the local community out there.

Pretty soon, she also became very fluent in Nepali language. To be fair, she had picked up the basics of the language while in the Unit with Ajai, but she truly mastered the language during her days in Nepal.

Unsurprisingly, Abhinav and Sanjana too took to the language like natives and before long, Nepali became the lingua franca in Shalini's household, with even routine day-to-day talks within the four of them happening in Nepali!

This way she covered a large number of interior areas of Nepal with Ajai. Having grown up amidst the hills of Dehradun and Mussoorie, she fell in total and unconditional love with the Himalayas all over again, including the friendly people that called Nepal their home.

Shalini developed a lot of intimate friendships with a large number of ladies in and around Dharan, once again thanks to her outgoing and social nature that perfectly synced with most of the locals out there.

Meanwhile, there was also a substantial Indian community in Dharan which was steadily building up at about the same time as Shalini and Ajai reached there.

Much of the reason for that was that a Multi-Specialty Hospital was under construction in Dharan at that time, as a goodwill act by the Govt of India.

The project itself had been conceived a few years ago when Mr Chandrashekhar was the Indian Prime Minister. He had a good rapport with Prime Minister G P Koirala of Nepal and had promised to build a hospital close to the India-Nepal border.

The location initially proposed was Biratnagar, but the Govt of Nepal was unable to find suitable land over there. Then fate intervened and it was realized that the British Army, which had a bustling Regimental Centre in Dharan were vacating it. That establishment included a 100-bedded hospital, including accommodation for the staff of that hospital.

Thus, it was a no-brainer that it would be the best place to set-up the proposed hospital. The hospital was called the BP Koirala Institute of Health and Sciences (BPKIHS) sited at Ghopa Camp, Dharan.

So a lot of Indian doctors, including quite a few super-specialists from AIIMS as well as engineers from the CPWD were there to set-up the hospital. Major Chaturvedi had also taken care to acquaint Ajai with them all before moving out of Dharan, leaving Ajai and Shalini to find their own space within that milieu.

All said and done, the Indian community in Dharan was fairly large and diverse as well when you counted the wives and children too. Of course, the Marwari business community was well represented in Dharan, with some of them having earned good riches thanks to their business acumen. They all looked up to Ajai, who was the representative of the Indian Embassy to them, akin to a 'mini-ambassador'!

Another benefit of such a large Indian community in Dharan was the local branch of the Delhi Public School which had followed them there! Thus, Abhinav and Sanjana's studies could proceed uninterrupted.

As days progressed, Ajai did end up facilitating a lot of their work with the Indian Embassy in Kathmandu, thus actually earning the sobriquet of 'mini-ambassador' that was earlier used in jest!

Even though his work was demanding, Ajai and Shalini went all-out in establishing personal bonds with the local community – both Indian and Nepalese. The fact that he was the lone Indian Embassy representative in Eastern Nepal gave him a natural head start, with him being akin to a VVIP in that area. But what endeared him and Shalini to the entire community out there was not their stature, but instead it was their warm hearts that welcomed everyone with equal affection.

In fact, many of the acquaintances made in the late 1990s in Nepal continue strong to this day, even after more than a quarter century.

Meanwhile, with the benefit of hindsight, Ajai could also see that destiny had been immensely kind to him in denying the earlier opportunity to get posted to Nepal in 1991, and delaying it to 1997 instead. What had transpired in this duration was that there was now a substantial jump in emoluments to army personnel in Nepal, just before Ajai joined. These amounted to the tune of more than Rs 1 Lac per month in addition to the basic salary as authorized in normal course of things.

This was a very substantial amount for a Major whose basic salary was Rs 11,600 in 1997!

Unsurprisingly, it gave Shalini and Ajai a *lot* of financial freedom.

This gave them a different perspective of shopping at the bustling market of Dhulabari on the Nepal side of Nepal-India border near Siliguri.

Earlier, while doing the Basic Mountaineering Course in HMI, Darjeeling, Ajai had visited this market as a tourist to pick up a lot of stuff that was otherwise not available in India. Now, Shalini and he would go there in a diplomatic vehicle for the same shopping, this time with a lot more money to spend.

And Shalini didn't hesitate in doing so, but with a good reason.

The house was new and needed to be made into a home, and that too as a home worthy of hosting senior diplomats, army officers as well govt officials including Ministers every once in a while.

They spent almost Rs 4.5 Lac on their first shopping trip to Dhulabari!

The shops there knew that Indian Army personnel from both sides of the border were some of their major clientele and were accordingly stocked, to be able to fulfill their typical requirements. Thus, they were able to get all their requirements from just a handful of shops on a single street despite spending so much.

Over time, Shalini was able to home in on to 2-3 shops and do her bulk of shopping at Dhulabari and as was her connection, soon she wouldn't even need to visit them in person any more. Instead she would just call them up on the phone and they would send her whatever she wanted (and often, whatever that they thought she *might* want as well!) to her in Dharan itself.

Shalini's home was ready as per her liking in record time, which was just as well because Dharan was one of the 'must visit' places for any Indian dignitaries visiting Nepal and as a Major's wife, she was soon hosting Service Chiefs, Ambassadors, other senior officers and once, even the Foreign Minister of India, Mr Jaswant Singh who was accompanied by General Ved Prakash Malik, the then Army Chief with their spouses and General Ashok Mehta (Retired).

She shone in her role as a hostess. Hosting prominent as well as other regular local guests did wonders to her confidence in her own abilities as well, having moved on from young Lieutenants and Captains as her guests to a much different crowd. In addition, she and Ajai would travel to Kathmandu often, where they would interact with the Nepalese Royalty and the top echelons of Nepal Army.

One thing that Lt Gen Ajai still remembers about those get-togethers at their Dharan residence is the way Shalini organized everything, especially the meals.

From a young girl who didn't know much about cooking less than a decade earlier, Shalini had now blossomed into a master of culinary skills! So much so that meals served by her were talked about by all that were fortunate enough to have tasted them.

Such was the expertise that she had gained that she could prepare a meal fit for a King, with practically no advance notice at all. Her kitchen was nothing short of a well-organized workshop where she practiced her culinary art.

She did have a cook to help her out, but his tasks were only limited to preparatory actions such as cutting and chopping vegetables, because when it came to cooking, she preferred to do it herself from beginning to the end.

She was highly methodical in the kitchen when it came to preparing meals for guests. So methodical in fact, that at times Ajai would end up wondering when did she cook at all!

Shalini would be up early in the morning and tell the cook how she wanted the preparations done with respect to cutting etc, while she prepared the *masala* for the dishes.

Thus working together, Shalini and her cook would have all dishes prepared in the morning itself, only needing to reheat them in the evening before serving. This way, she could be the perfect hostess by spending more time with the guests than in the kitchen.

Dharan's beauty coupled with Shalini's ability to be a fantastic hostess, made the then Indian Ambassador to Nepal, Mr KV Rajan and his wife fall in love with the place. He being a keen tennis player, the tennis court in the PPO Dharan was an added attraction and he would make it a point to have a couple of early morning games of tennis with Ajai and the doctors of BPKIHS, regardless of how late at night their social functions ended. *At least a few of his trips to Dharan were made with the underlying, unofficial reason being his longing to play a game or two of tennis in that beautiful place!*

Amongst all of her preparations, *Chicken Stew* was the most awaited one by guests and family alike. Reason for this was that it was Shalini's favourite dish as well, learnt from the best chef in the world – her own mother!

Pretty soon, it was the favourite dish of many folks in Dharan as well!

Shalini's transition from a novice cook to a true master of the art was a treat to watch for those who knew!

But once again, it wasn't all play and no work out there, lest someone get that impression!

Ajai worked really hard, staying away from home for at least two weeks each month, trekking nearly 80-90 kilometres to various Pension Disbursement Camps. And in addition, being from the 11th Gorkha Rifles which recruited primarily from Eastern parts of Nepal, he was amongst his own Regimental Ex-servicemen. So the connection with them was very deep.

In fact Major Ajai Kumar Singh was the first PPO from 11th Gorkha Rifles to have been posted to PPO Dharan in more than a decade!

Thus, going beyond the call of duty to ameliorate their issues was the most natural thing for Ajai and even Shalini to do. In case of Ajai, it mostly pertained to rectifying incomplete / faulty documentation which the Ex-servicemen from Nepal were very prone to do, while in the case of Shalini, it was mostly in terms of making them feel welcome whenever they travelled to PPO Dharan.

The PPO had a large and well-furnished dormitory earmarked for such visiting pensioners since there were hardly any lodgings available for renting in that part of Nepal at that time. Shalini took it upon herself to look after their well-being while they were there.

Thus, she would frequently visit the dormitory as well as the kitchen in order to ensure that not only were the visiting pensioners lodged comfortably but were also fed well. Of course, such visits would often get prolonged by her sitting down to chat with them over a cup of tea ever so often!

Apart from them, Shalini also similarly looked after the welfare of the small complement of staff at the PPO Dharan, comprising a handful of soldiers, clerks and medical personnel in addition to a sizable chunk of local employees as well.

With Ajai being on the move for nearly half a month every month, Shalini soon became an unofficial 'go to' person for many of the pensioners looking for resolution of issues.

Thus passed the blissful three years in Dharan, one day at a time. It was truly the best time of their lives for them all to be staying together as a family.

But Shalini's health woes continued unabated throughout her Dharan days as well. In fact, in a way, it became worse.

A couple of years prior, while Ajai was preparing for the Staff College Entrance Exam in Mussoorie, one evening when they were together, Shalini said to him that something was happening with her health and that she was unable to feel the left side of her body. She was losing sensation in parts of her body.

Ajai quickly called for a doctor and after a preliminary investigation he discovered that Shalini's blood pressure was very high, as much as 220/110. She was now also suffering from heart palpitations.

Thankfully that episode subsided after some time and Shalini was back to normal.

That was the first time she had such an episode. Unfortunately, it wasn't the last time, and such episodes continued through her days in Nepal as well. Over time, they realized that these were triggered by some emotional trauma, which could be in the form of an argument with Ajai, or any other such incident.

Those days, her youngest brother Amit was not doing too well in his studies and was also suffering from a lot of personal issues. Shalini was always very concerned about him, and he being her youngest sibling was very close to her. Naturally, Shalini would spend a lot of time worrying about Amit and whenever any negative news about Amit came, it would have a hugely negative impact on Shalini's health, often triggering fresh episodes of high BP and heart palpitations.

Typically, such episodes would subside within a couple of hours and her heart would be back to normal, with a normal blood pressure. Shalini would always seem in good health.

Naturally, they consulted many doctors over the years, but none were able to pinpoint the cause of these issues. Dharan gave them another opportunity to consult some of the best doctors of India who were right next door, and good personal friends as well.

These doctors too tried their best, but were unable to diagnose the problem. In fact, they found Shalini's heart to be absolutely fine. They even tested her for Pheochromocytoma, a condition that makes the adrenaline gland pump large quantities of the hormone in the bloodstream, affecting the heart. But that too was ruled out.

Ultimately, even though she kept suffering from these episodes, though not very frequently, even the super specialists in the BP Koirala Institute of Health and Sciences couldn't pinpoint the reason why.

Moreover, since these episodes would subside on their own after a short while, and her vitals would return to normal, neither did they prescribe any medicines to Shalini for keeping her blood pressure in check.

This was the way Shalini continued her Nepal days.

Gratefully, the blood pressure spike episodes were few and far between. So they carried on living their normal family life, making full use of the facilities and benefits that came with this diplomatic assignment in one of the most beautiful parts of the world.

The family would often move out on small treks amongst the many beautiful hills around their abode in Dharan. The kids being young, such treks would last just for a few hours, with Shalini packing lunch for them all to have at a suitable place, free from all distractions.

Then came the episode of perhaps *the* most adventurous trek for Shalini as she accompanied Ajai to yet another Pension Camp at a mighty remote part of Nepal in Diktel!

Since Shalini was accompanying, Ajai decided to take a flight to Diktel instead of the long, back-breaking road journey over non-existent roads. Diktel was a longish, six-hour long trek from the nearest landing strip at a place called Lami Danda.

A Twin Otter aircraft would fly there from Biratnagar, with tickets subsidized by the Govt of Nepal as a welfare measure for those staying in such remote places. It was an interesting set-up, with goats and hens accompanying human flyers in those small aircraft many times!

The airfield at Lami Danda had an unpaved, *kutcha* landing strip that doubled up as a pasture ground for the cattle. The normal drill was for the ATC to sound a siren just before the aircraft was to land so that the landing strip could be cleared of the many animals merrily grazing there!

The aircrafts were quite old, but in the hands of experienced pilots, there were hardly any issues. Hats off indeed to those pilots who would expertly enter the narrow valley that housed Lami Danda, needing to circle many times over to lose altitude for a safe landing. There was hardly any scope for error whatsoever. Hats off also to the passengers who would be scared to within an inch of life with the aircraft seeming to nearly crash into the hills before taking a steep banking turn as it approached and departed Lami Danda in that valley.

However, what made this one time especially memorable was due to a stubborn, non-cooperative four legged creature who decided to go on a strike!

What happened was that as always, with Shalini accompanying Ajai, the Secretary of the Zila Sainik Board had arranged for a mule for Shalini to ride on as they climbed up towards Diktel. Unfortunately, that particular day, the mule handler just couldn't coax the mule into obeying his commands. Seeing the animal so jittery, Shalini too decided she wouldn't be riding on it.

Now this created a Catch-22 situation for Ajai since the next flight out of Lami Danda was only after two days. Pretty soon, everyone concerned saw the writing on the wall – Shalini would have to cover the distance to Diktel on foot, with all others.

It was a case of really bad timing because the trek to Diktel was perhaps the toughest one in all of Eastern Nepal, with an uphill climb right from the word *go.* Enroute were 8-9 false crests that gave you a feeling of having reached the top of the feature, only to find yet another *top* staring you in the face!

Ajai was aware of the challenge facing Shalini because he had climbed that route earlier. He chose the best possible course of action – He didn't tell her about the magnitude of the effort that she had just volunteered to make!

In spite of Shalini realizing that Ajai wasn't giving her the correct picture, she also knew that there was no other option. Hanging on to the false optimism offered to her by her husband, she started the climb.

It was bright and sunny already by the time they commenced climbing, thanks to the leisurely speed of the Twin Otter that had brought them there and the time wasted by the mule.

The beginning of the climb itself was steep, stony and full of loose gravel, pretty much setting the tone for what was to come next.

Understandably, Shalini started slowly and chose to maintain that pace throughout the next eight hours or so! But jokes apart, through sheer grit and willpower, she kept on climbing without any complaints and with short breaks at regular intervals to catch her breath and rest her limbs.

Ajai too tried to make it a bit easier for her and kept on promising that the next crest would be the final one. After hearing this six or seven times, Shalini understood what he was trying to do, but still didn't complain, perhaps even to keep husband motivated so that he doesn't feel as much guilt for putting her through this difficult journey than what he already must have been feeling!

The little bunch kept on climbing, with Shalini dictating the pace.

Enroute, about halfway through, they encountered an old Nepalese couple on the track. When they saw the struggle that Shalini was going through, they very nearly *ordered* her to sit with them for a while and offered her a generous helping of curd and *sattu* that they were carrying.

Such were and still are, the beautiful people of Nepal that they just couldn't ignore the silent prayers which Shalini had been offering throughout this ordeal. They were not only able to hear her, but were also very happy to share the meagre rations which they themselves needed for their own sustenance.

It was almost as if the Almighty had Himself sent them there to help His favourite child, Shalini to carry on.

Suitably nourished as well as refreshed after the unplanned break in the company of the old couple, Shalini announced that she was good to recommence the trek. After offering profuse thanks, she and Ajai moved on.

The day's climb finally came to an end at about sunset, much to Shalini's relief. Ajai, while giving a massage to her tired legs, then told her that Diktel was still about three hours away!

Shalini had made her peace with this particular turn of events in her life and just gave a sigh and went off to sleep!

Thankfully, the next day's trek wasn't as difficult and the hills closer to Diktel were a lot more forgiving.

When she saw that the hospital where the temporary lodgings for Ajai and herself had been prepared required climbing down approximately one hundred steps to reach, Shalini, without a moment's hesitation, declared that she would not climb back up those stairs till the time they were in Diktel!

Thus every morning Ajai would plod up those 100 stairs for the Pension Camp while Shalini rested her tired body in the hospital! He would be back for lunch and later in the evening, once the camp was over for the day.

This way they were able to squeeze out blissful times of togetherness in each other's company in Diktel, without worrying about the house or the kids. She thoroughly enjoyed this time, catching up with a lot of reading while Ajai was away. In fact, after a couple of days of rest, she even relented to accompany him for a short sojourn to explore Diktel.

Once the camp was over, she decided she would once again walk back to Lami Danda instead of riding on a mule. Thankfully, it was mostly downhill and the trip was accomplished within a day and they were back in Dharan one day after that.

Unsurprisingly, the story of Shalini's heroic trek to Diktel became something of a folklore not just in Dharan but even in the diplomatic circles in Kathmandu itself, and was frequently the topic of discussion over many meals!

The trek to Diktel continues to be a highly challenging one even to this day.

The clock kept ticking through all this and days turned to weeks, weeks to months and months to years till one fine day Ajai got the orders for repatriation to India, having completed his three years in the assignment.

What made it even more memorable was the fact that nearly all family members were invited and hosted by the couple in Dharan, with their itineraries including exhaustive travels throughout Nepal, including visits to Kathmandu and Pokhara.

One particular guest who still remembers her visit to Dharan is Preeti, Shalini's sister-in-law. It so happened that she fell ill while in Dehradun and such was her condition that her hemoglobin count fell to an alarming level of 6. As soon as Shalini heard about this, she literally *ordered* her brother Atul to send Preeti to Dharan where she lovingly tended to her and ensured a speedy recovery for Preeti before sending her back home.

It was an emotional affair, bidding farewell to the place where their stay had not only been the happiest, but also the longest. Life went on and Shalini handed over her lovingly nurtured nest to the next occupants and accompanied her husband back home, not to her or his parents' place, but to his Battalion which was located at Ganganagar at that time.

08

THE AWAKENING: A NEW CHAPTER

Ajai joined his Battalion in Ganganagar as the Second-in-Command, or 2iC for short. Ganganagar was a fairly active station, with sizable numbers of troops there. Naturally, the social scene was equally hectic.

Shalini and Ajai's stay while in Ganganagar was short because the Battalion had already received orders to move to Siachen Glacier and Ajai being the 2iC, was to take the *Advance Party* there in order to set things in motion before the rest of the Battalion joined after a couple of months.

This time, with so much additional household items accumulated while in Nepal, they decided that Shalini and the kids would move to Dehradun but instead of staying with her parents while keeping their household packed, they would instead stay in a *Separated Family Accommodation* in the town.

When time came to pack-up the household in Ganganagar, Shalini found herself alone since Ajai was out in the deserts for a training exercise. This time she got her household packed single handedly, and even arranged for a truck to cart it all to Dehradun.

By the time Ajai came back, the bulk of the back-breaking labour had already been done, except for one small problem – Their household goods just wouldn't fit into one truck due to the amount of furniture they now had!

So finally, Ajai too got to do his bit and quickly arranged yet another truck for the balance of their furniture.

On the appointed day, the two trucks departed for Dehradun while Shalini and Ajai moved to Bhatinda from where Ajai was to catch a train for Jammu with the *Advance Party*, while Shalini would catch another train to Dehradun.

More drama followed (as always!) and Ajai just missed his train in which the rest of the *Advance Party* with Captain Pranav had moved, without him. He and Capt PCR Karki, who was to accompany him to Siachen, quickly rushed out in a jeep, hoping to catch the train at the next station.

Shalini found herself alone at the Bhatinda Railway Station, waiting for her own train that was still a few hours away. Thankfully, even though Ajai had quite the adventure, *just missing* his train at practically every station ahead, Shalini's journey to Dehradun happened without any such hitches!

For the initial part, she and the kids stayed with her parents while Ajai was processing a case for allotment of a suitable SF accommodation in Dehradun. Ultimately, that process was hastened when another officer from his Battalion, Major Karki (who himself had just got an SF accommodation allotted) informed him that there was a house near his own which was available immediately.

But as always, in this offer too there was a catch!

Maj Karki reported that the reason the house was available immediately was because no one was accepting it since it was in a very dilapidated condition!

Undeterred, Ajai took possession of the house and requested his Father-in-Law to help get it up to mark. One unintended benefit of this was also that Shalini could get certain things done in the house which she otherwise wouldn't have been able to, had it been in a *ready to move in condition*!

Once again, back home amongst friends and family, Shalini and the kids had a wonderful stay in Dehradun. This time, with Mrs Karki and her own kids too staying next door, there was a connection with the Battalion as well, in addition to many *Corridor Parties*!

As soon as Ajai was settled in his new location, prior to induction to the Siachen Glacier, he sent for Shalini and the kids to come and join him for a couple of weeks.

Accordingly, they landed up in Leh and after a couple of days of acclimatization, moved to Tangse to meet him. This route took them via the ChangLa Pass which was located at an altitude of nearly 18,000 feet.

During the course of travel, Shalini's blood pressure once again shot up, triggering the fears of another episode of uncontrolled palpitations. Medical personnel enroute advised to quickly get her to a lower altitude. Fortunately, she was already on her way to Tangse which was much lower in altitude than the ChangLa Pass and once there, her BP was back to normal.

She stayed with Ajai for almost two weeks during that trip.

It was another time of great bliss. There was a small rivulet full of fishes that flowed right next to their lodgings. Such was the abundance that the Gorkha soldiers of the Battalion could just scoop them out using their bare hands!

The day's catch would be roasted every evening for a sumptuous meal by a bonfire, trading stories and anecdotes amongst all officers and ladies that were there at that time.

When it was time for Shalini and the kids to head back to Dehradun, Ajai decided to take a longer route that would avoid the steep altitude of ChangLa Pass. Ajai decided to drive the Jeep himself, so that he could spend more time with his loved ones.

As always, the Almighty decided to add a bit of *spice* to this journey of theirs!

On the day of their travel it rained throughout, making an already picturesque drive even more enjoyable. The wipers on the vehicle turned out to be worn out and ineffective, making Ajai's job a lot more challenging.

Regardless of the plight of the driver, Shalini and the children thoroughly enjoyed the road trip. After an unhurried lunch at Chushul, the happy bunch recommenced their drive.

The going was slow, partly due to the rains and partly also because of the condition of the vehicle itself and the distance to be covered was fairly large. So naturally, when the daylight started to fade, they were still some distance away from their destination.

Now came another shock – The headlights of their vehicle were not working!

It was almost as if the Almighty was challenging them to a game of '*What Now?*'!

Thankfully, He had ensured that the non-functional headlights wouldn't be an issue, thanks to a bright moonlit night that ensured adequate ambient light for them to drive safely, even if slowly.

This part of the drive was along the mighty Indus River which kept them company throughout, guiding them gently.

It was fairly late in the evening when they reached Leh.

Over there, Lt Col IA Khan, a coursemate of Ajai's, had invited them over for dinner. Even though dead tired, Shalini made it a point of accompanying Ajai to his place. She wasn't one to decline, especially when she knew that they would have put in a lot of efforts to host them. That being said, the dinner was, understandably, a quick affair before she hit bed and was soon in a deep slumber.

The next day Shalini, along with Abhinav and Sanjana flew back to Dehradun while Ajai returned to Tangse, this time in a vehicle that seemed a bit extra empty, devoid of the presence of his loved ones.

Shalini made another trip to meet Ajai after a couple of months. This time, her journey to Tangse was planned via Chushul in order to avoid another bout of high BP like the last time.

But unknown to Shalini, Ajai had decided to surprise her by meeting her at Chushul where she was to halt for lunch. Not just that, he went a step ahead and actually hid in the guest room that was earmarked for her to freshen up before lunch.

Needless to say, the surprise was total and complete, even though Shalini would prefer to use the word *shock* instead of *surprise*!

She stayed for about 10 days with Ajai. With the rest of the Battalion having fetched up, it was nothing short of a reunion with them all.

This was to be her last trip because the Battalion soon inducted into the Northern part of the Siachen Glacier, which the army refers to as the NG (short for Northern Glacier).

Ajai, who was now a Lieutenant Colonel and the 2IC of the Battalion, was awaiting his turn to be inducted. The way things were organized, the Commanding Officer moved up with the first induction and the 2iC would induct when the second induction happened. This way the two senior most officers of the Battalion would alternate between the forward and rear echelons in order to keep things moving smoothly.

So here Ajai was, at what was referred to as the Forward Logistics Base (FLB), with the sobriquet of NG Tiger being the senior most officer in the NG.

Work at the FLB was equally critical, though, because upon them depended the hundreds of the men of the Battalion that were deployed in perhaps the most challenging battlefield anywhere in the world.

Despite that, Ajai had maintained a routine of taking a walk every morning and evening in order to stay physically fit. This was perhaps the only strenuous physical activity one could undertake in those insane altitudes.

The walk was not just physically invigorating, but the sights in that area were a joy to behold. The FLB had two beautiful lakes in the vicinity and a lot of flora and fauna that still managed to survive in those conditions.

And then it happened ..

While on one such walk, as Ajai saw the now familiar view comprising of about 70 kilometers of the glacier flanked by the mighty 20,000+ feet Himalayan peaks, something just clicked in his head.

A thought flashed ..

I am responsible for the territorial integrity of this area, and the well-being of the men that guard it. But standing here, looking at myself and my entire 'being', am I not absolutely insignificant in front of what the Almighty has created?

My presence in the midst of these towering and humbling edifices of His creation is not even worth a speck of dust in the larger scheme of things.

This was the moment of spiritual awakening of Lt Col Ajai Kumar Singh, humbled as he was with the enormity of His creation and the huge responsibility that He had chosen to bestow upon Ajai.

These thoughts made Ajai come to a realization that if he is to do justice to the responsibilities bestowed upon him by the virtue of his rank, he realized that he needs to align himself with a higher power in order to be able to discharge his duties in such diffi cult terrain and weather conditions.

They say that ascetics, who have renounced everything, are pulled to the mighty Himalayas. At that moment, Ajai realized the significance of why this was so.

There is something about the mountains, especially the Himalayas, that has such an effect on people. Standing in the midst of mountains as mighty as the Himalayas, one can finally realize how small and insignificant he is in the larger scheme of things. Once that realization sets in, the path to further spiritual progress opens up.

This is also partly the reason that people who have grown up in the hilly regions in the Himalayas seem so intrinsically happy from within. They are some of the most joyous and happy folks anywhere in the world. It is only and only because they know that the ego of Man is not to be taken too seriously, given that no creation of Man can ever match what the Almighty has created!

Lo and behold, the *Powers That Be*, opened up a path for him to follow not soon thereafter.

Ajai was visiting the Battalion's post at BilafondLa Pass. The company commander there was Major Pankaj Singh, who was Ajai's immediate junior in the Battalion.

The bond between an officer and his immediate senior or junior in the Indian Army is something that is simply out of the ordinary and transcends even the thickest of the blood relations at times.

So naturally, the two spent a large part of the night just talking.

During their conversation that night, Ajai shared his recent experience of spiritual awakening, which prompted Major Pankaj to suggest that he do a *Self Realization Fellowship* at the Yogoda Satsanga Society of India. It was a one-year programme of distance learning about *Kriya Yog* offered for a very nominal fee.

Major Pankaj was already undergoing the fellowship and showed the material he had received in the process. One look at it, and Ajai too decided to subscribe to the course, thereby embarking on his spiritual journey soon after the realization during the daily walk some time ago.

He started with the *Kriya Yog* offered by the Yogada Satsang Society. *The Autobiography of a Yogi* by Swami Paramahansa Yogananda who established the Society was amongst the first books that Ajai read as he commenced his spiritual journey.

Swami Paramahansa Yogananda was the disciple of Shri Yukteshwar Giri, who himself was from the lineage of Mahavatara

Baba, a renowned Himalayan Yogi and guru known as great avatar who is believed to be still alive.

There is an interesting story of Shri Lahiri Mahashay who was a clerk in the Military Engineering Services, posted in Ranikhet when he got a *darshan* of Mahavatara Baba at the Dronagiri Mountain. The Baba initiated him and he subsequently gave up his job and settled in Kashi, in furtherance of his own spiritual pursuits. Shri Yukteshwara Giri was one of his many illustrious disciples, in turn mentoring Swami Paramahansa Yogananda.

Shri Yukteshwara Giri had directed Swami Yogananda Paramahansa to spread the message of spiritualism in the West because he saw the West as bereft of the same, hurtling down the destructive path of meaningless materialism instead.

Back to the story of the NG Tiger, Lt Col Ajai Kumar Singh, who while exploring the path of spirituality, still had a job to do. But unlike earlier times, this time he was testing his faith as well.

Ajai wanted to ensure that the Battalion completed the tenure without a single weather-related casualty. Once at the Amar Post, which is one of the most challenging ones in Siachen, a soldier got very critically ill and the Battalion doctor called Ajai that he has to be evacuated forthwith.

This call came late in the evening. At that hour, there was no way a helicopter could come and evacuate that boy to more specialized medical care.

Ajai was firm in his resolve to avoid any weather-related casualties amongst his soldiers. But given the peculiar circumstances of that night, all that he could do was to pray for that soldier's well-being.

He kept praying throughout the night and was still in the midst of his prayers when at about 2:30 am the doctor called him again, saying that he couldn't feel the pulse in that soldier.

But unwilling to accept defeat, Ajai told the doctor to keep up his efforts at reviving the patient and that he *will* find a suitable weather window to get him evacuated.

When the morning dawned, weather conditions were marginal for helicopter flying. Ajai spent a lot of time on the military line to the base, insisting that the boy is critical and that even if there is a small window for an evacuation sortie, an attempt must be made.

And he kept praying.

And hats-off to the helicopter pilots who, realizing that a soul is in peril, decided to attempt an evacuation even in those marginal weather conditions, putting their own lives on the line.

Meanwhile the doctor told Ajai that he was able to finally detect a faint heartbeat.

Soon Ajai heard the unmistakable sound of a helicopter engine and a few minutes later, the doctor again called, saying the helicopter was there and that the soldier was being evacuated.

It was almost as if the Almighty had designed this as a test for Ajai's faith in Him. Ajai passed it with flying colours by never losing faith in the power of prayer .. in the power of a fervent appeal to Him.

That said, Lt Gen Ajai Kumar Singh still looks back at that night and often wonders who was testing whom!

A few months later when Ajai deinducted from the Glacier, he met the boy who was now hale and hearty, having been on the very verge of death earlier that year.

Thus ended the Siachen tenure, with not just professional satisfaction, but also a new beginning in the lives of Shalini and Ajai, thanks to his spiritual awakening. Shalini, as always, would follow in the wake of Ajai here as well.

With the benefit of hindsight, it can be said with reasonable confidence that the realization, or the awakening that Ajai found that day during his daily walks, was not a coincidence. True, that thousands like him would have seen the same sights of the mighty Himalayas, without coming to the realization that he did. But then, it would still be improper to call it a coincidence.

Reason for not calling it thus is that in the larger scheme of things, there are absolutely NO coincidences. Everything manifests at the time and place chosen for the same and it happened in the case of Ajai just as it had always been meant to.

It came at a time of immense joy, as Ajai would soon move on to command a sister battalion of his own regiment, and that too in Dehradun.

It also came at the dawn of intense challenges that Shalini and he would soon find themselves in, thanks to her medical condition.

In a way, it empowered them both not just to become good and benevolent leaders of their military family, but also to resolutely and more importantly, cheerfully face the immense challenges that were capable of easily breaking apart any individual.

They not just faced the challenges, they made sure that they were mere 'side-notes' in their journey of togetherness.

Shalini suffered through immense pain, but retained her smile throughout, right till her very last moment.

And Ajai carries on still, bearing the weight of immense responsibilities that come with a high rank, while staying focused on the ultimate goal, that of spiritual ascent of the soul.

09

THOSE WERE THE BEST OF THE DAYS...

Sometime in the first few months of the year 2003, Shalini and both kids were again in Leh with Ajai and the rest of the Battalion as they were winding up the Siachen tenure, soaking in the beautiful place and of course, the company of their beloved Unit personnel.

One afternoon as the entire family were relaxing in the 2iC's lodgings, Ajai received a much anticipated and much awaited phone call. The kids and Shalini remained quiet, as was usual whenever he received any official phone calls in his room.

But this time it was a bit different.

This time there was a sense of anticipation.

As expected, Ajai had a smile on his face as he put the receiver down and turned back towards his family.

'First Eleven', he said, and the entire room burst into shrieks of joy. A bunch of chocolates lying about were shared around amongst all four in celebration.

What had happened was that Lt Col Ajai Kumar Singh had recently been approved for the rank of Colonel after a Selection Board some weeks ago and had received a phone call from his dear friend Lt Col Atulya Solankey. Atulya had informed Ajai that he had been slotted to take over command of First Eleven Gorkha Rifles, a sister Battalion from the same Regiment.

It was a moment of great joy, for the command of a battalion is something that every officer aspires to, yet it was bittersweet because Shalini and Ajai's own battalion, 7/11 Gorkha Rifles was not due for a turnover and he was instead slated to take over 1/11 Gorkha Rifles.

This would mean a final farewell to Shalini and Ajai's parent battalion, and moving on to another one that they had never been to before. Given that both battalions were from the same regiment and with the same stock of soldiers, but ones that weren't personally known to Shalini and Ajai.

At another level, it was a thing of joy as well, especially since 1/11 GR had just moved to Dehradun.

Shalini was headed back home for the second time after marriage, this time as the First Lady of a highly decorated infantry battalion.

Even as congratulatory messages kept pouring in, Shalini's mind was already racing ahead. She and the kids were already living in a *separated family* accommodation in Dehradun and now she would need to shift to another, more suitable one closer to the cantonment.

She had to plan well because even though Ajai would take a couple of months to fulfill his responsibilities in Leh before he could reach Dehradun to take over command of the battalion, she was already there!

In this case the battalion was already well-settled in the location and being the CO's wife, Shalini would have to have her household up and running at the earliest in order to be ready to host the large numbers of social engagements that come with the job.

Thankfully, once Ajai took over command of the Battalion in May 2003 and got allotted suitable accommodation, the ever efficient Shalini did the unthinkable and declared her new home fit to receive the first of their guests in less than a week!

What followed were the best of the days indeed ..

Unsurprisingly, Shalini shone bright in her role as the *First Lady* of the battalion. True to her nature, she soon got to know the nearly 300 ladies of the officers, JCOs and other ranks of the battalion that were there in Dehradun, while also endearing herself to them all.

From being the elder sister to two brothers, Shalini had become the elder sister to nearly 300 sisters as well. She was just as fond of them as she was of her brothers.

Shalini was very fond of *her* ladies and they too reciprocated wholeheartedly. This showed in the way they all came together in organizing the various family-oriented activities as part of peacetime soldiering.

For the uninitiated, it might be pertinent to point out that whenever a typical Indian Army Battalion is deployed in a 'Peace Station', a large number of officers, JCOs and other ranks also get their wives and children to stay with them in order to get some years of family life.

However, typically, these ladies and children are not localites of that town / city and hence, need to be not only guided on occasion but also kept engaged in fruitful activities in order to make-up for the immense distance from their blood-relations back in their own villages.

This is all the more pronounced in the case of Gorkha troops since many of them actually hail from Nepal!

Thus, a typical infantry battalion of the Indian Army in peacetime is a really big and happy family. Being the senior most lady of the Battalion, it is on the shoulders of the CO's wife that the responsibility of keeping them engaged as well as happy rests.

The families were kept engaged with a plethora of formal and informal activities which entailed a fair amount of preparation. In addition, interested ladies were imparted skills in various disciplines at various institutes being run by the Welfare Organisation. There was also the day-to-day well-being of the ladies and their children that needed to be looked after by the CO's wife, duly assisted by wives of other officers.

This is the role Shalini found herself in, and soon carved out a reputation of being one of the most loved senior ladies in the Station.

She did have some experience of such a role while in Tibri some years ago. However, that was from the perspective of the

Adjutant's wife. The role of the maternal head of the Unit family was something that could not be taught, and yet, she seemed born for it as she settled down in her responsibilities.

Now, representing the Battalion ladies in various fora amongst her peers and wives of other senior officers, it was natural that there would be clashes of personalities at times. Being the gentle soul that she was, Shalini was never one to indulge in petty politics or score-keeping and kept her head down and did her best, whatever be the circumstances.

So much so, that at times it even meant additional workload on occasions. She would ensure that her ladies weren't unduly burdened and many times she chose to take on the extra tasks by herself, without delegating it further.

Thankfully, such instances were few and far between, yet they would put her under tremendous stress because she would hardly ever pass on the stress to the other ladies of the battalion.

Thus went on her life as the *First Lady* of the Battalion.

Ajai and Shalini had embraced their new battalion with all the love that their hearts held, and the battalion too reciprocated in equal measure. Overall, it was one big, happy family, with Ajai commanding the men of the battalion and Shalini looking after the ladies.

All of them worked really hard, and partied even harder!

An added advantage was that Shalini was back in her own hometown and with her family as well. Her father was by then, established as a big lawyer in Dehradun and her brothers were settling down in their own careers as lawyers.

Shalini's own reputation as an empathetic *First Lady* spread soon.

She had prepared herself well for the role through past experiences as a *fauji* wife in peace and field, with her husband and separated, in different Units and assignments. Through it all, she had been a quick learner, especially because she kept her eyes and ears open.

Her naturally affable nature endeared her to her new family right from the word go. She never put on any false airs of being the senior most lady of the Battalion, and instead, connected with all at a very human level.

As mentioned above, peace-time soldiering was often very busy and demanding, especially for the families due to the host of organized welfare activities. Thankfully for the ladies of the Battalion, Shalini was able to steer her flock through it all with great dexterity and grace.

She was also ably assisted by a good mix of ladies, from those that were experienced old hands with respect to army life, to totally green newlyweds as well!

Another key helping hand in all this was the Subedar Major of the Battalion, Deo Mani Rai. He was a war veteran and a decorated soldier, having earned a Sena Medal during an audacious operation in Assam in the early 90s. But here, part of his responsibilities included family welfare activities for the wives of JCOs and other ranks and he excelled in that as well.

Together, the men and women of the Battalion ensured that spirits were always high and everyone remained in good cheer always, at times even to the envy of others in the Dehradun Cantonment!

The Battalion created a niche for itself in the Station when it came to family welfare activities, thanks majorly to the naturally confident and outgoing Gorkha ladies who are ever-ready to adapt to new circumstances, ably marshaled by Shalini and the Subedar Major of the Battalion.

The cultural events that they showcased, the in-house entertainment programmes that they conducted and the enthusiasm with which they participated in the various Station-level and even Unit-level competitions, soon had everyone in awe of them

In spite of being busy, Shalini ensured that the plethora of activities didn't become a burden on the ladies who too deserved to be able to spend a good amount of time with their husbands. To that end, she wasn't beyond saying *no* either.

One such example came about pretty early during the Dehradun tenure.

The Battalion location had a very good *Motivation Hall* that also doubled up as a makeshift auditorium whenever occasion demanded. This was also the most suitable place for organizing central AWWA functions in the entire Brigade.

It so happened that the wife of a senior officer from Ambala was to visit Dehradun and wished to interact with the ladies of the Station. Naturally, the choice for venue fell on the Battalion's *Motivation Hall*, and ladies of 1/11 Gorkha Rifles put up a cultural programme for the guest.

That was hardly an issue, though.

However, what created a minor flutter in the Brigade ladies' circle was that when the Brigade Commander's wife called up Shalini on a Saturday and suggested a rehearsal of the cultural programme the next day, Shalini promptly refused!

Her refusal was prompted by the knowledge that Ajai had passed an order that no soldiers or families were to be involved in any additional tasking on Sundays in order for them to have the entire day as *family time.*

Moreover, the visit of the senior lady was still quite some time away, so Shalini was prompt and unapologetic in declining to have the rehearsal on a Sunday.

Somehow, it was not taken in the right spirit by the Brigade Commander's wife. This resulted in the venue for the event getting shifted to the neighbouring battalion of the brigade. But their own venue was in a dilapidated condition. Unsurprisingly, the event venue soon shifted back to the *Khukri Hall,* of 1/11 Gorkha Rifles.

Unperturbed and without any rancour or ill-feeling, Shalini went about organizing the event to the best of her abilities. She was at her proactive best and ensured that the event showcased the best that her battalion had to offer.

Unfortunately, the ill-feeling continued and in the words of Shalini, on the day of the event, the Brigade Commander's wife would still not talk with her. In fact, she appeared to just see through Shalini even when they were face to face!

Knowing Shalini and her no-nonsense attitude, it wasn't surprising that despite being the CO's wife and the custodian of the venue, she chose *not* to sit in the front row despite a seat earmarked for her, and sat in the second row with her own Battalion ladies.

In the end, this minor issue got tided over and the misunderstanding soon forgotten, thanks to Shalini just being her natural, endearing self.

Bottomline is that Shalini took a lot of pains in order to ensure that her ladies were well looked after. But despite that, she wasn't beyond administering adequate doses of *tough love* either, whenever the situation demanded. Resultantly, despite so many varied personalities, the ladies of her battalion hardly had any interpersonal issues amongst them.

She led her family by personal example as well.

One simple, yet profound thing that she did to that end was to ensure that she herself was always well-dressed. In fact, she would always dress up very fondly and with great care. Her reason for that was simple. She would say, *If I dress well, my ladies too will dress well.*

And dress well they all did!

This was borne merely by the fact that Shalini wanted to lead by example, and because her ladies were equally keen to *follow* her.

Such was the endearment that Shalini had earned in a totally new environment in a very short period of time!

On a personal front, the household responsibilities involved looking after two energetic teenagers who were not just in one of the most challenging phases of young adulthood, but also preparing for Class X and XII Board Exams respectively.

Shalini ensured that her kids were not neglected in the wake of her responsibilities as the CO's wife, especially since Ajai didn't have much time to devote due to his own commitments as the CO.

Moreover, the 16-year old Abhinav was also in the midst of a 'rebellious' phase for a while in this duration and needed to be handled with sensitivity as well as strictness, together.

Shalini handled it all pretty much single handedly and ensured that both her kids blossomed into beautiful young people.

This also meant that she had to push herself hard. Whenever there was a central welfare or social event being planned, Shalini would make sure that she took care of her responsibilities when the kids were away to school. She would invariably be back home before the kids returned and would be there with them throughout the rest of the day, ensuring that they ate in time and sat down for their studies soon thereafter.

Along with them, Shalini, at the prodding of her sister-in-law, also enrolled into a graduation programme in order to complete her own studies that had got interrupted due to early marriage.

However, instead of being shy or apologetic about the same, she took it as yet another opportunity to motivate her Battalion ladies using herself as an example!

She would emphasise the importance of education to them and that they should empower themselves to be independent and capable of running the household affairs when their husbands were away on field postings.

As a result, quite a few of the Unit ladies ended up completing their own schooling / graduation while in Dehradun.

Of course with her own kids in classes X and XII, they would all study together quite often, with Shalini doing her own assignments and solving equations as Abhinav and Sanjana themselves studied for their own exams!

Shalini staying up almost all night to study wasn't a very rare occurrence. Such was her devotion and passion to earn a graduate degree for herself.

That said, she was never fond of putting on too much make-up. A simple bindi and some lipstick and she would be ready for anything in file! However, one exception to this rule of hers was the Karva Chauth. On that day, she would go all out to be dressed, almost like a new bride!

A bright red saree would be her garment of choice on Karva Chauth, along with a full dab of sindoor. She would dress up very fondly, with her best ornaments adding on to her charm in addition to her *Mangal Sutra* that she wore everyday. Mehndi would be applied on her hands with great care and planning as well. All this, for the continued well-being and long life of her husband whom she loved so dearly.

At the same time, family commitments too were never-ending, with the bulk of Shalini's family in Dehradun, and Ajai's family in Roorkee, not very far away. She was not just handling the role of the *First Lady* of the Battalion, but also a daughter and a *Bahurani* as well.

Almost every weekend and sometimes during the weekdays as well, Shalini and her family would be at her parents' place for a meal since they didn't live too far from the cantonment. There were also the innumerable functions in the extended family which couldn't be skipped.

At times, however, Ajai would be unable to accompany them due to his own official commitments. Whenever asked about his absence she would very politely, yet candidly affirm that she was there to represent them both since Ajai had huge responsibilities and commitments by the virtue of being the head of an even larger family.

In essence, Shalini was living that phase of her life not for herself, but for so many others. Not that she was complaining about it, but it did end up with her ignoring her own health, with a really unfortunate outcome.

In between, she would have episodes of headache which gradually turned into occasional bouts of intense migraine. She would try and manage these with painkillers, but unknown to anyone, she had high blood pressure which was only diagnosed much later.

Yet, life in Dehradun continued unabated. The entire household as well as the families' part of life in the Battalion revolved almost entirely around Shalini, who too had immersed herself totally into it all.

Through it all, she never once complained because she knew that as a Commanding Officer, Ajai's was an onerous responsibility. She was aware that during that appointment, his primary responsibility was towards his Battalion and that she would have to be the primary caretaker of the family.

Shalini was a great support to Ajai, whatever be the situation. Her total and unwavering support made Ajai's job that much easier, on the personal and social fronts as well. Together, they were the ideal *First Couple* for the battalion, and it showed in how the battalion itself responded to them.

It wasn't *all work and no play* either. Especially not with them being in Shalini's home town!

Many evenings, Ajai, Shalini and the kids would be going out visiting the town. At times, other officers and ladies of the battalion too would accompany them and it would become a great social event, many times an impromptu one!

Together the team of officers and their ladies, all bonded extremely well during that tenure.

The happy team had a magical impact on not just the way they overcame whatever challenges that came their way, but also the way they were seen by the other Battalions and higher headquarters in the Station.

One very fine example of this camaraderie in action came by during the Raising Day celebrations of the Battalion in September 2003. Having done with the in-house functions with the troops and their families, it was now time for inviting all officers and ladies of the Station to the Battalion Officers' Mess for dinner.

The ladies, duly marshalled by Shalini, had worked really hard in decking up the Mess for the occasion. As they were finishing, dark monsoon clouds started appearing in the skies above.

Everyone was praying for Lord Indra to spare them from showers at least till the time the Mess function was done. However, He refused to oblige and just 30 minutes before the time for guests' arrival, a heavy downpour commenced.

It was possibly the heaviest downpour of that year's monsoon!

So much so that Shalini and Ajai had to literally wade through a mini-river that was flowing furiously right by the entrance of the Mess!

Instead of getting disheartened by this turn of events, the team of officers, ladies and other ranks of the Battalion rose to the challenge and reworked the administrative arrangements in record time.

Fortunately, Ajai had had the foresight of having a small waterproof Shamiana erected by the entrance of the Mess, which proved to be a great saviour!

Incidentally, it wasn't just the team of the Battalion that rose to the challenge, the guests themselves too were not cowed down by the *minor* inconvenience of the intense downpour.

It was partly to do with the fact that 1/11 GR was one of the most renowned and respected Battalions in the Station, known for their famous victories in the relatively recent Kargil War, as well as for their large-hearted hospitality.

At some level, it might also have been due to the curiosity amongst at least a few of the invitees to see how the Battalion would deal with this sudden turn of weather.

Unsurprisingly, almost all invitees made it a point of showing up for the dinner!

There was no way that the sitting arrangements outside in the lawns could be made use of due to the rains. Even the chairs that were laid out for that purpose were drenched due to the suddenness of the rains. So the Mess was choc-a-bloc with a sea of humanity that night!

The waiters entrusted with looking after the guests had no way to navigate this sea with their trays, or even to ensure that everyone was served. So a new method came into being – drinks and snacks were circulated by the guests themselves, with a tag of *to whom it may concern!*

One of the first orders passed by Ajai that night was for the Battalion's in-house band to start playing some music. Soon the gifted musicians of the Battalion had everyone in their thrall, including perhaps Lord Indra himself, for the unceasing tip-tap of raindrops only added to the melody of the lovely numbers being dished out by the band non-stop!

The next act by Col Ajai Kumar Singh that evening had everyone holding their breaths. What he did was to walk up to the Chief Guest of the evening, Major General Gangadharan and his wife, and ask them to join Shalini and him on the dance floor!

Once the Chief Guest and his wife were on the dance floor with the hosts, everyone else too joined in pretty soon and resultantly, the rainfall was soon forgotten. There was much joy in the air and sarees dirtied by the rainwater and slush was a small price to pay.

In fact, quite a few ladies walked up to Ajai before leaving the Mess, jokingly threatening to send their dry-cleaning bills to him for reimbursement!

That evening was unlike any other Mess function anywhere in the Indian military. Far from being perturbed or disheartened by the weather, the infectious enthusiasm of Shalini, Ajai and their entire team soon had everyone having the time of their lives!

In fact, more than two decades later, everyone still remembers that crazy evening in the 1/11 GR Officers' Mess!

Of course, professionally too the Battalion excelled and for the Training Year 2004, they stood 2nd in the overall Division Championship comprising a large number of events keenly contested by nearly 20 Battalions.

The wives of the soldiers of the battalion also played a major part in the way 1/11 GR developed a formidable reputation in the Station. As is typical of Gorkhas, they had a keen sense when it came to living well, yet within their resources.

Each and every Gorkha lady of the Battalion maintained not just their home, but also their humble kitchen gardens and common areas in a manner befitting a queen! Even their kitchens used to be so spic and span that at times visitors wondered if they even used them at all!

Any and every visitor to their colonies and quarters went not just impressed, but overawed at the way they lived their lives. Of course, the happy little Gorkha kids running about in joy only added to the happiness quotient all around.

Needless to say, Shalini's own gentle guidance too had a role to play in channelizing the efforts of the ladies of the battalion thusly.

At the same time, Shalini continued to thrive in her happy little world, but she also continued to face her fears with aplomb and near disdain.

One of her biggest fears was that of water. She was very scared of entering water and naturally, couldn't swim at all. When the Battalion organised a picnic by the banks of the Holy Ganga River in Rishikesh, Shalini, being the Chief Hostess, very confidently chose to sit right in the front of the raft when time came to experience the joys of rafting in the rapids of Ganga.

Of course, an ever watchful Ajai right by her side played a major role in giving her that confidence!

The one indulgence which she permitted herself through it all was shopping for her own home that she and Ajai would often talk of constructing in Dehradun when he would retire!

She would very fondly scan the markets for the best of the showpieces for her future home, even though Ajai's retirement was more than two decades away! Her tastes were such that not a single *paisa* was wasted on vain stuff, but on things that she and Ajai could proudly display in their home.

All of it would promptly go inside a box, to be opened when the home was constructed!

Much of the stuff that Shalini so fondly collected for her home is still intact and in those same boxes, even as Abhinav is currently overseeing the construction of their house in Dhaulas, Dehradun.

Another favourite activity of hers was baking! Having started practically as a novice, Shalini would soon learn how to bake the best of the cakes, thanks to her precious notebook, full of cake recipes collected from various sources. Tell her any type of cake – Banana, Fruit, Chocolate, Pineapple – and she would quickly open up her notebook and look up the relevant recipe. Then she would follow each recipe perfectly, measuring every ingredient with great precision and monitoring various timelines equally diligently.

The results were always stunning!

That notebook with all of Shalini's cake recipes is now in the possession of Sanjana, who helped churn many a cake batter for her mother in her younger days!

Like all good things, the Battalion's tenure in Dehradun too soon came to an end, albeit a bit earlier than anticipated. Having spent less than two years in Dehradun, orders came for the Battalion to move to Kashmir Valley for an operational deployment.

The *Advance Party* had already moved ahead under Lt Col JS Rautela in the month of Sep 2004. Soon, it was time for the rest of the Battalion to move as well. The date for the move was 11 Nov 2004.

Ajai had decided to give his final orders for the move in the Battalion Mandir Grounds. After the *Puja*, he addressed all his troops and passed other relevant instructions to them. Also gathered there to bid farewell to their menfolk were all the ladies of the Battalion, including Shalini.

It was a very emotional moment for all who were present there that morning. Not only were they leaving a cherished peace station where they had created so many happy memories, but they were leaving it much earlier than they had expected to. But then, such are the exigencies of military service.

For the ladies of the Battalion, it was the beginning of yet another separation from their husbands, who were going out to yet another highly active and challenging field location.

Naturally, they were all very emotional.

Despite her own emotional state where she would once again be staying away from Ajai, handling two kids who were blossoming into young adults, all on her own, Shalini chose at that moment to discard her own worries and instead, be the rock of support on whom *her* ladies could lean for support.

She gathered her flock around and reassured them that she would continue to be there to support them as most of them wound up their own households to head back to their own native places.

Even though just her presence was enough, these words from Shalini went a long way in assuaging the fears of not just the ladies, but their husbands too, as they commenced the long road journey to the troubled Kashmir Valley.

She had always been very regular with the daily *pooja*. However, ever since Ajai assumed command of his Battalion, the intensity of her daily *pooja* too increased, since she now had the well-being of a much larger family to pray for.

Her day would begin with the Gayatri Mantra. She would do a '108 *Mala Jap'* every morning before she ate anything. Now, with Ajai and his men headed back into the thick of counter-insurgency operations, her prayers for their well-being only increased further.

As luck would have it, it being the winter season, infiltration from Pakistan Occupied Kashmir was generally non-existent. So after the initial *Pre-Induction Training* near Srinagar, the Battalion was ordered to go to a training area near Udhampur for further training.

Towards the end of the training, an unexpected and heavy bout of snow blocked the only route into the Kashmir Valley and the Battalion ended up spending an additional three weeks in the training area itself.

Not one to let go of this opportunity, Shalini, along with both kids, promptly reached Udhampur, where Ajai had arranged a stay in a beautiful Govt run resort near a lakeside.

The family was together again, after a separation of three months.

In this duration they also found time to visit the Mata Vaishno Devi Shrine. Here again, Shalini faced up to one of her other big fears – that of riding a pony on a hill trail! While going up to the shrine, she bravely sat on the pony, but on the return journey downhill, the pony gave her a few *extra* scares and she decided it was safer to come down walking!

Once the snows melted and Ajai left with his Battalion for the Kashmir Valley, Shalini returned back home to Dehradun to once again look after the kids as well as her Unit ladies that were continuing to stay on in Dehradun.

At the same time, she continued to worry, and pray for the safety of her husband and other men of the Battalion, for they were deployed in a highly active area near the line of control and partly in the hinterland as well. Almost every day there was news of encounters with terrorists in that part of the Kashmir Valley and she would sit glued to TV, searching for more details.

Thankfully, the Battalion HQ location had reasonably reliable telephone connectivity. This ensured that during this field tenure, instead of daily letters, they would speak every evening for 30-60 minutes.

During these phone calls, Shalini would often complain of headaches and migraines.

Looking back after all those years, with the attendant benefit of hindsight, Lt Gen Ajai Kumar Singh never fails to implore the ladies within the vast military family to take care of their health. He maintains that in their zeal to look after their husbands and children, ladies tend to ignore medical issues that may turn out to be life-threatening in some cases. It is a fair assumption that heeding his advice would have actually helped save at least a few such ladies from major medical issues in life.

Shalini and the kids visited the Battalion twice, including once during their school's summer holidays. They got to see the Kashmir Valley in one of its most untouched parts – Trehgam – where Ajai's Battalion HQ was located.

However, this was also a professionally challenging time for Ajai. The snows had melted and infiltration had picked up, requiring the battalion to be forever vigilant.

In this time, Ajai would move to the line of control with the rest of the Battalion, leaving a small rear detachment in Trehgam. However, there still were adequate windows of opportunity available for Shalini to visit him whenever he returned temporarily to Trehgam.

Once again, those were good times of togetherness. Ajai remained busy, while Shalini and kids would take long walks within the beautiful (and secure) Trehgam Military Station. Further, there was an Army Dog Unit within the Station which the kids loved to visit every day, to see the Military Dogs being put through their paces in an operational area.

At the same time, they weren't all cooped up inside the secured military premises throughout. Here too, Ajai had earned enough goodwill and made enough friends that he and the family got to taste Kashmiri hospitality in their homes on quite a few occasions. Of course, local shopkeepers in Trehgam and Kupwara were only too happy to showcase and sell their wares to Shalini!

Then there were two memorable trips to Srinagar and Gulmarg as well, though Ajai himself couldn't accompany them there.

One such trip was timed in a way that Shalini and the kids would see off Ajai as he climbed up the famous Shamshabari Ridge, enroute to the Line of Control.

It was yet another parting within a parting, still they made it into a celebration. The place from where Ajai would start his climb was a tiny hamlet called Kralpora. The family drove up with him all the way till there to see him off.

Once there, instead of bidding farewell right away, they decided to have an impromptu picnic by a nearby stream, enjoying steaming hot tea with pakoras, before Ajai finally moved on to his destination.

This was perhaps the first time that the kids saw their father move out on an operational move. Consequently, Sanjana wasn't quite able to comprehend as to why her mother was crying at seeing him go. She asked Shalini the reason for her tears, when Ajai was *merely going out for a trek!*

Yes, the kids were sheltered from the realities of the counter-insurgency operations that their father was leading his Battalion in.

Shalini quietly wiped her tears and with a smile, nodded to Sanjana and replied, '*Yes, you are correct. He is going for a trek.*'

Her prayers for the safety of Ajai and all men of the Battalion continued apace.

The second time when Shalini came to visit Ajai, she had an unexpected adventure of her own, giving her another perspective of the conditions under which her husband and thousands of other soldiers carried on with their soldierly tasks!

She was to travel in a taxi along with the military convoy from Srinagar to Trehgam. Unfortunately, due to a landslide enroute, the convoy got stuck. Since Shalini was travelling in a private taxi and not strictly bound by convoy protocols, Ajai could do some coordination with military units enroute and got her taxi moving singly via a series of detours.

The driver was a local Kashmiri and very reliable, however, due to the conditions in Kashmir as prevalent at that time, Shalini was very apprehensive throughout the journey and due to the still nascent mobile phone network in the area she couldn't even be in continuous communication with Ajai. She only breathed a sigh of relief when she finally reached Trehgam late in the evening!

What this experience did was to give her a feel of the Kashmir Valley as an outsider, devoid of the inherent security that military presence all around provided her.

This experience was to stand her in good stead just over a decade later when Ajai commanded a division sized Counter-Insurgency Force in the same area. Unknown to her at that time, these frequent trips to Trehgam and that one day travelling practically alone in the Kashmir Valley with a local driver, gave her an excellent perspective and empathy towards the people, who too were suffering immensely due to the poor security situation in the area.

Ajai commanded the battalion in Trehgam and thereabouts for nearly 18 months before handing over reins of the Battalion to his successor.

Thanks to his professionalism and Shalini's continued prayers, the Battalion performed exceedingly well even in those challenging circumstances.

This was also duly noted by the hierarchy above Ajai and he was rewarded with a Sena Medal for Distinguished Service and also nominated for the prestigious *Higher Command Course.*

He left the Battalion in April and was granted two months' leave before reporting to the Army War College for the course that was to commence in June. It was a perfect ending to what was to be their last separation while Shalini was still alive.

However, it was also a bittersweet ending to those times for Shalini.

Given the strict hierarchical structure of Indian Army ranks, vacancies for promotion to higher ranks are limited. To that end, Ajai getting nominated for the *Higher Command Course* was a good indicator of his future prospects.

At the same time, there were others in the Station who did not get nominated. This included husbands of a few of the ladies who stayed in Dehradun and were good friends with Shalini.

The *Higher Command* nomination put a lot of *saltiness* in some such friendships by changing the equations between them to some extent. The ladies whose husbands didn't get the nomination, found themselves somewhat resentful of Shalini. Over time, Shalini found her to be isolated within her closest of social circles in Dehradun.

To be fair, it is basic human nature in light of paucities and over time, that resentment / saltiness melts away. The pure soul that Shalini was, she too forgot, forgave and moved on with time. But while it was happening, she just couldn't come to terms with it.

It was as if she had suddenly become an alien to some of her best friends and confidants.

Happy as she was for Ajai's nomination, she was also taken aback by the change in attitudes of some of her closest friends.

Thus ended what was possibly the most beautiful time in the lives of Shalini, Ajai and the kids – on a mix of high spirits as well as heartbreak.

To some extent, it set the pace for what lay ahead for them all.

Shalini's deteriorating health, the gravity of which was still not fully understood by them all, would soon result in a shocking diagnosis which would change their lives forever.

What had just ended was indeed the best of the times ..

10

WHEN HOPE TRIUMPHED!

At the end of his command tenure, Ajai got a windfall in terms of two months' leave before he was due to report to the Army War College for the Higher Command Course. These two months were spent with family in Dehradun and thereabouts.

One requirement in that duration was that of a new car for the family. They were looking at various options of a sedan, but true to past precedence, fell in love with a Ford Fusion MUV and pretty soon it became a part of the family. Its first trip was to the famous Daat Mandir on the outskirts of Dehradun, where the car was blessed by the Deity!

Interestingly, the Fusion still soldiers on in Dehradun, even at nearly two decades of age, thanks to the blessings of the Deity and of course, the excellent care it received, and continues to receive from Abhinav!

As was the norm, the family chose to drive from Dehradun to Pune (as Abhinav was starting his graduation studies in Pune) and then thereon to Mhow. Thanks to Ajai's long leave, the family was able to accompany Abhinav to Pune and get him settled in his new surroundings.

That also meant that Sanjana had quite a comfortable ride in the backseat of the Fusion as they undertook the long road journey to Mhow!

Mhow, a quaint little town close to Indore, is considered as the Mecca of military training in the Indian Army, with three major training establishments running dozens of courses each for officers and other ranks. A course of instruction in the Indian Army not only enables officers and men to grow professionally, but also gives them a break from routine work in their battalions. Plus a course of instruction is a much welcome 're-introduction' to civilization for those deployed in remote, far-flung areas along the borders.

As a result, Mhow always exudes a very festive and welcoming vibe.

It was the same vibe that welcomed the family when they reached the Army War College and quickly set up home in their allotted accommodation in C-35 block within the campus. It was a home that would give them shelter for the next year or so, as Ajai went about his course.

The best part about the Higher Command Course is that officers attending it are of similar seniority, give or take a year or two. In Ajai's case, there were a lot of coursemates nominated for the course. These included Col BS Raju, the one who was the first guest hosted by Ajai and Shalini after marriage. He rose to be the Vice Chief of Army Staff, later moving on as the South Western Army Commander before retiring in 2023.

Within Ajai's own block of four houses were Col Rajinder Pathania, an Engineer officer, occupying the first floor with him, while the ground floor flat was occupied by Col Upendra Dwivedi, who is the Chief of Army Staff. Col Manoj Pande (Former Chief of Army Staff) also did the same course and was staying a few blocks away. Col Dwivedi was a coursemate of Ajai's while Col Pande was two years senior to them both.

Officers being of similar seniority meant that their wives and kids were also of similar age groups and that, coupled with the long duration of the course, resulted in excellent bonds being formed amongst them all. This only added to the charm of the course.

This extended Higher Command 'family' would also turn out to be an unexpected blessing when Shalini's illness would be positively diagnosed a few months later. It was almost as if the Almighty had choreographed even the minutest details of Shalini's journey through this lifetime so as to ensure that even when she was in pain internally, the external circumstances were such that she would have all the help and support she needed to soldier on through it.

Sanjana was admitted in Class XI in the APS nearby, along with many of her friends, old and new, by the time Ajai started with the course after a week of setting up home.

Despite the busy schedule, the Higher Command Course did provide an excellent opportunity for officers to spend time with their families and socialize among themselves as well. As a result, the bonds formed during this course were lifelong indeed, not just within officers but also within the ladies and even the children.

The aim of the course being to broaden the intellectual horizons of participating officers to prepare them for tenanting higher appointments subsequently in their careers meant that there were a lot of talks by pioneers / leaders in various fields.

For the ever-enthusiastic Shalini, this was another opportunity to learn and at the same time, share. The ladies bonded very well indeed and did a lot of things together, learning from each other.

Shalini's new interests while in Mhow at that time included painting, at which she steadily improved. Of course, refining her cooking skills continued to remain equally important. Also, she got introduced to Mata Nirmala Devi's Sahaj Yog programme through one of the ladies there. She joined them in their meditation sessions.

At the same time, the then Commandant of Army War College, Lt Gen Kapoor was a proponent of Sahaj Yog and had given a talk about that to the officers attending the course. Resultantly, Ajai too got introduced to it and on occasion, joined Shalini in practicing the same.

The Almighty knew what lay ahead .. it was a difficult path that they would soon be treading together .. He was doing His best to strengthen them both for what was coming their way. After all, Shalini was just as dear to Him, as she was to everyone else!

The Higher Command Course was a lively gathering of like-minded souls who, with a good amount of time at hand, liked to socialize almost every day. Soon Shalini and Ajai's hospitality was such that their house became the hub of social life for the course members. They would host the varied groups of their peers, apart from attending the many parties that they themselves would be invited for!

One such evening, when they were at the home of an Air Force officer on the ground floor of their block, having a cup of tea with him and his wife, Shalini suddenly felt very giddy along with heavy perspiration and sweating. She told Ajai that she wasn't feeling very well and they came back to their home upstairs.

When her symptoms persisted, Ajai rushed her to the Military Hospital in Mhow. The doctor on duty ordered a battery of tests and administered medications. After Shalini's condition stabilized, he suggested that she be brought again the next morning to see the Medical Specialist.

They saw the Medical Specialist the next morning where Ajai told him about the episodic high blood pressure issues of Shalini, including the fact that they would mostly be triggered by some sort of emotional traumas or stressful situations, lasting for a few hours before subsiding on their own. He also informed the doctor about Shalini often complaining of intense headaches during the time when he was in the field. He told him that she assumed these were migraines and would take a lot of painkillers whenever that happened.

The doctor absorbed all this information and decided to check Shalini's blood pressure, even though she was feeling quite fine at that moment. To their surprise, her blood pressure was still high.

Next, the doctor dropped another bombshell. He said that Shalini had been having consistent high blood pressure for all those years and that without treatment, that might have had an adverse impact on her internal organs. He said he wanted to check her retina, heart and kidneys.

The tests were duly done. Thankfully, the first report to come told them that her retina and heart were functioning just fine. But before the report of the kidney test could come, Ajai had to leave for a Forward Area Tour with the rest of the Higher Command Course.

Thankfully, Shalini wasn't alone back home in Mhow. Her sister-in-law, Preeti was visiting at that time.

The reports of the kidney test came in this duration, while Ajai was in Srinagar with the rest of the course members. Shalini and Preeti could only see the parameters written on the report, but didn't know what it meant.

Wanting to get some clarity on the same, Preeti called up a doctor back home in Dehradun that evening. When he heard that Shalini's Creatinine level was 4.6, he gave her the devastating news.

Shalini's kidneys were heavily damaged, he told her.

Shocked, Preeti kept this to herself and decided to take Shalini to another local doctor in order to get a second opinion.

Together, they both went to a hospital in Mhow and met the specialist there.

The moment he saw the report, he looked at Shalini and exclaimed in a highly unbecoming manner for a doctor – '*How the hell are you still alive?*'

Shalini went numb, even as the doctor continued speaking. Her eyes filled with tears, but she didn't cry.

After a few moments, she just got up and left the doctor's chamber. Preeti tried to hold her hand and keep her there but Shalini was in a different zone altogether.

Preeti didn't follow Shalini out right away. She stayed back to give a piece of her mind to the doctor for being so insensitive. After administering a good scolding to the now speechless doctor, Preeti quickly rushed to join Shalini.

On the way back, Shalini remained absolutely silent. Preeti tried to make small talk, but then she also just let her be. She knew that Shalini needed some time to come to terms with what she had just learnt.

Upon reaching home, she just went and grabbed a broom and started sweeping the floor, cleaning the already clean house, as if to wish away the news she had just heard.

Preeti saw this and tried to console her, saying that nothing will happen and asking her to just sit down and relax. However, Shalini was still in shock and for the first and only time, shouted at Preeti.

'*Get Out. I am absolutely fine and I will prove it to everyone*', she shouted.

Undaunted, Preeti gave her the space that she needed at that moment. She started calling up a few more doctors that she knew, trying to get their opinions as well. However, they all too told her the same thing.

The first medical advice on the way ahead also came via this flurry of phone calls when one of the doctors advised to have meals without salt.

This gave some semblance of hope and Preeti prepared the next meal without salt. She also decided to eat the same food along with Shalini. But the very first, tasteless morsel that she ate, once again told Shalini that life was no longer the same.

In a fit of anger, she threw her plate away.

Preeti was stunned.

This was a side of Shalini that no one in the family had ever witnessed. In fact, this was NOT Shalini at all. Throughout her life, she had been just like her name – Shalini. The battleground of thoughts in her mind, more so with Ajai literally 1000 miles away, was something that she was struggling to come to terms with.

The moment that plate hit the ground, it was as if something switched within her, and Shalini was back again. The first thing she did was to hug Preeti and offer her sincerest apologies for her behaviour towards her sister-in-law.

Shalini then told her, '*Come what may, I will remain happy and not seek anyone's mercy.*'

This was indeed the true face of Shalini – resolute, empathetic and apologetic despite her own troubles.

Preeti too put up a brave front, reassuring Shalini that things will be fine, despite knowing deep within that it may not actually turn out that way. But she did what she had to do.

To this day, Preeti remembers the face of Shalini in that moment. This is an unfortunate memory that just refuses to leave her. That said, things might have been even worse had she not been there in Mhow with Shalini when she found out about her condition.

From that moment till Shalini's last day, Preeti never saw Shalini sad or perturbed or even complaining that she wasn't well, whatever be the state of her health. This was the fortitude that Shalini summoned for the long battle that lay ahead.

That said, Preeti has never been able to summon the courage to go to Mhow ever again.

Preeti had another, equally difficult task to do. She had to inform Ajai as well as Shalini's parents. She summoned the courage to do so, while at the same time, leaving the details of what transpired in the hospital with that doctor.

Meanwhile Ajai was meeting an acquaintance in Srinagar Cantonment when he received a call from Shalini who told him about the Chronic Renal Failure that she had been diagnosed with and that she had been advised to commence dialysis right away. Further, the doctors had advised to start looking for a kidney donor as well, preferably from amongst Shalini's blood relations.

Lt Gen Ajai Kumar Singh still remembers that moment.

Life was at its best. Everything was beautifully in the place it should have been. Srinagar was exceptionally beautiful at that time of the year. And then came the call about the serious medical condition that his wife had been diagnosed with.

He was shocked beyond belief. It was as if life suddenly took a 180 degree turn out of the blue.

To accept this fact and its likely future implications was a herculean task for Ajai. However, the strong and ever-empathetic woman that Shalini was, she was still worried more about Ajai than herself. No wonder that she only chose to break this news to Ajai after she herself had come to terms with it, so that the shock on him doesn't get unmanageable.

Lt Gen Ajai Kumar Singh remembers fondly that even when telling him about her diagnosis, Shalini seemed in control of the situation and more importantly, her own emotions. Of course, she was still in shock, but her efforts to reconcile with the situation and start looking ahead seemed to have already kicked in.

Shalini wouldn't be giving up without a fight. The fight she put up till the very end is something that is still talked about with awe and admiration. She would ultimately yield to her fate, but on her own terms.

Naturally, Ajai rushed back to Mhow to be with Shalini. Upon reaching home, they spoke at length about the implications and the way forward.

The Military Hospital in Mhow didn't have a Nephrologist. Ajai took some leave and took Shalini to the R&R Hospital in New

Delhi, leaving behind Sanjana and Abhinav (who was home on a short break) in Mhow on their own.

Even as the kids enjoyed the relative freedom of having the entire house to themselves, Ajai and Shalini sought an urgent appointment with the Nephrologist in R&R Hospital.

As luck would have it, the specialist they landed up with was Col Ashok Hooda, who just happened to be the Regimental Medical Officer posted with 7/11 Gorkha Rifles when Ajai had gotten commissioned into the Unit. In fact, on Ajai's first day in the battalion, his bed had been placed in the Regimental Aid Post itself, which was the 'office' of (then) Capt Hooda!

Having seen so many fortuitous coincidences in Shalini's life thus far, she and Ajai were hardly surprised at this latest blessing in the form of an old friend who just happened to specialise in a field of medicine that she needed the most. The Almighty was definitely testing Shalini, but at the same time, He was ensuring that her journey ahead was facilitated as well.

Shalini must have been born with a load of good karmas from her past life that despite all the challenges, she was never helpless or without hope.

Naturally, Col Hooda did the best he could under those circumstances. But given the situation, apart from minor lifestyle related advice, he could only reinforce what Shalini and Ajai already knew, i.e., dialysis to commence without any delay and to start searching for a donor. He also said that given Shalini's age, the chances of a successful transplant were really good for her.

Hope restored, they returned to Mhow.

Of course, life had changed for good. Now it would be Shalini's medical condition that would dictate the future courses of action.

Shalini was determined to live life on her own terms. After the initial shock, she had come to terms with her condition and instead of despondency, she responded with acceptance. She decided that the best way forward was to face the situation head-on, instead of wishing it away.

Shalini had realized that there still was quite a bit of life to be lived, and more importantly, so many responsibilities that needed to be taken care of. Both kids were at an age where they would soon be testing their own wings while Ajai himself was at the cusp of greater things in his career. They all needed her as an anchor in these crucial phases of their lives.

It would be fair to say that in her scheme of things, she just decided that she simply *has* to be around for her family. She just couldn't leave without fulfilling her responsibilities.

Meanwhile, Ajai was coming to terms with this new reality and had already started looking for reliable nephrologists in the nearby town of Indore, finally moving on to what he thought was the best option.

Not taking any chances with Shalini's health, the couple decided to consult two different nephrologists simultaneously.

Both advised commencement of dialysis forthwith.

In the midst of all this, the kids were initially kept away from this news. But pretty soon it was time to tell them both. In a way it got preempted when upon returning from school one day, Sanjana heard her mother crying in her room.

Even to this day she remembers faintly hearing her mother between her sobs, saying .. Why did this happen to me? What have I done? Why me? What is wrong with me? My kids are still young ..

Yes, there were weak moments as well but those continued to be few, and most importantly, extremely private, shared only with her husband, if at all.

The room being locked, Sanjana knocked on it and Ajai soon opened the door to let her in. By the time Sanjana entered, Shalini had wiped her tears and the crying had stopped.

Sanjana was straight to the point, asking what happened. To this Shalini said nothing happened and that she was just a bit unwell. Feeling reassured, Sanjana told her mother that it will be fine and that she shouldn't worry. Saying this, she went off to her evening tuition classes.

That night, when Sanjana returned back from tuition, her parents sat her down and told her that there was something wrong with her mother's kidneys. At about the same time, Abhinav too was told about this over a phone call.

At that moment, both kids failed to realize the gravity of the situation facing their mother. That realization would set in slowly as the days progressed.

Abhinav still remembers the first trip that he made to Mhow a few weeks after hearing of the news. To him, his mother seemed perfectly fine and just as she always had been. This was a small consolation for a young man living away from his parents' nest for the first time in his life.

Come to think of it, this resilience was exactly what made Shalini so exceptional through all her trials and tribulations. She had decided that her kids would not see her as being sick, and made it a point to be always wearing a smile whenever they were around, regardless of the pain she was in.

Life went on ..

Shalini and Ajai started reading about her ailment from whatever sources they could find. Shalini took refuge in the Sahaj Yog practice that she had recently started. Now she became fully immersed in it, seeking refuge in the vast realm of spiritualism.

It didn't take long before the rest of the officers and ladies in the Higher Command Course came to know of Shalini's condition. After the initial wave of shock, the entire course got together as one big family and played a pivotal role in helping Shalini and Ajai come to terms with the new reality.

They did it by just being themselves and treating each other the way they had always done – with extreme kinship, camaraderie and understanding. It was one big, boisterous and happy family who also doubled up as a wonderful and selfless support system.

They just and never felt the need to leave Shalini out of their routine activities, giving her just the right dose of extra energy that she needed.

At the cost of repetition, it is perfectly clear that the Almighty chose just the right place and the right time to make Shalini aware of her medical condition so that she could come to terms with it in the shortest possible time frame and be able to soldier on.

In the initial days and months after she was first diagnosed, the ramifications of her condition were not immediately evident and for most part, Shalini continued to feel quite normal.

This led Ajai and Shalini to jointly decide to hold off dialysis for the time being. This was not a foolhardy decision, mind you, but a well-considered one. They decided to seek alternative treatment options to delay taking recourse to dialysis for as long as they could.

Thus began their journey into the world of spirituality, yoga, meditation, pranayama and naturopathy. They both studied a lot. They were a team, fighting this ailment together .. working towards their future, together.

They also read a lot. One particular book that made a world of difference to both Shalini and Ajai was *The Power of Positive Thinking, by Norman Vincent Peale*. This book was recommended to Shalini by one of the ladies from the Higher Command Course family itself.

Shalini found this book to be an ocean of motivation and ended up reading it a number of times. It would be fair to say that she found great strength in that book and it served to reinforce her decision to look ahead with positivity and optimism.

In the initial days, she was fairly convinced that her condition could be reversed and if not, then at least controlled so that she could continue to discharge her responsibilities. This is what kept her going.

In the midst of this, Ajai managed to home in on to an excellent Yoga instructor in Mhow itself for Shalini and she started doing Yoga every evening. Thanks to the well set and predictable schedule of the Higher Command Course, Ajai too started doing Yoga with her regularly.

He also started reading a lot of self-help books as also books on spirituality in order to seek answers that weren't very easy to come by otherwise.

This mutual fight against the deadly medical condition of Shalini also changed their relationship, making it more intimate, more understanding.

They maximized the time spent in each other's company, almost as if trying to make the most of what was left, even if they didn't know it consciously. They both understood what is important in life and what are the frivolous issues not worth their time, limited as it already was.

They started enjoying each other's company all over again, this time with an even deeper connect.

They also decided to live life as normally as they could.

This meant a *lot* of outings since Shalini was very fond of it!

They went shopping, sight-seeing or movies almost every day. In fact, very soon it would turn into a weekly ritual of seeing the 'first day first show' of new movies every Friday, followed by a meal outside!

The frequency of visits to places of religious and / or spiritual significance also increased. There are a lot of such places in and around Mhow. The visits to Omkareshwar Mandir and the Kaal Bhairava Mandir were particularly memorable and enriching ones.

The underlying belief deep in the minds of Shalini and Ajai was that allopathic intervention could be delayed through alternative methods. And it actually happened exactly this way.

Along with yoga, pranayama, naturotherapy etc, Shalini also focussed on lifestyle changes in order to ensure that her Creatinine levels don't go too high. She reduced protein intake and also limited excess physical activities in order to limit the levels of Creatinine in her body.

Visits to the Military Hospital were very frequent because they wanted to keep her body parameters under constant monitoring.

Managing Shalini's medical condition became the focal point of their lives. But that did not prevent them from living their lives either!

They continued to be part of all social events, partying hard along with the rest of their peers. But the highlight of their social life was their marriage anniversary, for which they took a really bold decision with respect to the celebration.

They decided to invite the entire Higher Command Course – all officers and ladies – to their three-bedroom govt accommodation!

This was something that was practically unheard of, with such gatherings either restricted in numbers or done outside in larger venues. But then it wouldn't be Shalini and Ajai's story if they followed the crowd!

Of course, their next-door neighbours too opened up their house in anticipation of the swell of humanity that was expected that night. The fact that theirs being first floor houses, they also had fairly large terraces that too were put to good use!

On the night of the gathering, both houses and terraces were filled choc-a-block with fellow officers and ladies. Needless to say, it was pure commotion, and everyone enjoyed it thoroughly. This event still gets talked about today, nearly two decades later!

During all of this, there were numerous trips to the R&R Hospital in New Delhi, as well as trips to both the Nephrologists in Indore every Sunday. The couple was taking absolutely no chances whatsoever with Shalini's ailment.

It was also with an unsaid aim of reinforcing their own resolve of not letting Shalini's medical condition prevent them from being themselves.

Meanwhile, a quick survey was also underway amongst the immediate family members to find a suitable donor. Even though most were willing, unfortunately there was no suitable individual on Ajai's side of the family, including Ajai himself, who had a matching blood group with Shalini.

It was a big setback since at that time transplants of kidneys were limited to donors and recipients of the same blood group. Over the years, though, medical science has thankfully evolved and found a way to do so. However, at that point in time this was just not possible.

On Shalini's side too, despite matching blood groups, most suitable donors had some or the other medical issues that prevented them from donating their kidneys to Shalini. This also included both her brothers, Amit and Atul.

Since Shalini's symptoms were manageable at that time, there was no criticality of finding a donor even though the search continued. That said, things still became dicey at times.

On one such occasion, as Shalini and Ajai were headed back to Mhow after yet another check-up at the R&R Hospital, as soon as the flight took off, Shalini started feeling unwell. Ajai realised that it was yet another episode of High BP and palpitations. Not taking any chances with her health, Ajai requested the flight to return back to Delhi so that Shalini could be rushed to medical care.

Thankfully, the flight landed back in Delhi soon and Shalini was rushed to R&R Hospital, where Col Hooda was already waiting for her. He administered immediate remedial treatment and soon her parameters were back under control. But he still wanted to admit her for a couple of days in order to keep her under observation.

Shalini put her foot down and said she didn't want to get admitted in the hospital. After trying to convince her for some time, both Ajai and Col Hooda gave up. Shalini and Ajai went to

Ajai's elder sister's residence in Janakpuri where they spent the next couple of days.

Having sought and received a couple of days' extension of leave, it was time for Ajai to report back to Mhow. Before the flight, they met Col Hooda once again and he gave Shalini some medicines to ensure her blood pressure stays manageable for the duration of the flight.

Despite all this, Shalini and Ajai continued to make the most of each and every moment of togetherness. Together, they started treading on the path of spirituality with even greater vigour in order to try and understand the world beyond the conscious one that we normally feel and see. Another book that made a great impact on Shalini and Ajai in this duration was *The Secret*, by Rhonda Byrne which became very dear to Shalini.

Taking everything in their stride, the couple continued living their life and before long, the Higher Command Course was on the verge of culmination. With this came the all-round excitement and anticipation of the future postings of course members that would shortly be announced.

This added another dimension to the management of Shalini's condition as far as Ajai was concerned. With a fairly well-set routine and support system in Mhow about to get left behind, he mulled over his future and decided that Delhi would be the best place to seek his next billet, and accordingly put in a request for the same.

As was the procedure, the Colonel Military Secretary-1 (Col MS-1) from Army Headquarters came to interact with all army officers attending the course to seek their preferences for the next place of posting and to discuss their placement as per vacancies available.

When Ajai's turn came, he was candidly told that as per his profile, Ajai would be considered for a posting in one of the higher headquarters in Rajasthan. In any case, as per the policy in vogue, no officer would be going to New Delhi right after the Higher Command Course. Ajai told him about his peculiar requirements but didn't push beyond a point, preferring rather to let destiny take its own course.

However, the very next day the same Col MS-1 who had vehemently declined Ajai's request for a posting to Delhi, called him again and told him he would try to oblige Ajai as a special exemption.

It so transpired that the previous evening, the Col MS-1 had joined one of his close friends doing the Higher Command Course for a drink and during the conversation, Ajai's name popped up. That officer managed to convince Col MS-1 that if anyone from the course deserved to get posted to New Delhi, it was Ajai, due to Shalini's condition.

The Almighty had placed yet another angel in just the right place and the right time, to pave the way ahead for Shalini!

Ajai followed up with the Col MS-1 a few weeks later and was informed that a suitable billet had been found for him in the Military Operations (MO) Directorate. He further told him that even though life in the MO Directorate was incredibly busy, he had been able to place Ajai as Col MO-12, enabling him to focus on Shalini's treatment.

Ajai couldn't thank him enough. Not only did Delhi provide the best possible facilities for Shalini's treatment, their families in Roorkee and Dehradun too were that much closer.

Soon the course ended and Shalini, Ajai and Sanjana were in Delhi. Needless to say, the Mhow household too was packed under direct supervision of Shalini!

The beauty about a Delhi tenure is that at first, it is very unsettling for any newcomer! You are practically on your own and have to hunt for every single thing initially before you get used to the 'different' way of life there. So it was for Ajai as well.

He reported physically to the Adm and Coord Branch of MO Directorate even though he was still on leave that had been granted at the end of the course. That done, his first priority was to find a suitable temporary accommodation because the waiting period for permanent accommodation was quite long. Accordingly, he was advised to apply for a two-room set with a kitchenette in the Army Battle Honours Mess (ABHM, in short), which would likely be available fairly quickly. In addition, he also put in an application for a temporary accommodation in Shankar Vihar

Having applied for the accommodation, and with leave still ongoing, the trio headed out to Roorkee and Dehradun to catch up with the rest of their family members. During the few days spent in Dehradun, Ajai called up an officer in the Adm and Coord Wing of MO Dte to check the status of his accommodation and was told that the prospect for an early allotment seemed bleak despite his request to be treated as a special case due to Shalini's medical condition.

It was at this moment that Ajai decided to seek the indulgence of a senior officer from his Regiment to put in a favourable word.

Thankfully, that recommendation worked and a two-room set in ABHM was allotted to Ajai. Then, as if the Almighty was merely teasing them, soon came the news that the temporary accommodation that they had applied for in Shankar Vihar as a special case, had also come through!

The choice was natural.

The family quickly settled in the relatively spacious temporary accommodation in Shankar Vihar post Ajai rejoining duty after completion of his leave. That it was fairly close to the R&R Hospital was an added bonus as well.

Once again, Shalini didn't let her medical condition come in the way of ensuring that the house became a welcoming *home* for her little family. Sanjana too, was a huge help in this settling down period, which was a welcome change noticed by her parents who were quite used to her being the younger child. But then, it was fair to assume that this was her own coping mechanism to deal with her mother's condition even though she didn't let it show.

Over the coming years, both Abhinav and Sanjana would rapidly evolve from young, rebellious teens to mature adults as their mother kept fighting her battle against her own medical conditions.

Meanwhile, Ajai realised that MO-12 too was a lot of work, with it dealing with a new and still evolving field. However, given the fact that his desk hardly had any files that were *urgent,* he was still able to find adequate time to spare for Shalini's treatment.

MO-12 at that time was dealing with a very new domain and the work, though mostly without any crazy deadlines, was still very challenging. Ajai had to study a lot to get on top of this new tech domain that he was dealing with.

In spite of being a new domain, there were no sudden criticalities in his branch, unlike in some of the other branches of the MO Directorate. So he was able to devote adequate time to the health concerns of Shalini and pretty soon, trips to the R&R Hospital became a regular feature. At the same time, a second opinion was taken at the AIIMS.

Shalini was soon registered for a cadaver donor programme at both the R&R Hospital as well as the AIIMS.

That apart, life went on as normally as it could.

The couple continued with their busy social life, inviting friends and family over to their place as well as getting invited for meals with friends and family. The semblance of normality carried on, as much for themselves as also for the children who were just about beginning to understand the seriousness of their mother's condition.

Ever so often, they would get reminded that their mother wasn't well. One such instance happened in Dec 2008 when Shalini declined to go to a New Year Party at the DSOI. Sanjana was aghast, not able to believe her mother would decline to go to a party!

She tried convincing her to go with them, but Shalini was steadfast in her refusal, finally telling Sanjana that she wasn't feeling very well. At the same time, she was firm that her husband and daughter must go.

Consequently, it was only Ajai and Sanjana that attended the New Year Celebration.

Since Shalini's symptoms were not yet very severe, Ajai and she had decided to try and manage them with alternate therapies for as long as they could, before the inevitable allopathic intervention would be needed.

They decided to actually *learn* these alternative therapies instead of relying upon other practitioners whose talents and credentials couldn't be easily verified. So they learnt Pranic Healing and also did a Psychotherapy course together over a few weekends.

Despite the outward normalcy, Ajai continued to have apprehensions and worries about the future. He believes Shalini too had these worries but managed to keep them hidden behind her naturally happy persona and an ever-smiling face.

In the opinion of General Ajai Kumar Singh, his wife just steeled herself. He thinks that she willed herself to live on in order to be around for the children in their crucial years wherein she would have to play an important role, even if it meant living in pain and discomfort.

In order to cope, Ajai took up running after a break of quite some time and started practicing Meditation. Every morning he would practice Meditation and run 3-5km and sweat profusely. This mental and physical diversion helped him cope and sustain with the rapidly mounting challenges in his and Shalini's life.

Slowly and inevitably, Shalini's medical condition became more and more challenging, exacerbated by low protein intake. Life became increasingly uncertain as Shalini grew weaker by the day.

Her blood pressure continued to be erratic, though the palpitation episodes were still only occasional. Plus her Creatinine levels too were a cause of concern, even though by avoiding proteins and restricting her physical activities, Shalini kept it between 4 and 7.

What also played a key role in sustaining her through this was her regular yoga practice, pranayam, the ever-positive attitude towards life and a social life that was as normal as her circumstances permitted.

Their challenges did not go unnoticed either. Ajai would often be asked by one or other of his colleagues as to how he was managing his wife's medical condition while in such a challenging appointment.

Invariably, Ajai would reply that it was not he, but Shalini that was managing it all and that contrary to conventional wisdom, it was she who was giving him the strength to carry on.

In short, Shalini had simply normalised everything, including her illness. After that initial panic (which itself lasted barely a couple of hours), she had gotten hold of herself for the sake of her family. This gave them all the strength to face the future head-on.

In a self-fulfilling cycle, Ajai's own support gave Shalini a lot of strength as well.

The duo had found a perfect balance between life and illness, it seemed.

That said, it wasn't that Ajai wasn't worried.

The truth was, in fact, quite the opposite.

Deep within, he had a lot of worries about the dark inevitability that the future held. It would be fair to say that the same held true for Shalini as well. However, for the sake of each other and most importantly, for their children, they lived their lives as normally as they could.

Ajai continued to worry, even while asleep. In fact, his sleep was extremely fitful, because Shalini herself wasn't able to sleep comfortably due to her condition. During such episodes, including palpitations, all that Ajai could do was to hold her in a tight embrace, ask her to breathe deeply, and *will* her to get better. Thankfully, it would work and within a few minutes Shalini would fall back to sleep.

However, Ajai would still be edgy throughout the night, even checking her Blood Pressure regularly. Such was the worry that even if Shalini turned in her sleep, Ajai would be instantly awake to make sure she was still breathing.

The worries were quite real, and in order to not get overwhelmed by them, Ajai too had to find an outlet, just like Shalini had done by not feeding her own worries.

This he did in the form of Meditation and the daily runs every morning, come sun or rain, not missing even a single day. He also read a lot of spiritual and self-help books, including the

Shrimadbhagvadgita, The Power of Positive Thinking, The Monk Who Sold His Ferrari, The Secret and Vivekachudamani, to name a few. In addition, he did the course of Self-Realisation Fellowship (SRF) by the Yogada Satsang Society (YSS), besides practicing Kriya Yog and Twin Heart Meditation.

It helped him retain his own sanity and to stay mentally strong.

Their life continued unabated, especially their movie routine that had started in Mhow. With Delhi offering much more opportunities, Shalini and Ajai became almost fanatic in their pursuit of 'First Day First Show' of any new movie getting released.

Over time, they even managed to game the system of the various multiplexes in Delhi and came to a realization that come what may, PVR Naraina would *always* have tickets available, partly due to its relatively obscure location, and pretty soon, they were regulars there, not in the least due to its proximity to Delhi Cantonment!

With online show bookings slowly becoming more and more normal, the pursuit of tickets also became that much easier.

It did not matter whether a movie was good or bad or what its ratings were. Shalini and Ajai were always willing to give it a try. It was their one, much awaited escape from reality as well as a time in each other's company without any worries.

Their usual Friday routine comprised a movie and a meal at some nearby eating joint. This done, they would be ready to welcome the weekend!

At the same time, they kept trying to manage her symptoms through alternative means in their quest to delay surgical intervention for as long as possible. With Ajai being busy and only able to spare time on weekends, Shalini went ahead on her own as well, learning Reiki Healing and ultimately becoming a Reiki Grandmaster as well.

This helped her not only physically, but also spiritually by helping her put at least part of her issues in some context beyond scientific explanations.

Regular visits to the Nephrologist, Col Hooda & Lt Col Ranjith Nair continued. During each and every such visit, Col Ashik Hooda would admonish Ajai and Shalini for delaying the dialysis. He just couldn't fathom why Shalini was so adamant on continuing to live her life with such blatant disregard to medical advice.

Shalini was quite adamant in not signing up for dialysis, at least not at this stage, despite Col Hooda's warnings about implications on her health.

Ajai was firm that he will not force Shalini to undergo any invasive medical procedures against her will. However, he continued to gently remind her that this was the ultimate approach and the most rational one as well.

Ultimately, Shalini agreed to have an AV Fistula done in her arm in order to facilitate dialysis.

This would be the first of 17 surgical procedures she would be subject to before finally deciding to leave her body. Come to think of it, she was absolutely right in choosing to stay away from surgical intervention for as long as she could.

This was not to say that she had absolutely rejected an allopathic intervention altogether thus far. Nothing could be farther from the truth.

Shalini had become quite used to surgical needles, with most of her visits also resulting in drawl of blood samples or some IV injections.

With IV, sometimes the doctors would prefer to put a 'butterfly' for subsequent use that would remain for at least 2-3 days. It would hurt a lot, especially in case the nursing staff entrusted with the task were not very proficient and took multiple attempts to find the blood vessels, especially when the bone was so nearby.

Shalini bore through all this pain with a smile, even if with tearful eyes at the same time.

However, all said and done, the ultimate long-term solution was a transplant. Even though Shalini had been registered for a cadaver transplant at both AIIMS and R&R Hospital, certainty of it happening anytime soon was still doubtful.

With all these things playing in Ajai's mind, there were various other options as well that he was looking at. In fact, he had already sounded out the extended family for potential donors. Further, amongst the various scenarios going through his mind, Ajai had even thought of getting it done in a foreign country despite the complexities of logistics and cost involved.

Talking about cost, it soon dawned on Ajai that in case a transplant through a living donor from the family had to happen in a private hospital, he should also have some cash readily available.

In less than a month of this thought coming to his mind, he had sold off their house in Dehradun.

It was a beautiful house, ideally located with a beautiful lawn, a kitchen garden, a beautiful, long driveway and a majestic view of the mountains. But when it came to the question of Shalini's health, the decision to sell it off came quite naturally and easily.

The wait for a kidney for Shalini continued.

Sometime in this duration, Ajai sat down with both the kids individually and had a heart-to-heart talk with them about their mother's condition, the prognosis and the way ahead just so that they don't find themselves in the dark, especially in these times of uncertainty about their mother's future.

Sometime soon thereafter, Abhinav announced that he wanted to donate his kidney to his mother. However, Shalini nixed that demand in the bud by flat-out refusing to accept a kidney from her son, preferring to wait for a cadaver kidney instead.

Ajai was in constant touch with the AIIMS as well as the R&R Hospital. One of the key suggestions that he received from them was to always be ready to rush to the hospital with Shalini at zero notice in case a cadaver kidney ever became available, because the window for a successful transplant would be very short.

Accordingly, they stayed within Delhi throughout, not knowing when they might receive the much awaited phone call from either of these hospitals .. till one fine day they decided to make a quick weekend trip to Roorkee and Dehradun

Shalini wanted to visit home after so many months of being so near yet so far. It was on precisely that day that the Almighty decided to test her.

They were just short of Roorkee when Ajai's phone rang. Thinking nothing of it, he answered it. The voice on the other end gave them the much-awaited good news – A cadaver kidney with matching blood group was available at R&R Hospital!

However, the timing couldn't have been worse. Had it been just a few hours earlier, Shalini would have been barely 10 minutes away from the hospital. But now, it would take at least three to four hours.

Not wanting to give false information with such a critical thing as a cadaver kidney, Ajai informed the person at the other end about this and told them that they are turning back right then.

He drove back as fast as he could, even taking risks that he would otherwise never even have dreamt of, and reached R&R Hospital within three hours.

However, by the time they reached there, the doctors had already started preparing another patient for receiving the kidney. Shalini and Ajai were told that due to complexities of testing kit and the fact that the surgical teams just couldn't have waited this long due to the extremely limited window available for the handling of a cadaver kidney before it became unsuitable for a transplant.

Left with no other choice, Shalini and Ajai returned home.

However, there was no sense of dejection in either of them. They just accepted the situation, knowing that this particular kidney was never meant for Shalini.

Perhaps *that* was the reason that the Almighty chose that day for them to decide to travel out of Delhi.

Regardless of it all, it was hardly surprising Shalini chose to take this turn of events in her stride instead of getting dejected. She had never been one to be gloomy, whatever be her challenges.

This was the glue that kept their little family from falling apart despite such a huge challenge. Despite her critical health condition, Shalini continued to be the glue that held her flock together.

Life kept going on.

Pretty soon, there was yet another test that came their way. That day when Sanjana returned from school, her mother wasn't there. She quickly checked and realised that her dad's car too was not there in the garage.

She was old enough to put two and two together, and realized something was amiss. Yet, she had no way of knowing because she didn't have a mobile phone. So, she waited.

But the young and worried teen that Sanjana was, it took just 30-40 minutes before she got restless and borrowed the mobile phone of her father's buddy and tried calling him up.

There was no response from her father's end.

The clock kept on ticking and after about three hours, she tried calling again, but with the same result as earlier.

Later in the evening, seeing her pacing back and forth in the garden, the neighbours grew concerned and came over to check on her. She told them she was worried and they tried to convince her that her father had just taken her mother for a routine checkup and that they would be back soon.

But Sanjana was hardly convinced. She kept worrying for her mother, crying throughout.

Ajai and Shalini returned home after 11pm that night, to find their tearful daughter outside the home on the road. The moment she saw them return, Sanjana all but flung herself at her mother, holding her in a tight embrace, shooting one question after another amidst her sobs.

What had happened was that earlier that day, Shalini received a call from AIIMS about another cadaver kidney getting available but she had refused to accept that kidney. However, Ajai had shared his number with them and they called him up thereafter.

Fortunately, Ajai happened to be free when they called and was able to answer the call. He was just as surprised as the person at the other end of the call when he heard that Shalini had refused.

Regardless, he promised that Shalini and he will reach AIIMS right away.

He then called up Shalini on the way back home from office, asking her why she refused. Shalini chose not to reply to this. Ajai just told her that they should still go to AIIMS and at least go through the process so that they know what lies in store when the moment comes.

As far as the decision to go ahead with the transplant or not in this case, Ajai told Shalini that he would not force her and that whatever she decided would be endorsed by him as well.

Convinced, Shalini was ready to move by the time Ajai reached back home.

The transplant coordinator was already waiting for them when they reached. There was a large battery of tests that had to be done right away and soon Shalini and Ajai were literally running from one part of the huge AIIMS campus to another, trying to stay on top of it all.

It took great effort to get all tests done in time, especially since Shalini wasn't in the best of physical condition to run around from one department to another. It was the perfect testimony to her grit and resilience that she managed to do so over a prolonged period of time, despite knowing that she wasn't going to accept that kidney.

All test reports were submitted to the transplant coordinator well in time. Then came a short wait while the staff at AIIMS analysed the test reports of all potential recipients for the kidney.

At the end of it came the best news that Ajai had heard ever since Shalini's condition was first diagnosed.

Shalini was the best match amongst them all to receive the kidney, they said, and asked to wheel her in for the surgery right away.

And then Shalini refused to accept that kidney once again.

Ajai was not very happy and called up Shalini's parents to try and convince her. When they failed, he called up his old friend from Nepal days, Dr Nalin Mehta who too was in AIIMS at that time. Even Dr Nalin and his wife, Dr Namita were unable to convince Shalini.

Meanwhile, apart from Ajai, even the staff in the Nephrology Department of AIIMS were taken aback at the refusal by Shalini. To them all, it was as if she was refusing the very lease at life that was there just for the taking. They had never encountered such a patient before who had gone to immense pain and suffering, then spent many hours rushing from one department to another for all those tests, only to refuse a kidney for which she was the best match.

However, they too failed to convince Shalini.

Despite so many well-meaning people trying to convince Shalini to take this god-sent opportunity, she was firm in her refusal.

Ajai was crestfallen and even a bit angry at Shalini. But he knew that it was her body and her decision, and if she was not willing, there would be a good chance that the body too would reject the transplanted kidney.

He still hadn't asked Shalini the reason for her refusal.

So Ajai went to the nephrologist and conveyed Shalini's decision. He still remembers that moment vividly, even 16 years later. The name of the specialist was Dr Guleria. He was quite literally, aghast on hearing this.

Bewildered, he told Ajai that having been in this specialty for nearly two decades, he had seen the things people were willing to do in order to *get* a cadaver kidney. And now here was Shalini, actually refusing one.

He sent for Shalini as well in order to try and convince her himself. But Shalini was firm in her decision.

In the end, because they couldn't wait any longer, the staff at AIIMS just accepted her decision and wheeled in the next best suited patient for the transplant.

On the way back home from AIIMS, Ajai was no longer angry at Shalini. In fact, that anger had been momentary and had vanished once he accepted Shalini's decision. But a sense of dejection still remained.

Some time later when he asked Shalini why she had refused, she said that she had been told that one of the other likely recipients being evaluated for the cadaver kidney was a young girl.

Somehow, Shalini just couldn't get herself to prioritise her own need over that of a child and had already made up her mind to reject the kidney the moment she heard about the other likely recipient.

Physically, at that point in time Shalini was in a relatively fine condition and thought that she could sustain a bit longer without a transplant. Hence her decision.

Here again was that pure soul, full of empathy and compassion for another soul she didn't even know, but still decided to help out. Knowing the way Shalini was, neither Ajai nor anyone else in the family were upset when they found out the reason. To them, it was just Shalini being .. well .. herself!

Thankfully, they later found out that the transplant surgery for that child was successful.

The wait continued.

Meanwhile, Sanjana too had left Delhi to pursue her own graduation at Wigan and Leigh College, Pune and now Shalini and Ajai had a truly empty nest. Of course, friends and family in Delhi and thereabouts made sure that there were enough people around them at all times.

Not wanting her condition to dictate her daughter's education plans, Shalini had actively encouraged Sanjana to seek to pursue her dreams even if it meant leaving Delhi for that. Thus encouraged, Sanjana sought and got an admission in the Wigan and Leigh College in Pune. Abhinav, already being in Pune also played a key role in convincing his sister to make the move.

Sanjana would ultimately put her own career on hold and move back to Delhi in order to take care of her mother. It should read But that was still about half a decade away.

Some weeks later, there was another cadaver kidney that became available at the R&R Hospital and Shalini was once again rushed there, but this time the doctors found traces of high blood sugar in the kidney and Ajai and Shalini both rejected the kidney, even though compatibility tests had come out good.

Their reasoning was clear. If Shalini was to get a transplant, she should rather wait for a healthy kidney instead of risking a major surgical procedure with a kidney that was less than healthy.

This time Ajai and Shalini both declined the transplant and decided to wait some more.

The fact remained that time was ticking by and Shalini's condition gradually got worse over the next few weeks and months. In fact, her Creatinine levels rose alarmingly to nearly 20. This was a level at which a patient cannot reasonably be expected to live anymore.

But then, this was Shalini, who just refused to give up and hung on.

Those days were not easy. Due to all those toxins in the body that the kidneys couldn't filter out any more, her skin turned dark and quite frequently, boils would erupt on the skin, bursting after a few days and expelling the toxins that would otherwise have been done by the kidneys.

Shalini's condition kept on deteriorating and unfortunately, unlike the first three instances, no cadaver kidney seemed to be available any more.

Alarmed, Ajai sent an SOS call to the family and pretty soon, Shalini's parents were in Delhi, aghast to see the condition of their daughter.

As news travelled back home, Shalini's youngest brother Amit offered to donate his own kidney to Shalini.

Apart from the intense love that he had for Shalini, it was also almost as if he wanted to repay Shalini for saving his own life not too long ago.

Unfortunately, being a patient of hypertension, Amit too was ruled out as a potential donor, much to his disappointment. Similarly, her brother Atul and others too were ruled out.

Now they needed a miracle to save Shalini because without a transplant, she wouldn't survive much longer.

A miracle was exactly what happened!

As Shalini's father slept that night, he once again saw his father, his grandfather and his grandmother in a dream. They gently admonished him and told him to go back to his village and meet a cousin of his, Brij Pal. Brij Pal will donate his kidney to Shalini, they said.

Continuing the conversation with his father and grandparents, Shalini's father let out a gentle chuckle and replied that he met or spoke with Brij Pal nearly every day and that he never once said that he would want to donate his kidney to Shalini.

To this, he got admonished once again and was saw told to just go and speak with Brij Pal.

This was the point at which he woke up with a jerk. The time was 4 O' Clock and even though a bit too early in the morning, yet he was wide awake, thanks to the realization of a possibility of getting help for his daughter.

Mr Yash Pal couldn't help but wake up his wife as well, with a simple sentence – *'Utho, abhi gaanv chalna hai'* (Get up, we have to go to the village right away). When she queried why, he told her about the dream about Brij Pal being the donor of a kidney for Shalini.

That is all that Mrs Pundir needed to hear, before she rushed to get ready.

Mr Pundir next woke up his driver, Rohit, and even before the sun rose, they were out of their Dehradun house and headed to their ancestral village.

But that was not the end of the miracle!

As soon as they entered the village, the first face that they saw was that of Brij Pal. Naturally, they stopped to meet him. As if it wasn't already too much of a coincidence, the first words out of Brij Pal's mouth were, 'How is Shalini doing?'

Yash Pal truthfully replied that Shalini is on the deathbed because they are unable to find a kidney donor for her. Brij Pal was stunned. He had seen Shalini growing up and the very thought that the little girl whom he knew and was so very fond of was now counting her days, was overwhelming for him.

He was speechless and simply walked away from that place without saying anything.

Shalini's parents just stayed there, foxed, not knowing what to do when about 10 minutes later Brij Pal returned back. He had taken a bath and gotten ready.

Then he spoke the second sentence of the day to Yash Pal.

'Bhai Saab chalo, mein Shalini ko kidney de raha hoon.' (Come, I will donate my kidney to Shalini.)

Yash Pal was stunned upon hearing those words, He told Brij Pal that he would be so indebted that he would do anything for him, even give up his own life if Brij Pal said so.

A minute later, they had started for Dehradun.

Strange indeed are His ways.

Enroute to Dehradun, Yash Pal called up Ajai and gave him the good news. Then he asked to check from the R&R Hospital regarding the tests that needed to be done by the donor.

Once he got the list of tests, he took Brij Pal to a Pathologist in Dehradun and got them done that same day. Needless to say, all his test results came out favourable and he was cleared to donate his kidney.

Come to think of it, there was no other possible outcome of the said tests. In fact, those were a mere formality for the sake of the mortal world, especially when he donating his kidney to Shalini was already ordained by the Almighty himself.

Now that he was cleared to donate his kidney, Brij Pal made a very unusual request to Shalini's father. He requested that he be permitted to stay in Dehradun itself till the time a date for surgery is fixed.

His reason was very simple and at the same time, very profound as well.

He did not want any impediment to come in the way of saving Shalini's life. He just became over-protective about himself.

Brij Pal had made up his mind and didn't want to change it at any cost and his cousin Yash Pal was only too happy to continue playing host to him in Dehradun.

After a few days in Dehradun, Shalini's parents drove down to Delhi with Brij Pal. There he was once again tested by the doctors at R&R Hospital and yet again, cleared to donate his kidney to Shalini.

Now all that was needed to be done was for the Medical Ethics Committees of both UP and Delhi to clear the transplant.

They had a key role in all such instances to ensure that no unethical or illegal means of gratification / pressure were used to get people to donate their body organs. They do a lot of diligent investigation, including through the police as well as banks in order to rule out any cause of concern with respect to the motivation of the donor / recipient.

Yash Pal, after herculean efforts, was able to get the 'Okay' from the Medical Ethics Committee of UP.

But apparently, Ajai being in the profession of arms turned Shalini's case to be a challenging one for the Medical Ethics Committee of Delhi as well as Shalini's family.

Since Shalini had been away with Ajai wherever he had been posted, the questions by the Committee members to the donor regarding basic details of when and how much he had interacted with her and other such details had Brij Pal truthfully telling them that he hadn't seen her in a very long time.

This was a clear red flag for the Committee members.

Continuing with their line of investigation, they called Shalini next. Being very weak and in a wheelchair, Ajai also took the opportunity to walk in as he pushed the wheelchair.

Now it was Ajai's time to acquaint the members of the Medical Ethics Committee with the realities of life in the army. He was able to make them see the reality that being posted in different parts of the country and even abroad for three years, they hardly got time to see their extended family.

He further highlighted the fact that annual leave, though generous, cannot usually be availed fully due to service commitments as well as to prevent a break in kids' education. He told them that despite commanding his battalion in Dehradun for nearly two years, he could only visit his own home in Roorkee, which was hardly 40 minutes away, barely twice and that too for not more than two days at a time. In fact, one of these visits was actually clubbed with a professional engagement in the nearby town of Purkazi, else he might not have visited home a second time at all.

He further reiterated that here they had a patient who needed a kidney and a donor who was prepared to give his own kidney voluntarily and without any expectations of gratification in lieu and that if they didn't permit the surgery to go ahead then the patient is as good as lost.

Thankfully, the Committee members got convinced and cleared the organ donation for Shalini.

Things were now set for the much-awaited surgery and an appropriate date was decided.

Sanjana and Abhinav also came over to Delhi ahead of their mother's surgery, as did practically the entire extended family from Roorkee and Dehradun. It was quite a gathering at their residence a night before the surgery.

Before being taken to the hospital for the surgery, she told Ajai to take care of the kids. She also spoke with the kids and asked them to take care of themselves and lead a good life.

This broke something inside of Abhinav. His assumed persona of a rebellious teenager suddenly crumbled and he became a little child all over again, crying out of fear for his mother's life. He cried throughout the night.

Sanjana herself too prepared for the big day, deciding to be beautifully decked up in a bright, orange coloured suit so that her mother sees a bright and colourful sight as she regains consciousness.

In their own way, both kids were dealing with their mother's condition even as they continued to take their own tentative steps into adulthood.

However, the surgery itself wasn't without its own share of 'excitement'.

Apparently, the date chosen initially was not the best date for the surgery.

Now this wasn't as per the medical science, but from the worlds beyond. What happened was that one night prior to the originally scheduled surgery, Shalini's father was once again visited by his father and grandparents in a dream and they told him that the next day wasn't auspicious for the surgery.

Once again, Yash Pal wondered how might it be possible to reschedule the surgery at such a late stage, but he only got smiles in reply from his ancestors!

However, they had taken care of things on their own as he soon found out.

Next morning when he reached the hospital he met Ajai and the first thing that Ajai told him was that the surgery couldn't take place that day because the donor had come down with fever!

The surgery finally took place when higher powers ordained it and the kidney was successfully transplanted. Counting all minor and not so minor surgical procedures that she had undergone thus far, this would have been her eighth or ninth surgery since her diagnosis.

Shalini regained consciousness that same evening and was in fine health, but Brij Pal took a bit longer to recover from the surgery. Thankfully, he too made a full recovery.

Such was the genetic match that it was almost as if Shalini had received a kidney from a twin. This ensured a perfect transplant and assured acceptance of the kidney by her body, resulting in good life of the transplanted organ as well.

Shalini's grandfather and her great-grandparents had indeed found the best possible solution for a fresh lease at life for her.

Thus started yet another phase in Shalini's life .. with a new kidney and a reinvigorated zest for making the most of her life.

Little Shalini, younger brother Atul and mausi

Young Shalini, in the marriage of her uncle.

"Destiny's first chapter: Shalini meets Ajai, a moment that unknowingly set the course for a lifetime of memories."

"Embracing the joy of the moment, Shalini skates through life with a childlike spirit and a heart full of joy."

"Shalini stands strong, her heart heavy with unspoken fears, sheilding Abhinav and Sanjana with a mother's unwavering courage as Ajai embarks on his perilous mission."

The Family time - Flag Staff house Bhuj

Celebrating 25 years of love and togetherness

"Life blossoms anew. Shalini's first outing post her transplant to Surajkund.

Celebrating Sanjana's bday with Doofus and Daisy- where she is, the love follows.

"Shalini and Ajai, standing tall like the Eiddel Tower' Europes Panoramic tour.

Taking a breathtaking view of the iconic London Bridge, where every moment felt like a dream

The Golden couple amidst the Golden dunes of Dubai.

"Shalini in her role as the Principal of the Army Regimental play school 11 GRRC, Lucknow

The radiant smile telling the story of strenght, positivity and an unyeliding resolve.

The smile says it all - Happy parents with the groom.

"Pure joy, endless laughter, and a family bond shining bright for the new chapter - at Abhinav and Sukritis wedding

"Shalini and the family groove together atop the Rath at Abhinav's wedding.

"Celebrating love, unity and new beginnings - at Abhinav and Sukritis wedding

In her favourite glassroom - at Sharifabad, Kashmir valley

Even the birds felt her love and care - with the bulbul at Sharifabad, Kashmir valley.

"Conquering fears, one wave at a time. During the marriage of Air Marshal Chandrashekar's daughter.

A beautiful moment - at Punakha Dzong

"Shalini, Ajai and Akshat, who was soon to marry their daughter Sanjana - cherishing the warm moments of what would be her last Diwali.

Sharing moments of love and laughter - Kiranti House, Lucknow.

"Shalini, radiating joy and nostalgia - in Lucknow to attend regimental get together.

Triumph of the spirit - First day first show.

The last party at Rorkee celebrating the promotion of Ajai.

Celebrating the 60th marriage anniversary of her beloved parents.

"Shalini at Terra Woods - Abhinav's venture cherishing the success of kids.

She continues to live on as our guardian angel guiding us with her love and care.

11

A NEW LIFE!

Much to the pleasant surprise of everyone, Shalini's recovery commenced almost as soon as the new kidney was transplanted. The first sign of this was her skin that rapidly started recovering its normal shade as the new kidney started filtering out the body waste.

After so many months and years of uncertainty and other struggles, this was indeed a welcome sign and reason enough to rejoice. However, there still remained a lot of work to be done by Ajai, Abhinav and Sanjana as there would continue to be a lot of health-related challenges for Shalini in the near and far future, primarily due to the immunosuppressants that she would be taking in order to help her body accept the donated kidney.

The immediate challenge was to prepare the house for her arrival after immediate post-surgery care was done in the hospital.

The trio of Ajai, Abhinav and Sanjana quickly got to work, in getting their government accommodation ready for Shalini. It was a typical house in a typical military enclave – House No 180, Dhaula Kuan 2. This was a first floor house that would now transform into a sterile environment for Shalini.

The work began with a deep cleaning and fumigation of the entire house, whereafter a glass screen door was installed by the Military Engineering Services in Shalini's room.

Meanwhile, back in the hospital, Shalini continued to recover, no doubt helped by her cheerful nature and the happy knowledge that the transplant had been successful. After about two weeks in the hospital, she was ready to come back home!

When she had last left home, Shalini's weight was down to 46kg and her skin had turned dark, covered with sores and boils that were excreting the waste which the kidneys were unable to. But now, when she returned, she was totally transformed!

It would be wrong to say that she was 'normal'. In fact, there was still a long road to recovery ahead of her. However, she was on the mend and definitely in a much better condition than she had been earlier. And most importantly, she was extremely happy to be back home!

The home too suddenly seemed to come alive with the happy aura of Shalini soon permeating each and every nook and cranny!

During her first few days back home, Shalini stayed alone in the room created for her. Even the immediate family members would stay away in order to minimize any chances of infection. Even food and water were just pushed inside the room with minimum disturbance. Even the two pet dogs learnt fairly quickly to keep away from Shalini in those days!

Thank God for the glass door, though, that enabled them to see each other!

On the rare occasion when someone needed to enter her room to clean it up or for whatever other reason, they would diligently sterilize themselves and the clothes they were wearing.

Slowly, the days passed. Ajai made it a routine to stay in that very room with Shalini upon return from office after taking a bath and sterilizing himself to the extent he could.

Over time, even this routine relaxed a bit because firstly, Shalini was healing fairly well and secondly, this was not the way she would live her life. The periodic hospital visits for follow-on check ups also slowly helped normalize things. Yet, they were all very clear in their minds that they had to take all possible precautions due to her weakened immunity.

Seeing their mother recovering fine, Abhinav and Sanjana reluctantly returned to their colleges in Pune and resumed their graduation sometime in this duration.

The doctors had given her very strict instructions to watch what she ate and drank and to wear a mask whenever she moved out of home. Shalini followed these instructions diligently and wearing a mask soon became second nature for her.

As was typical of Shalini, she didn't take these instructions as some imposition on her and instead, took them as a ticket for liberty! Liberty, to slowly start living her life again and to enjoy the things that she loved.

As the winters approached, the house below Shalini and Ajai's was vacated by their neighbour, Brigadier Mukherjee. Though, army accommodations getting vacated every two or three years is a fairly regular occurrence due to tenure durations being such, in this particular case what was different was that the house lay vacant and unallotted for quite some time.

Taking this as an opportunity, Ajai and Shalini made full use of the beautiful lawn that Brig and Mrs Mukherjee had so lovingly created in the now-locked house!

It was almost as if the Almighty had decided to gift a lawn for Shalini to enjoy the beautiful sunny winter afternoons of Delhi!

On Sundays, Shalini and Ajai would spend bulk of their mornings and afternoons on the lawn of the vacant house downstairs. That exposure to sunlight also helped Shalini heal faster.

It was at about this time that their two dogs - Shelly, the female Labrador and Wai, a stray that Abhinav had adopted - also started to gingerly come to her, still maintaining their distance. Much as she loved them both, Shalini just couldn't play with them anymore the way she used to earlier.

However, to their credit, the dogs displayed how perceptive they were when it came to Shalini's health. It was as if they knew instinctively that something was wrong with her, and did their best to take care of her in their own way.

Once they realised that Shalini was not well, they took special care of her. They would never trouble her and were extra affectionate with her. When she was in a playful mood, they would happily play with her but the moment they sensed that she was tired and wanted to rest, they would just as quickly tone down.

They were constant companions to Shalini before and after her transplant, especially due to long absences of Ajai during office hours. The dogs instinctively knew the power of physical touch and would constantly be by her side, mostly by her feet, with their bodies in physical contact with Shalini as if to soothe her.

The dogs did not just keep her company especially when Ajai was in office, but kept her entertained as well! Wai was a stray little pup that Abhinav had picked up during a road trip to Goa some years ago. As the little pup grew, they realised it was part German Shephard or some similar breed. Resultantly, Wai loved to run, and she soon made a really interesting game of it while in Dhaula Kuan.

Since the family stayed on the first floor, whenever Wai would come out on the terrace, the stray dogs would start barking. Wai would wait for that to happen and then as if to challenge them, she would go down and take all those dogs out for a chase around the Dhaula Kuan 2 colony!

Wai was so fast that none of the dogs could even come close to her. After two or three rounds of the colony at full speed, she would climb back to the terrace and stare back at them, mocking!

All this made for great entertainment and amusement for Shalini as well, and life gradually 'normalized' for her and her family.

Through this all, she was very particular about her medications and other precautions that doctors had advised her about.

Slow and steady, the beautiful moments started making a comeback as Shalini and Ajai came to terms with the new normal. As a family and as a couple, they started enjoying life with a renewed zeal.

They gradually started going out on leisure trips within Delhi and some time later to Roorkee and Dehradun as well. Sanjana too remembers the first shopping trips that she took with her mother after more than a year.

Life was good again, and soon, as is typical of an Army job, Ajai got fresh posting orders to proceed to the 11 Gorkha Rifles Regimental Centre in Lucknow as the Deputy Commandant sometime in mid-2009, after a three year long tenure in Delhi.

It wasn't entirely unexpected since Lt Gen GM Nair, the *Colonel of the Regiment*, had called up Ajai and sought his willingness to go to the Regimental Centre. Of course, in such cases, a request is as good as an order and there was no way Ajai would even think of saying no. The Regimental Centre was in Lucknow where there were good medical facilities for Shalini also helped make the decision. Of course, going back to the cradle of the Regiment was an additional incentive as well.

The household in Dhaula Kuan 2 was packed up accordingly and the staff was dispatched to Lucknow by truck. As always, Shalini and Ajai drove down to Lucknow in their trusty Ford Fusion. The only difference this time was that this was the first posting where they were driving in without any of the kids, with both pursuing their graduation studies in Pune.

The just concluded Delhi tenure had been a defining period in Shalini's as well as Ajai's lives. They had gone in with uncertainty and apprehension about their future, had made strenuous efforts individually and together to overcome the massive challenges facing them, and thankfully, had emerged victorious and at the same time, transformed.

It was nothing short of miraculous that they had survived a tenure that could have very easily turned devastatingly ugly. This in itself is a great testimony to Shalini's grit and sheer willpower that she manifested her recovery and bore immense pain and suffering in order to ensure the same.

She had *chosen* to live on till her children were settled and her husband too was set in his career. It was her doggedness and perseverance in pursuance of this aim that carried her through such difficult times that might have devastated a lesser mortal.

Throughout it all, Shalini remained positive and optimistic and it showed on her ever-smiling face. While leaning on Ajai and the rest of her family for support, she herself too kept giving them hope.

In a way, it wouldn't be wrong to say that her cheerful demeanour had some sort of a placebo effect on her caregivers as well, for the doctors and nurses in the Army Hospital R&R too were suitably charmed and enamoured by this patient who never let her life-threatening condition come in the way of a smile.

So in a way, during the road trip to Lucknow Shalini left behind not just the city of New Delhi but also a very difficult chapter of her life. Befittingly, the entire drive saw monsoon clouds and the occasional showers of rain accompanying them along with beautiful weather, as a portend of happy and pleasant times ahead.

This was not to say that there would be no challenges. But just that life would be much better for the next few years than it had been for the past few years.

It was quite late in the evening by the time they reached the Regimental Centre in Lucknow. One of the Battalion Commanders was there to receive them at their guest room.

Incidentally, it was the same guest room where Ajai had stayed nearly 25 years ago after the successful culmination of a mountaineering expedition to Mt. Rathong in Sikkim. Of course, the guest room itself had changed drastically since then!

Since it was quite a few years since his last visit to the Regimental Centre, Ajai decided to quickly change to games dress and go for a walk around the Centre to soak in the essence of the very cradle of his Regiment as well as to get acquainted with the roads and tracks within it.

As Ajai went about exploring the Regimental Centre, Shalini too wasted no time and got busy opening up the household stuff they had carried in their car, and started converting that guest room into her temporary home.

In the case of Shalini, it was also uniquely symbolic because after marriage, she had come first to Ajai's Battalion instead of his ancestral home. This time, coming to the Regimental Centre after a major life event too was something quite similar, as she commenced yet another new phase of her life's journey.

Thus began the new chapter in their lives, akin to a homecoming to the place from where Ajai's Regimental journey had begun. As mentioned earlier, it was also *different* in that both kids were now young adults and exploring the world on their own in Pune, away from their parents.

In a unique turn of events, the Regimental Centre didn't have a Commandant posted at the time Ajai reported there, so he had to don the hat of the Officiating Commandant for quite some time. Accordingly, Shalini too settled into her new role as the head of the ladies' part of the Regimental family and together, they pretty soon had a happy family going about their business in Lucknow.

In a way, Shalini was equally busy if not busier than Ajai because Lucknow, being a major military station, had a lot of organised activities for the ladies. With the 11 Gorkha Rifles Regimental Centre being the de-facto workhorse of the Lucknow based Central Command, a lot of such responsibilities came in the lap of Shalini.

Unsurprisingly, she was more than up for the job that called upon her to invest a lot of her time, Shalini was practically everywhere, marshalling her ladies and ensuring things happened the way they needed to. Her days were busy but happy nonetheless, and pretty soon, the ladies of Regimental Centre established a solid reputation in the ladies' circles in Lucknow.

Ajai was also happy to see his wife up and about, after almost three years of having had to curtail her natural instincts and being confined to her house or hospital. In the middle of all this, they never forgot the medical precautions that Shalini had to take. The Command Hospital being nearby also helped in her periodic check-ups by the Nephrologist posted there.

The check-ups were very regular and Shalini would undergo an entire battery of tests every month or so. Yet, she never complained and those who didn't know about her medical history could never had guessed what this jolly and happy lady had been through and what she was still going through.

A few months in, came the news of the posting of Brigadier Anil Chauhan (now the CDS) as the Centre Commandant.

Ajai could finally shed some responsibilities that had come on his shoulders due to him officiating as the Commandant. However, there was no such relief for Shalini because Brig Anil Chauhan came single, with Mrs Chauhan unable to join him in Lucknow!

So Shalini continued in her role as the seniormost lady of the Regimental Centre. Hers was a really busy social life, with frequent Family Welfare Programmes, Ladies' Meets and the added responsibilities of coordinating such events with other senior ladies of the Command Headquarters as well as the Command Hospital.

Thankfully, she was in a good physical condition and continued to religiously follow the medical advice that she had been given.

One of her passions was gardening, and with the Regimental Centre blessed with beautiful gardens and lawns, Shalini really came into her own as far as gardening went.

So much so that on one occasion some seeds were specially procured from Kolkata and the gardeners and other staff specially trained and all gardens in the Regimental Centre were carefully and lovingly tended to under Shalini's watch.

This was really fortuitous because the social scene in Lucknow also comprised of a plethora of gardening competitions as well! And those who had seen Shalini tend to her gardens were not at all surprised when thanks to her efforts, the Regimental Centre made a clean sweep of most of the prizes across practically every category in the Garden Competition!

In fact, there is a much-cherished photograph of Shalini sitting at the steps of the Auditorium after the concluding ceremony of the competition, with all the trophies and medals won by the Regimental Centre under her stewardship.

Where an ordinary mortal might have given up, Shalini thrived in discharging the responsibilities that had fallen on her shoulders in that tenure. As always, she was never seen without that characteristic smile on her face and spring in her step. Her enthusiasm was infectious and it brought out the best from all ladies that she was responsible for guiding through various tasks.

While Shalini made it look easy, but fact remains that getting so many ladies to function together was quite an achievement, especially because officers and ladies in a Regimental Centre come from all battalions of the Regiment and in most cases, have never served with or known each other before that.

Hats off indeed that Shalini ensured a happy team of ladies in the Regimental Centre. Of course, this also meant that Shalini had to go the extra mile ever so often, but she did it without any complaints, always aware of the larger goal of having a happy family in the Centre.

Those nine months that Shalini and Ajai spent in Lucknow passed this way in a state of near-perpetual bliss.

As always, they also played host to a steady stream of friends and family and their home was almost always hosting someone or the other.

In the midst of this, however, there was a sad incident wherein Wai got bitten by a snake and died as a result. She was a naturally inquisitive dog and would often wander to the small jungle area behind the Deputy Commandant's bungalow into which Shalini and Ajai had shifted.

The area was known to be inhabited by a large variety of snakes and scorpions. During one such sojourn, Wai came back crying in agony, unable to use her hind legs properly.

It was quite apparent that she had been bitten by a venomous snake and was soon unable to walk at all. She was in immense pain and crying bitterly. Ajai rushed home from office as soon as he heard about this, but there was hardly anything he could do.

Despite their best efforts to help her, Wai died in agony within a few hours.

Wai was a beloved member of the family and the entire household was devastated at this sudden and unexpected turn of events. That night, hardly anyone in the household had a proper meal. But unknown to them, there was yet more agony to come their way pretty soon.

Next day, Shelly too passed away.

She had no ailments and was in the prime of her age. It appeared that she just couldn't bear the loss of her closest companion and decided to leave her own mortal body as well.

While devastating for the family, losing yet another beloved pet within 24 hours of the loss of the first one, it was also poignantly profound at some level. That companionship and love between two dogs of different breeds who had been constant companions for the past many years of their lives, meant that when one died, the other too chose to die.

This was indeed something to be cherished, regardless of the immense pain at the loss of those two faithful companions.

Befittingly, Shelly too was laid to rest right next to the spot where Wai's mortal remains were buried. The site was next to the gate leading to the fish pond and mango orchard right in front of the KIRAT HOUSE Commandant's official residence, just across the road.

Naturally, that gate became quite a landmark for Shalini as well as Ajai and whenever they passed by, they would look in the direction of the two mounds underneath which their dogs were peacefully at rest. In later years too, even after they had moved out of the Regimental Centre, no visit to Lucknow was complete without visiting that site.

Thankfully, their abode already had another dog by then – a Pug named Doofus that belonged to Sanjana which had been gifted to her by one of Ajai's school classmates, Anil Sally, from Saharanpur.

Sanjana had taken the Pug with her to Mumbai as she cut short her graduation and chose instead to start her career as an Assistant Director in the film industry. However, due to her frequent absence during shoots, she was unable to look after Doofus. And Pugs being companion dogs, it wasn't good for his emotional health either.

Resultantly, she decided to leave her dog in the care of her parents in Lucknow and that is how Doofus the Pug came to be Shalini and Ajai's companion.

Even though the Lucknow tenure was relatively short due to Ajai's promotion, Shalini still made it a point to go about exploring as much of the city as she could. Though Ajai couldn't venture out much due to his official commitments, Shalini managed to see quite a bit of Lucknow on her own, or with other ladies of the Regimental Centre.

She shopped to her heart's content and she ate to her heart's content too, making sure to become a lifelong authority on two of Lucknow's signature offerings – garments and non-veg gourmet food!

Some time in this duration came the good news of Ajai getting approved for promotion to the rank of Brigadier. Naturally, there were celebrations all around, but there would still be some time before he could be placed in command of a suitable brigade as and when a vacancy arose.

Initially, he was earmarked for taking over command of Uri Brigade, located in the Kashmir Valley. Ajai was quite happy with this, because he would be going back to his old hunting grounds of Uri and thereabouts. Further, Uri Brigade is pretty much a show-window brigade of the Indian Army, located as it is in a very crucial part of the Kashmir Valley.

However, this would entail leaving Shalini behind, which was a matter of concern for Ajai. Moreover, his mother too wasn't very happy to see him go back to Kashmir.

It seems that her prayers were answered because one afternoon out of the blue, Ajai got a call from Lt Gen GM Nair, the Military Secretary in the Army Headquarters. The Military Secretary heads the branch that looks after postings of officers.

Gen Nair besides being a fellow Regimental officer who too had commanded 1/11 Gorkha Rifles, just like Ajai, was also the Colonel of the ELEVENTH GORKHA RIFLES. However, this afternoon he was calling both as a Regimental senior as well as the Military Secretary. He came straight to the point and told Ajai that for some reasons, Uri Brigade was not working out for him.

Then he asked Ajai whether he had ever been to Bhuj!

Ajai understood what he meant, but couldn't ask directly. So he informed Gen Nair that yes, he had been there one time while doing the Higher Command Course.

This is how the call ended. Ajai knew that he was now more likely to go to command the Brigade in Bhuj rather than Kashmir. Instead of feeling bad about it or trying to influence the decision somehow, he chose to accept it as destiny and decided to accept what came his way.

Of course, his mother would be happy and Shalini too would be able to stay with him in Bhuj.

With the benefit of hindsight, it can safely be said that this intervention by fate was for the good of all concerned!

Unsurprisingly, Ajai soon got his orders to take over command of the Indian Army brigade in Bhuj. It was to be an entirely new experience, not just with the unique geography of the area, but also because of other factors due to it.

But as always, this move too had the usual *twist*!

Apparently, the Army Headquarters had rushed Ajai's posting without realising that the incumbent Brigade Commander still hadn't completed his mandated reckonable Annual Confidential Reports in that appointment!

So they did the next best thing – they granted some leave to Ajai before his joining!

On his part, Ajai too decided to reach the place much earlier than his scheduled date of reporting so that he could unhurriedly get acquainted with the area and also get ample opportunity to learn from the experiences of the incumbent Brigade Commander. So he spoke with the incumbent, Brig RS Rathore and with his concurrence, started for Bhuj a couple of weeks before his official joining date.

Of course, this time too, Ajai and Shalini chose to drive down to Bhuj in their trusted Ford Fusion!

The household had been duly packed up and Ajai's parents moved back to the family home in Roorkee. Both kids too had by now moved to Mumbai to pursue their respective careers.

So it was just Shalini and Ajai by themselves for the next few days as they drove down to Bhuj. And of course, little Doofus who too was on his first long drive!

First halt during this journey was Jhansi. It had been raining very heavily that day and they had to wade through ankle deep water to get to their guestroom!

Not keen to miss this opportunity, they decided to visit the Jhansi Fort. Thus, after a quick freshening up, they were off to the historical fort. It was a mesmerizing evening, with the beautiful Light and Sound Show that brought out the rich history of valour associated with the Rani of Jhansi.

At the same time, it was also a sight to see Shalini, despite her own physical and medical issues, keep up with Ajai despite a punishing schedule of the past few days and a long drive that day.

The large numbers of steps & the walk at the Fort didn't deter her either. All in all, it was a memorable evening. Early next morning, they took off for the second leg of their long drive, this time to Kota.

Thankfully, the only plan they had for the evening in Kota was to hit bed early and sleep off some of the fatigue of the accumulated past few days!

Waking up refreshed the next morning, they started early because the plan was to hit Udaipur – the Lake City. Brig RG Patil, a coursemate and a good friend of Ajai was commanding the Udaipur Brigade at that time. Upon reaching there, Shalini and Ajai checked into a beautiful guest room on the first floor overlooking the Udaipur Lake. In the evening, they were invited by Brig Patil for dinner at the Flag Staff House. It was a wonderful evening indeed, spent catching up with old times. Post dinner, they both returned early after soaking in the night view of the Udaipur Lake.

Bhuj was their destination the next day. It was a beautiful drive .. almost as a sign of how things would be for the next many months for which they would be calling Bhuj as home.

The road was wonderful, thankfully the traffic was also not very bad and most importantly, the monsoon weather was just perfect for such a drive!

The weather enroute was especially memorable .. full of clouds and pleasant temperatures, as if Mother Nature too had decided to be at her best for welcoming Shalini and Ajai to their new abode.

Sometime in the afternoon they found a small hut surrounded by a clump of trees where they decided to halt for lunch. It was a leisurely and unhurried lunch by the roadside that they enjoyed thoroughly and then just as they packed up and started off again, it started raining.

Pretty soon, it went from a light drizzle to a heavy downpour. It was as if Mother Nature was waiting for them to finish their meal in peace before letting go of all that moisture that was there in the clouds above!

It was the heaviest downpour that Ajai had ever seen, accompanied by high winds as well. So much so that even the road was barely visible. Yet, they drove on, albeit at a much reduced speed.

The delay enroute only gave Shalini and Ajai more time for themselves!

The weather gradually let up and got milder as they reached Bhuj. Once again, it was as if Mother Nature had let go of her fury just so that their first view of the salt wastelands in that part of the country was unimpeded and suitably impressive!

Finally they reached the Bhuj Military Station at about 4:30 pm and were guided to their allotted guest room. Over there, the DQ of the Brigade, Lt Col Jagbhan Singh and his wife were waiting to receive and welcome them to the Station.

Amongst the many *firsts* that Shalini and Ajai experienced while over there was seeing a Flamingo egg that had been placed in their guest room!

After exchanging pleasantries and calling up the incumbent Brigade Commander, Shalini and Ajai settled down in the guest room for a relaxed evening. It was important to be well rested before they dived into the life in Bhuj from the next day onwards!

Weather in Bhuj was wonderful. In the evening, it was almost like a natural air conditioner, with cool winds blowing inwards from the sea every evening as the hot air over the land rose and pulled in the sea breeze.

They would stay in the guest room for the next few days before Ajai assumed his new rank and took over command of the Brigade.

This duration was well spent by Ajai in getting briefed about the Brigade and visiting the various parts of the area of responsibility.

In an interesting turn of events, the Deputy Commander in the Brigade was Col Om Gulia, a coursemate of Ajai's, In fact Col Gulia was also approved for the next rank and was keen to take over the Bhuj Brigade before destiny intervened and Ajai was diverted in his place.

Col Gulia, being an old friend, ended up taking Ajai through the paces in a very methodical and clear manner even as he found himself diverted to take over the Brigade in Pune.

It was a very satisfying turn of events in which Col Gulia instead of having to take over command of the Bhuj Brigade, ended up in Pune where his daughter was studying at that time.

While Ajai was busy with the professional aspects, Shalini too started exploring the cantonment and the areas outside it in steadily expanding concentric circles. Along with that, she also started getting to know the ladies of the officers and jawans that were posted in the Station and various issues pertaining to the Station infrastructure and families that would merit her attention as the First Lady of the Station.

Time flew by and soon it was the day Ajai was to pick up his new rank as a Brigadier and take over command of the Bhuj Brigade. Shalini and Ajai had decided that he should be *pipped* in the ancient Shiv Mandir within the garrison.

Pipping is the military term for removing the current ranks from the shoulders of an officer on promotion and putting on new ranks.

On that day, the outgoing Brigade Commander and Shalini *pipped* Ajai with the ranks of Brigadier in the presence of the Almighty Lord Shiv.

Thus commenced what is remembered as the fondest tenure by both Shalini as well as Ajai.

It was a really challenging, yet professionally satisfying as well as enriching command tenure for Ajai due to the unique topology of the area and the unique structure of the Bhuj Brigade.

With that came a beautiful and majestic *Flag Staff House,* i.e. the official residence of the Brigade Commander. It was the best such house that they had stayed in thus far. Being a duplex house, they not only had two huge lawns and a whole orchard to themselves, but also a wonderful sit-out in the two large balconies on the first floor.

For Shalini, that house was love at first sight and she immediately set-out making it into their cozy nest for the next couple of years.

As they settled down in the new abode, Shalini and Ajai came to realize how big a blessing Bhuj was for them, especially considering that the original plan was for Ajai to be commanding a Brigade in the Kashmir Valley!

Not only were Shalini and Ajai together, but Bhuj also had a well equipped Military Hospital with a Medical Specialist posted there. Further, there was a daily, direct flight to Mumbai in case Shalini's medical condition needed access to a bigger hospital.

And then there was the very air in Bhuj that was greatly therapeutic in its own right. Bhuj is known for its vast salt plains in the vicinity of the Arabian Sea. So the air in the area is always laden with salt. Add to that the daily evening sea breeze and the sheer amount of salt hitting the body is quite high.

This salt laden air ends up cleansing the bodies and to a large extent, even the very souls of the people who come in regular contact with it. Needless to say, Shalini thrived in it.

The Flag Staff House was a double storey bungalow with the kitchen, drawing room and one bedroom on the ground floor and two bedrooms including the master bedroom on the first floor. Then there were the lavish lawns and a huge orchard as well.

All in all, it was a huge property. Shalini had fallen in love with it at first sight. She never ever got bothered with the constant running around that she would have to do in the house. In fact, as always, this house too was set up in record time and was ready to welcome its first guests within two weeks of Shalini setting foot in it!

At the same time, she got busy getting to know the ladies of officers and jawans in the Station. Such was the bonhomie that she created, that ladies of the then battalions of the Bhuj Brigade, which included one battalion each from the Kumaon Regiment, the Mahar Regiment and the Jammu and Kashmir Light Infantry, still remember those days under the wings of Shalini with great fondness.

Needless to say, the Bhuj Brigade was one large, happy family during the time Shalini and Ajai were there. Come to think of it, this is also what made it a formidable fighting formation – one with excellent camaraderie and professionalism. It came as no surprise that the Bhuj Brigade excelled under the command of (then) Brig Ajai Kumar Singh, SM.

As always, Shalini also ventured out to Bhuj town frequently and pretty soon, was a masterful repository of knowledge about the local art and handicrafts of Kutch in general and Bhuj in particular, in addition to making quite a few acquaintances amongst the local citizens of the town itself.

She shopped to her heart's content and not just for herself, but for her entire family.

In the meanwhile, Abhinav and Sanjana too were taking their own first steps in their respective careers in Mumbai and would often visit their parents in Bhuj whenever time permitted.

Those were some really carefree and blissful days for Shalini and Ajai, even if in a relatively remote and unknown part of the country.

Shalini was a seasoned veteran in her own rights when it came to matters pertaining to families and their welfare in a relatively large formation like the Bhuj Brigade. Her experiences in Dharan, Dehradun and Lucknow had moulded her into a *mother hen* who would go any distance when it came to ensuring happiness of her flock!

Not just content with keeping them happy, Shalini also took it upon herself to upskill the wives of the jawans who normally come from relatively humble backgrounds. Skill training was one of her key focus areas while in Bhuj.

She would very often be visiting the wives of jawans in their housing complexes to see what they were in need of, or many times, to just have a cup of tea with them.

Bhuj, being a relatively small town, didn't offer many avenues for outings to the military families posted there. With Shalini and Ajai leading from the front, the Military Station itself had such a vibrant social life that no one in particular missed it very much.

However, Shalini's medical condition still imposed a lot of caution. Even though she was in reasonably good health, both physically and spiritually, she had to make frequent trips to the Military Hospital for routine checkups.

Unfortunately, the Bhuj Military Hospital didn't have a nephrologist posted there. But, the young Medical Specialist, Major Arjun was a big boon.

In order to help him treat Shalini, Ajai would be in frequent contact with Col Ranjith Nair, the specialist who had treated her in Delhi. In turn, Col Nair would advise and guide Maj Arjun as he strove to ensure that Shalini remained as healthy as she could.

It was a nice little ecosystem of caregivers who were happily at work to ensure Shalini continued to make the most of the new lease of life that she had been given. Which was just as well, because Shalini did have the occasional health issues.

However, the most dramatic and alarming health scare of that tenure happened not with Shalini, but with Sanjana!

The timing too couldn't have been any worse. It happened when most of the brigade were out for a major exercise. It so happened that in that duration, Sanjana landed up for a weekend trip to Bhuj, making good use of the overnight bus service from Mumbai.

Together, mother and daughter headed out to the Mandvi Beach which was about one hour away from the Bhuj Military Station. It is a beautiful beach and was a favourite picnic spot for Shalini and her flock, especially since the Maharao of Kutch was happy to share his private beach with Ajai and his family.

On this particular day things took a turn for the worse when Sanjana got stung by a Jellyfish in the water. A jellyfish sting can be very dangerous in certain cases, and in this case it seemed to be affecting Sanjana very badly and she started to lose consciousness.

Shalini made frantic calls to Ajai even as she tried to keep Sanjana awake. However, Ajai was unable to do much since he, with most of the brigade, was hundreds of kilometres away.

Instead he advised Shalini to rush back to Bhuj and at the same time, called up the doctor and requested him to rush towards Mandvi.

This might just have been what saved Sanjana that day.

Shalini ensured that Sanjana stayed conscious throughout the one hour or so that it took for the doctor to meet them enroute. Thankfully, he was able to administer emergency treatment and stabilize her enough to be able to reach the Military Hospital where she stayed admitted for the next few days before making a full recovery.

The second major medical scare of the tenure pertained to Shalini. Once again, Ajai was out in an exercise and not available in Bhuj. During the exercise, he got the message that Shalini wasn't too well and that the doctors were of the opinion that she needs to go under specialist care in the navy hospital in Mumbai, INHS Ashwini.

However, there was a catch here.

Shalini, who was in any case fearful of flying, was just not willing to undertake a flight without Ajai, especially in this state. This was despite the fact that Sanjana was in Bhuj and willing to fly to Mumbai with her mother.

Ajai once again had to come up with a solution from about 200 km away.

His proposed solution was simple and efficient.

He suggested to the doctor to give her an Alprax that would calm her nerves and enable her to undertake the short flight to Mumbai. Further, coordination was carried out with the airport authorities in Bhuj to facilitate her check-in and other formalities so that she has minimal hassles.

Thus flew Shalini and Sanjana from Bhuj to Mumbai with Abhinav waiting for them there.

Shalini was taken straight to the hospital from the airport itself.

She had a running fever and was extremely weak. As soon as she reached the hospital, she was admitted and put on drips even as the doctors rushed to manage her situation. They were taking absolutely no chances due to Shalini's recent medical history.

The doctors at INHS Ashwini were at par with the best available anywhere in the country and Shalini was in safe hands. Sanjana lived more than one hour away from the hospital and it being a totally new setup, Shalini was reluctant to be alone in the hospital without any family around.

So the young Sanjana came up with a masterstroke.

She requested the doctors to admit her too in the hospital on some pretext!

Thankfully, the doctors saw the merit in her suggestion and soon mother and daughter were admitted together in the hospital in Mumbai. This not only saved Sanjana a two hour long round trip every day, but it also enabled her to look after her mother 24/7 for the few days that she was undergoing treatment out there.

Shalini was finally fit enough to be discharged in about a week's time and she flew back to her home in Bhuj, this time on her own!

Meanwhile Ajai continued to be in the exercise area with his brigade. It was a major exercise and they validated a large number of concepts and fine tuned the already well-oiled fighting formation that the Bhuj Brigade was.

For this exercise, the troops had worked long and hard. Befittingly, it called for an appropriate de-brief as well, where the senior hierarchy from the Division headquarters was also expected to be present including the Division Commander, General Iqbal Singha himself.

At the end of the exercise, the brigade quickly re-oriented themselves to play the perfect hosts for all who were expected to come over for the debrief. It was to happen somewhere in the Kutch region where the Bhuj Brigade created an entire 'Tent City'.

To be fair, they *had* to make arrangements for all the officers who would be coming over, due to the sheer remoteness of the area and lack of any hospitality infrastructure whatsoever. All that they did was to do it in military finesse!

The result was on totally expected lines! The officers from the Division headquarters stayed for a couple of days extra just to soak in the nature and the unique landscape of the Rann of Kutch.

This was followed by Shalini and other ladies of the Brigade too joining their husbands for a few days in the tent city, before it was wound up and the officers and men returned to Bhuj for some well-earned family time!

Sometime in this duration, Gen Singha made an official visit to Bhuj, with Mrs Singha too accompanying him. The itinerary prepared for the General and his wife included a breakfast hosted by Ajai and Shalini in the lavish lawns of their Flag Staff House.

Now Ajai being a Gorkha officer, typical Nepalese dishes were staple fare that was prepared whenever guests came over. This time too was no different .. until it became a *lot* different from other times!

What happened was that Mrs Singha, not very familiar with Nepalese cuisine, mistook a *Dalle Khursani* for a cherry and ate it whole in one go!

Dalle Khursani is a really hot Nepalese red cherry pepper chilli that is mostly cultivated in the Eastern part of Nepal, Darjeeling,

Sikkim and Bhutan. It is really easy to be mistaken for a cherry for someone who has never seen it before. *Dalle Khursani* is usually consumed in very small quantities along with the food.

That morning, to the horror of Ajai and Shalini, of all the people in the world who could have made that mistake, it just *had* to be the wife of the GOC and that too in their very home!

To cut a long story short, all hell broke loose the moment Mrs Singha took the first bite, and it took quite some time to get things under control! Thankfully, to their credit, General and Mrs Singha laughed it away and the breakfast as well as the rest of the visit continued as planned.

Bhuj was also the tenure where Shalini and Ajai completed 25 years of marital bliss. It was a momentous occasion and the staff officers of Ajai's brigade took it upon themselves to ensure it was celebrated in a befitting and grand manner.

The planning was done with true military efficiency and catered for anything and everything that one could think of. Naturally, it was impossible to keep this 'operation' a secret, but even then, one part was kept well hidden from the 'bride' and the 'groom'!

That evening in Shalini and Ajai's Flag Staff House saw them perform a *Nikaah*, presided over by the Maulvi of the 12 Jammu and Kashmir Light Infantry Battalion that was part of the brigade. True to the festive spirit, the officers and ladies of the brigade divided themselves into the groom's party and the bride's party and played their role to the hilt!

After the mutual *Kubool Hai* by the bride and the groom, the celebratory fervour assumed a different energy all together and bottles of wine and champagne were popped open!

A cake descended from the heavens above for the bride and the groom to cut. Well, actually it was lowered manually from the tree house in the garden of the Flag Staff House, but no one was bothered by such technicalities on such a momentous occasion!

Sometime in the middle of this, came the surprise gift that the bride and the groom had no clue about. It was the result of that secret operation which had been underway for the past few weeks.

The gift was a montage of memories from the very beginning of their married life. In order to prepare for this, Sanjana and Abhinav had been taken into confidence by the brigade officers and photographs from Shalini and Ajai's marital journey were obtained without their knowledge, including some photos that were still packed away in their boxes stored in Delhi!

These were then woven into a beautiful montage of memories which was signed by all officers of the brigade. This montage has since adorned the walls of Shalini and Ajai's room in each and every place that they have called home.

As the night progressed, the bride and the groom were called upon to sing a couple of songs. The most applauded song that night was *Ek Pyar Ka Nagma Hai*, that perfectly summed up their togetherness!

Dinner happened after 1 O' Clock in the night and by the time the last of the guests left, it was almost dawn!

Thus continued life in Bhuj!

No wonder it was and continues to be, a fabulous and highly cherished tenure for Shalini and Ajai. In a way, it marked a *Coming of Age* for both of them together as a couple, as well as individuals.

Having emerged from a truly difficult time wherein the very life of Shalini was on the brink, they revelled in each other's company as if to make up for the lost time and also to make the most of whatever time together that was left.

More than that, the fragility of mortal life had nudged them both, together as well as individually, on a path of spiritual learning. As they immersed themselves deeper and deeper into this ocean, they started enjoying each and every moment of their lives with that much more vigour and intensity. And it was inevitable that this sense of content and joy pervaded amongst all those who came in their lives, professionally, socially or personally.

While Ajai commanded the officers and men of the brigade, Shalini too kept her flock of ladies in a happy and congenial environment. There was the occasional challenge, but Shalini was a no-nonsense head of her own family and knew how to handle any issues with tact and maturity, thus ensuring a healthy climate throughout. Her motherly touch ensured that the families in the Station were always in good cheer and taken good care of.

It is thus no wonder that not just Shalini and Ajai but in fact, all those who were there in Bhuj with them at that time, remember that tenure with a special fondness in their hearts.

They worked hard, and they partied harder!

So much so, that in the year 2023, that family from Shalini and Ajai's time in Bhuj once again came together in Bhuj for a weekend of reminiscing and remembering that amazing tenure. The current team of the Bhuj Brigade played host to their predecessors from more than a decade ago and saw them revel in each other's company all over again.

Being in Bhuj offered another unique opportunity to Shalini and Ajai. Mount Abu was not very far away, especially during routine travels to the Division Headquarters in Ahmedabad. Now, Mount Abu, apart from being a popular tourist destination, is also home to Rishi Vashisht Ashram where a holy fire has been kept burning for many centuries.

It is believed that the clan of Chauhan Rajputs to whom Ajai belongs, originated from this fire. So it was a pilgrimage to what is perhaps the holiest site for the clan to which Ajai belongs. During the visit, prayers were offered to the holy agni over there, followed by a period of meditation wherein Brigadier Ajai Kumar Singh soaked in the essence of his warrior ancestors who had emerged from the same agni.

Then there was a historical Shiv Mandir near a beautiful lake that too was visited during that trip. In a unique turn of events, 2/11 Gorkha Rifles, with whom Ajai had served two decades ago, was located in Mount Abu during that time and they were glad to play host to Shalini and Ajai during the trip.

Back home, Kutch itself offered so many beautiful and historical places to visit. Apart from the Rann itself, there was the Koteshwar Mahadev Mandir where Ravan is said to have put down the Shivling given to him by Lord Shiva himself due to Lord Vishnu's *Maya.*

Then there was a gurudwara at Lakhpat where Guru Nanak Dev ji is believed to have halted enroute to Mecca during his travels. The famous Dwarkadheesh Mandir dedicated to Lord Krishna too lies in the Saurashtra Peninsula just South of Kutch.

In fact, the Lakhpat Gurudwara Sahib is actually being looked after by the Army Engineers complement of the Bhuj Brigade due to the sheer remoteness of the area.

Another unique legacy of Indian civilization that Shalini and Ajai got to visit was the Mandir of Rishi Dattatreya at Kala Dungar. Kala Dungar is a small hill accessible by a beautiful elevated road that runs truly straight over the vast Rann of Kutch, almost like a runway. The unique aspect of this road is that during high tide, there is a shimmering lake of sea water on both sides of it!

Legend has it that at Kala Dungar, Rishi Dattatreya used to feed the wild animals in that area, mostly jackals. It is said that once when he did not have anything to feed to the animals, he actually cut his limbs and offered them.

Kala Dungar also offers a unique vantage point from where one can see miles upon miles of the Rann of Kutch.

Another landmark in the area was the Dhordo Village, which is the last village of Kutch and also the site of the unique Rann Festival every year in December which is a major event on the world tourism calendar. Shalini and Ajai would visit the festival every year, with Shalini shopping to her heart's content each time!

It was a really fruitful tenure for Ajai as the Brigade Commander in Bhuj. Amongst the many things that he was able to accomplish was the creation of a museum in the Bhuj Garrison, for which he requested the Maharao of Kutch to donate some artefacts. The other accomplishment was the creation of a War Memorial in Bhuj Garrison.

By then Ajai and Shalini had established an excellent rapport with the Maharao and the Queen of Kutch and they readily agreed to this request. Further, Ajai also extended an invite to them to visit the Bhuj Garrison since it was on the land that earlier belonged to the erstwhile State Forces of Kutch before partition and amalgamation.

The Maharao and the Queen readily accepted the invite and on the appointed day, arrived in Bhuj. They were hosted by the brigade in a befitting manner and Ajai personally conducted them around the garrison after a sumptuous lunch at the Flag Staff House. The visit included a *darshan* at the Shiv Mandir in the garrison which was originally established and consecrated by the Kutch State Forces.

Such was their bond with the Maharao and the Queen that Ajai and Shalini had a standing invite to visit the private beach of the Maharao at Mandvi whenever they wanted. This was one thing that they made full use of whenever they got an opportunity, regardless of the fact that Shalini had a mortal fear of water!

Yet, they spent some beautiful evenings at the beach that was practically untouched by tourists. It was a befitting private beach to the Maharao of Kutch, with pristine, white sands. Many sunsets were watched by Shalini and Ajai and their family in this wonderful setting.

The Rann itself was just as untouched, thanks to the sheer remoteness of the area. There too, the officers and ladies of the

Bhuj Brigade would often go for picnics, especially on moonlit nights when it would transform into a magical landscape, with just whiteness all around and absolutely no other frames of reference whatsoever.

With the clean airs, clear skies and natural beauty of the area accepted as a matter of fact, even an evening in the lawns or terrace of the Flag Staff House would become a picnic, especially when entertaining guests.

In the midst of all this, life threw yet another challenge at Shalini.

She was called upon to give a PowerPoint Presentation on the AWWA related activities to the wife of the new Division Commander during her visit to Bhuj!

Of all the challenges that Shalini had faced thus far, this seemed to be the one that got her worried the most, because she had never ever given a formal presentation before in her life!

But then, as President of the local AWWA Chapter, it was a legitimate task for her to brief the President of the immediate senior AWWA Chapter. Realizing that there was no use worrying, Shalini got down to preparing for the dreaded presentation!

It wasn't as if she wasn't already on top of the job, but just that the sheer novelty of this task had Shalini a bit anxious. However, as was typical of her, she prepared hard and on the appointed day, she delivered a presentation that would have put even a seasoned veteran to shame!

Time in Bhuj passed at a rapid clip and soon it was time to bid farewell, when Ajai received orders to relinquish command at the appointed date and after a short break, to move back to the Regimental Centre as the Commandant.

It was an emotional farewell for Shalini and Ajai as they finally drove out of Bhuj on the appointed day, retracing their route to Lucknow from where they had come to Bhuj not very long ago.

As Bhuj receded in the rear-view mirror, they couldn't help but reminisce about the days that had just gone by. Even the word 'Fabulous' didn't seem adequate to describe the tenure in Bhuj. The overriding feeling that came to be associated with that particular tenure was one of happiness, coupled with content.

Shalini had been mostly healthy during that tenure, barring a couple of medical scares. She had gone about discharging her own unofficial role as the senior most lady of the garrison with grace and dignity and was able to make a lot of difference in the lives of her flock.

Ajai too was content as he looked back at his time as the head of a fairly large family that the Bhuj Brigade was at that time. It had been a happy and professionally satisfying tenure for him too.

But as always, it was time to move on. Even though they headed back to the Regimental Centre, this time both their roles and responsibilities were different.

In a delicious turn of events, where earlier Ajai had officiated as the Commandant for a long time before (then) Brig Anil Chauhan (later, CDS) came in as the Commandant, now it was Ajai's erstwhile company commander, Col Pankaj had been officiating as the Commandant for the past few months, waiting for Ajai to come and take over the mantle!

Ajai and Shalini moved straight into the Commandant's Bungalow upon arrival at the Regimental Centre and as always, were settled soon thereafter.

It was a spacious and sprawling bungalow and being the Commandant's earmarked residence, it was well-kept as well, regardless of lack of occupation for the past few months after the previous incumbent had moved out.

Their stay in Lucknow this time would last hardly a few months. Yet, Shalini and Ajai together would still leave an indelible mark regardless of the short stay.

The coming few months back in the Regimental Centre would also be very blissful, but at the same time, fate was working hard to reclaim Shalini for the heavens above. Her new lease of life would hereinafter be pulling hard at the tether.

Yet, Shalini continued her remaining journey unperturbed, choosing not to be cowed down by fate, living life on her own terms with that beautiful smile always on her face.

12

HER LAST INNINGS...
ON THE FRONT FOOT, AS ALWAYS!

This particular tenure in Lucknow was homecoming in more ways than one, especially for Ajai since the Bungalow that he now occupied as the Commandant was the Officers' Mess of the Regimental Centre when he was commissioned nearly three decades ago, along with two other coursemates 2/Lt Atulya Solankey & 2/ Lt PS Patil at that time, accommodation being in short supply, the trio had stayed in a tent pitched in the sprawling lawns of the Mess under a majestic banyan tree, which still stands at the same spot today.

That tree was akin to a *time capsule* that had stood still while three decades of Ajai's military career had seemingly flown by. So naturally, Shalini and Ajai spent a good amount of time in the company of the grand old tree as Ajai regaled Shalini with the stories of the two weeks that he and two more young officers, who were not so young now, had spent in its shade.

Life moved on without waiting for such nostalgic moments!

Ajai got busy with the nitty gritties of overseeing the training of the very future of his Regiment which was renowned for some of the best soldiers and some of the best battalions that the Indian Army is blessed with. Meanwhile, seeking to live her life on her own terms, Shalini too assumed the position of the Principal of the Pre-Primary School that the Regimental Centre ran for the little ones of their troops.

As was natural for her, Shalini shone bright in this role and pretty soon, the little school was in high demand all across the Lucknow Cantonment!

Since it was a Regimental school, i.e, run by the Regimental Centre of which Ajai was the Commandant, he flat-out refused to pay any salary to Shalini! She replied that she wasn't seeking that in any case. This concluded the *interview* of the school Principal by the Centre Commandant!

Ajai was aware that not only would Shalini be happy looking after the school, but also that given her naturally affectionate soul, she would take good care of the tiny tots of the school as well.

He was perfectly right in his assumption. Shalini was happy, the kids were happy, the teachers and admin staff were happy and the entire school itself was soon one big happy family!

Salary or no salary, one of the 'perks' that came with her role as the Principal was an office of her own for Shalini. With the Regimental

Centre responsible for the school, the Centre Commandant, i.e. Ajai would often drop in to take stock of things over there!

Of course, in the case of Ajai and Shalini, these 'inspection' visits would happen fairly often, whenever Ajai was able to find some time from his own busy schedule. It was a novel experience, with Shalini sitting on her chair and Ajai across the table from her, having tea in her office!

On a more serious note, Shalini's impact on the way the school functioned, was phenomenal. The school progressed really well with Shalini at the helm and to add to that, she loved each and every moment of it. It was a win-win in every possible way for all stakeholders.

At the same time, she continued to handle her various other responsibilities with great dedication as well, be it that of a wife, a mother, a daughter in law or even a hostess for the various social functions at their residence. Through this all, she continued to take care of her medical condition as well.

Those were some pretty busy months for Ajai as well as Shalini since the 11 Gorkha Rifles Regimental Centre was thickly involved in a lot of activities, professionally and socially, in addition to their own mandated task of training recruits for the Regiment. In addition, they were also the head of the family for a large number of officers posted to the Centre and their wives.

Through it all, she still kept up with the routine check-ups with the nephrologist posted at the Command Hospital nearby. Apart from that, there was no indication that she had gone through a major medical issue hardly a few years ago. Nothing about her gave it away, and people went about enjoying her hospitality and her company without having the slightest clues of the battles that she had fought thus far and that she was still fighting.

Shalini wasn't one to complain about her pains, or for that matter, let it hold her back from living her life!

She hosted a large number of social gatherings at her home. Amongst the most memorable ones was the get-together of the *One-Star Club*, i.e., all Brigadier ranked officers in Lucknow. It was the talk of the town for quite a while! Then there were the countless Regimental reunions and get-togethers as well, where large numbers of veterans would come over. During one such party, Abhinav was with his family and had invited his friends over. One of his friends, having never met his mother, asked him who this one girl is. Abhinav realising he is talking about his Mom, bewildered and amused, replied that she is his mother. The family had a hearty laugh over it.

One particular draw towards Shalini's parties was the *Laal Maans* that she would serve to her guests. She had perfected this difficult recipe during her days in Bhuj and put it to good use in Lucknow, which is a culinary paradise in its own right.

Another advantage of being in Lucknow was that it was relatively close to their hometowns of Roorkee and Dehradun. Needless to say, there was a steady stream of family members who too kept visiting them in Lucknow.

In fact, Ajai's parents also spent quite a bit of time in Lucknow, partly also due to his father's medical condition that needed specialist care.

All in all, life in Lucknow was busy but at the same time, quite happy as well. It did mean that Shalini had absolutely no time to get ill either, and she made sure of it by taking good care of her health!

Her affiliation with Ajai's Regiment – The Eleventh Gorkha Rifles only grew stronger during her days in Lucknow. Being the *First Lady* in the very cradle of the Regiment, she came to know practically each and every soul associated with the Regiment, be they retired or still serving, and her fondness and love for them only grew further.

So much so that just a few weeks before her demise, there was a reunion function at the Regimental Centre which she insisted on attending despite her fragile health. Her words to Ajai were – 'I don't know about you, but I am going to Lucknow for sure.' Naturally, Ajai had to accompany! Thankfully, her health remained good throughout that trip. It was almost as if she <u>willed</u> her health to hold good as she bade farewell to her beloved Regiment before she moved on from this mortal world.

Pretty soon, Ajai received the news about his nomination to the prestigious NDC (National Defence College) Course in New Delhi, thanks to his many achievements while commanding the Bhuj Brigade and it was soon time for Shalini and Ajai to leave Lucknow for Delhi.

Thankfully, this time the move was without any 'surprises' that had so come to characterize their journeys to new postings!

They were allotted a house in the heart of Delhi in the Raksha Bhawan Complex on the Kasturba Gandhi Marg, barely a stone's throw away from the famed India Gate. As always, Shalini wasted no time in setting up her new house and began yet another beautiful chapter in their journey of togetherness.

Post looking after the house and then spending the afternoon with other ladies, now she would be ready to quite literally *go to town* with her husband! This was the most awaited moment for Shalini.

What helped was the fact that Raksha Bhawan was bang in the heart of Delhi and a lot of theatres and other hubs of cultural activities were close by as were many renowned restaurants too.

Naturally, a *lot* of movies and plays were watched by Shalini and Ajai. Then there was the really hectic social life characterised by the coming together of so many batchmates from across all three services, some of whom were seeing each other for the first time after nearly three decades. The bonhomie amongst the officers and ladies was absolutely fantastic and infectious.

In fact, evening get-togethers would frequently carry on past midnight with the officers and their families ending walking to the India Gate for ice-cream before calling it a night!

This time Sanjana too decided to make a career shift and moved to Delhi to be with her parents, partly to explore a new career in the news media and majorly, to look after her mother. She worked on some television serials in the Noida Film City while simultaneously completing the work on projects that she was handling in Mumbai. This was also the tenure where Abhinav would make his family meet his future wife Sukriti.

Over time, Shalini and Sanjana became more of friends than a mother-daughter duo. Sanjana not just took it upon herself to look after her mother's health but also kept her in good humour throughout the day. She also became a permanent companion to Shalini on the various shopping trips all over Delhi!

The course involved a lot of travel, including a couple of foreign trips as well. Since Shalini was unable to make the trip abroad with Ajai and rest of the course members during the Higher Command Course due to her recently, this time he ensured that she was healthy enough to accompany him whenever he travelled abroad.

One such trip was to Kenya and the UK, with Kenya being the first destination. There was much excitement within the family for them to be able to travel abroad together after a long time. However, as they got around to taking stock of their finances, they realized it would be difficult for the kids to accompany them.

Abhinav and Sanjana, realizing the issue, decided to not press their parents to take them along. But somehow, Shalini and Ajai gave the situation a fresh look and by the next morning announced that the children too could accompany them, even though only for the Europe leg of the trip.

The atmosphere in the house turned 180 degrees from disappointment at night time to absolute ecstasy in the morning!

Accordingly, on the appointed day, course officers and their families embarked on their trip to Africa and Europe, with Kenya being the first halt. It was an absolutely novel experience, especially for the ladies, many of whom were travelling as part of an official delegation with their husbands for the first time. Right after checking into their hotel in Nairobi, Shalini and Ajai decided to go exploring the city.

Here came the usual *adventure* that was so characteristic of the many travels that Shalini and Ajai undertook together!

Despite having been cautioned in the initial briefings to not venture too far from the hotel, the couple just couldn't resist the lure of adventure and went exploring, looking for a good place to enjoy local cuisine. To cut a long story short, they had a good meal alright, but it was a really scary experience too, given the reputation of Nairobi in those days as a crime infested city with numerous instances of mugging and other violent crimes. The atmosphere they encountered was really scary and the way people in the streets looked at them, didn't help calm their nerves either.

All in all, it was an exciting meal, but they didn't dare repeat this again while in Nairobi!

The first few days were filled with official engagements wherein the Indian delegation got to interact with the highest echelons of the Govt of Kenya, meeting a large number of their highest ministers. Then there was a visit to the Wildlife Museum in Nairobi. It was truly one of a kind wherein the visitors were acquainted with the rich biodiversity that Kenya is blessed with.

After this came the much awaited excursion to the world famous Masai Mara Reserve and the adjoining Serengeti National Park. The officers and ladies were taken there in a bus from Nairobi. The journey itself was quite mesmerizing and they reached their hotel sometime in the evening.

The hotel itself was quite stunning, with beautiful views of the protected wilderness all around, thanks to the elevated piece of land that the hotel was built on. Shalini was absolutely thrilled to be there and after a quick freshening up, she made a beeline for the terrace from where miles upon miles of wilderness was visible. And unlike Indian forests where it takes a fair amount of effort to catch a glimpse of wildlife, here the sheer abundance of wildlife meant that they were literally surrounded by many species of local fauna.

They went out on the much awaited safari the next day. The highlight of that was the glimpse of a lion in its natural habitat. Naturally, the safari guides followed the lone male lion who ambled along with a gait befitting the king of the jungle. In fact, that particular lion seemed keen to show off to the two-legged visitors from India because it soon climbed a rock, stood there exactly like a King and as if to further underscore his status, let out a mighty roar as well.

That done, the visitors were soon treated to yet another aspect of life in the jungle wherein a lioness suddenly burst forth from nearby, in hot pursuit of a herd of Wildebeest. She caught and killed one but just as she started eating it, she was surrounded by a pack of hyenas who forced her off her hard-earned meal!

One interesting part of this encounter was that there were a few in the group who could not bear to see such gore and blood. But not Shalini! She was right up there, enjoying the cycle of life and death unfolding before her eyes.

She could not wait to get back to the hotel and get connected to the internet so that she could get on her daily video call with both her children to tell them about the exciting day that she had had in the Masai Mara!

Not happy that Abhinav and Sanjana were unable to join them for the Kenya leg of the trip, Shalini had made it a point to make videos and keep sending to them, in addition to frequent video calls to show them the sights and the vistas that she was seeing. Thus, even if virtually, Abhinav and Sanjana were as much part of that trip as were Shalini and Ajai.

The Kenya trip soon came to an end and the entire delegation flew to London on the appointed day. London was where Shalini and Ajai would catch up with Abhinav and Sanjana who would have landed a couple of hours ahead of them.

In order to make the trip as economical as possible, Ajai had reached out to Col Madan Gopal, who had been his Commanding Officer many years ago. It just so happened that Col Madan's son was based out of London and despite being out of town in that duration, he had left his house keys for Abhinav and Sanjana, both of them his childhood buddies, to be able to stay there during the visit. The house was well stocked with essential necessities so that they were not unduly hassled. As for Shalini and Ajai, they stayed in the hotel booked for the course members.

The kids couldn't have asked for a better arrangement. Together, they explored as much of London as they could, unencumbered by their parents!

Of course, whenever the parents got time from their official engagements, they too were right there with the kids!

The highlight of the London trip for Shalini was getting to watch 'Romeo and Juliet' with Ajai at the London Opera House. Apart from that, they explored as many of the iconic London monuments / landmarks as they could, given their tight schedule. They made it a point to experience the London Tram, the buses and even took a ride in the iconic London Taxis, along with a walk by the Thames River. As part of the official itinerary, they even got to visit Westminster where they were addressed by Lord Karan Bilimoria, the son of Lt Gen Bilimoria.

The official part of the trip soon finished in London. Hereafter, Ajai had taken some leave to explore Europe with his family. They had booked themselves on a scenic tour of Europe.

As always, this holiday too began with a mighty scare!

The plan was for Shalini and Ajai to meet their kids at the designated pick-up point for the tour bus. However, due to a comedy of errors, Abhinav and Sanjana ended up taking the wrong local bus because Sanjana wanted to travel in the famed Double decker and got delayed in reaching the rendezvous point with their parents. But thankfully, even the tour bus was somehow delayed and they were able to reach the designated point just in time to board the bus!

The tour bus had seven other families from the NDC Course booked for the same tour, plus a few more tourists from India. So it became a de-facto NDC tour all over again!

The bus took them to the ferry point on the English Channel where instead of requiring the passengers to deboard, the bus just drove on to the ferry! This was yet another novel experience for

Shalini and kept her distracted from the fact that now there was no solid ground beneath her, except for the ferry!

Jokes apart, Shalini was making conscious decisions to face her fears so that even if they did not go away entirely, at least they would be more tolerable. This is exactly what happened during the ferry ride as well wherein she enjoyed a meal with her family, sitting on the upper deck of the ferry, unperturbed.

The tour took them to Germany, Belgium, Switzerland and France. It being a guided tour, basic administrative requirements were already taken care of. The bus would halt at designated places for lunch and usually by evening they would reach their destinations so that they had time to change and explore the various towns and cities that were part of the tour.

Interestingly, most of the Motels that they stayed at, were owned by Indians and thus, Indian food was never far whenever they craved it.

The tour was hectic, but Shalini took to it with gusto and thankfully, managed her medical condition in a way that there were no issues whatsoever. Together, the family soaked in the sights and sounds and tastes of the beautiful Western Europe. Of course, there was the seemingly endless shopping too!

The final leg of the tour brought them to Paris where they had booked an apartment right in the heart of the city, on the banks of the Seine River and very close to the Eiffel Tower. The few days spent there were really memorable.

The accommodation, though a bit costlier than other options, was ideal for the family. They each had their personal space and the luxury to cook meals to their tastes instead of relying on expensive food from restaurants. The Seine River as well as the Eiffel Tower were just a short walk away and so was the world famous Louvre Museum.

The Louvre Museum is the one that houses the priceless Mona Lisa painting. Once there, they finally saw the craze the visitors had for the painting. So much so, that they found many visitors crying when they finally saw the painting.

That said, the Louvre Museum was a huge repository of many other priceless artefacts as well which Shalini and Ajai went on to explore. But it was here that yet another fundamental difference between the long married couple came to the fore – Where Shalini was content with taking one glimpse of an artefact and moving on, Ajai was keen to stay and study them in detail.

Shalini could never bear to wait for Ajai to take his time reading more and more about each artefact and would do her best to pull him to keep him moving. She succeeded often, but there were times when Ajai would simply refuse to budge! Thus, they completed their tour of the world famous Louvre Museum!

Days in Paris were really leisurely, which was a welcome break from the hectic few weeks in Kenya, London and rest of Europe. Alas, it was soon time to board their flight back to New Delhi. But it being from the Charles de Gaulle International Airport, this airport was yet another famous landmark that the family was looking forward to seeing. To say that the experience at the airport was underwhelming, would be an understatement. But that was exactly how it turned out to be for them, especially after having seen so much of the new Terminal 3 of the Indira Gandhi International Airport in New Delhi.

Their next trip abroad was to Bangladesh. This time Shalini and Ajai travelled without the children. Once again, it was yet another memorable trip wherein their hosts left no stone unturned in order to ensure that their guests had a memorable visit. While their husbands were busy with official engagements, the ladies were conducted around Dhaka so that they could spend their husbands' money on various handicrafts and such likes. Needless to say, they did not disappoint their Bangladeshi hosts and contributed quite a bit to the local economy during the trip, with Shalini loading herself with some well chosen silk sarees, among other things.

However, the high point of this visit was the trip to Chittagong where the visiting officers and ladies were taken in military helicopters by the Bangladesh Army. It was a wonderful excursion for not only did the visitors get acquainted with Bangladesh Navy infrastructure at Chittagong and the very competitive textile & garment factories but were also able to enjoy themselves on the beautiful beaches there. They also got to take a ride in the local rickshaws that were uniquely decorated.

However, with the benefit of hindsight, the biggest satisfaction that Lt Gen Ajai Kumar Singh (Retd) derives from that Bangladesh visit was the fact that Shalini and he got to travel together in a military helicopter. This is because she was no longer in her mortal form when she would be authorised to travel in military aircraft with him when he was the GOC-in-C of Indian Army's Southern Command. It seems that the Almighty had indeed ensured that they get at least one such opportunity in this lifetime of togetherness.

This is not to say that Shalini did not suffer medical challenges during the NDC days. In fact, she suffered from two major issues – a bout of Tuberculosis followed by a bout of Hepatitis. Both of these would lead to major adverse impact on her already stressed body as the years progressed, especially the Hepatitis C that she caught. This was because even though there were medicines to treat this ailment, due to her grafted kidney, the medicines could not be administered. It was a Catch-22 situation because they knew that Shalini's liver was gradually deteriorating but there was nothing that they could do. However, refusing to give up, Ajai did some research of his own and found out a new drug in the USA that could help Shalini. Accordingly, the authorities at the R&R Hospital procured that drug and Shalini finally got free of the Hepatitis C. But sadly, her liver had already suffered a lot of damage by then. It was barely functional to take care of her body's day-to-day functioning, but couldn't take any additional load, including that of anaesthesia for any further surgeries.

To add to the steady stream of bad news on the health front, at about that same time the doctors also discovered that Shalini's grafted kidney was showing signs of impairment, meaning that it too was steadily losing normal functionality.

Yet, at that particular time in her life during the NDC days, it was almost as if Shalini *chose* to treat them as minor setbacks in her quest to enjoy life to the fullest, which she did with great gusto.

Life in Delhi continued apace, even as the course was swiftly approaching its culmination. As the end of course loomed nearer and nearer, everyone was eagerly waiting to hear about their next places of postings. Once again, when the list of postings was declassified, Ajai found that the MS Branch had taken care of Shalini's medical condition and given him a billet in the Army HQ itself. Thus, they would be able to stay in Delhi for the next few years as well.

In yet another stroke of benevolence from the heavens above, they got another unexpectedly lucky break when they were given an opportunity to choose any accommodation of their choice in the newly constructed multi-storeyed residential complex in Delhi Cantonment called Sekhon Vihar.

Naturally, Shalini and Ajai chose Flat No. 202, signifying the date of their marriage, i.e. 20 Feb! They, along with many of their NDC batchmates were soon the first occupants of their respective flats and the bonds that were created during the NDC Course, continued apace in the new neighbourhood as well.

Ajai soon joined the Army HQ as the Deputy Director General Discipline and Vigilance (DDG DV). This was a key appointment wherein he was handling a large number of sensitive cases, each of which demanded due diligence, because of legal implications involved. As a result, Ajai would leave home at about 8:15 am and could only return by 6 pm, at times even getting delayed by up to two hours. Then there were occasions when he would keep busy in the office till past midnight. Fortunately, such occasions were rare.

However, he was secure in the knowledge that Shalini was just about 10 mins of drive from the R&R Hospital in case of any medical emergency. Thankfully, her health continued to be generally good and the only visits to the hospital were mostly for routine check-ups.

One good thing about Ajai's new appointment was that even though he was quite busy during the week, weekends were generally free. Ajai had started long distance cycling during the NDC Course and he continued with it on weekends, at times clocking nearly 150 km during a single ride. In addition, he had taken up long distance running and successfully completed the Airtel Delhi Half Marathon.

Meanwhile, Shalini was busy with life in Delhi, now with Sanjana too giving her company. Meanwhile, the *First Day First Show* ritual of Shalini and Ajai too continued uninterrupted. Every Friday evening Ajai would make it a point to leave office early and Shalini and he would go for whichever was the latest movie in town, followed by a meal. This more than made up for all the time that Ajai had to spend away from Shalini due to his busy office work!

In this duration, they also found time to visit their Battalion, 1/11 Gorkha Rifles, which was located in the quaint little town of Binaguri at that time. It was a befitting occasion as well – the 57th Raising Day of the Battalion on 01 Sep 2016. This was her first visit to the Battalion in six years and she thoroughly enjoyed herself, reconnecting with her Unit family all over again in the beautiful climes of Binaguri. They spent three blissful days in the Battalion, away from the hustle and bustle as well as the pollution of Delhi.

This was to be Shalini's last visit to the Battalion that her husband had commanded in her hometown. Thankfully, she was in good health and able to make the most of it, soaking in the essence of the Battalion that had been their home for the nearly three years that Ajai had commanded it.

Sometime soon after the visit, as expected, Ajai got approved for promotion to the rank of Major General and was soon earmarked to take over command of the elite Kilo Force in Northern Kashmir Valley. It was headquartered in the beautiful town of Sharifabad, close to Shalateng and was almost like an island, with the huge Hokarsar Lake close by.

As always, Shalini too accompanied her husband for their next stint in their journey as part of the Indian Army fraternity, this time in the relatively active hinterland of the Kashmir Valley. What was different here was that accompanying them was Capt Abhay Joshi from 1/11 Gorkha Rifles, who was to be the ADC to Maj Gen Ajai Kumar Singh during the Kilo Force tenure.

As the GOC Kilo Force, Ajai was authorised an ADC to look after his day-to-day programmes and other such aspects. But as was to be expected, the hardworking but soft-spoken and docile Abhay soon became part of their family, almost like a second son!

Sharifabad days were some of the best and most blissful days in the life of Shalini and Ajai where they both left their respective marks, Ajai with his professionalism and Shalini with her empathetic and caring nature.

The environs in and around Sharifabad were pristine, with nature offering its very best to them, untouched by human interference. The air was absolutely clean and the weather too was equally beautiful.

While Ajai got straight down to the business of handling the insurgency in that area in his own way, Shalini and he together also started looking at developing the Sharifabad Garrison in a holistic manner. What enabled this endeavour was the fact that not only were Counter Insurgency Forces such as the Kilo Force well funded, but also because the GOsC had much greater freedom to plan and expend such funds, along with the benefit of the Military Engineering Services and the Garrison Engineer directly under them.

To a large extent, Ajai's predecessors in Sharifabad too had done their bit. The Garrison had come up beautifully over the past many years. It had a Nature Park in the middle and an abundance of orchards with hundreds of apple, almond and cherry trees which would transform the landscape in a matter of days during the spring season when they bloomed.

And then there was the Flag Staff House that bore witness to the unique imprints left by all those who had lived there before. Past GOsC had done various improvements to their abode, ranging from extensions to creation of glass walled rooms to creative use of woodwork that Kashmir is renowned for. It had a huge lawn as well, which suited Shalini just fine.

Ajai would have to travel a lot to keep up with various operations in the Kilo Force's area of responsibility, as also to meet his troops that were deployed all over. Yet, he made it a point to be back home in Sharifabad by evening so that Shalini and he could spend some time together. It would be a rare occasion indeed when he would stay overnight in some subordinate headquarter location.

Meanwhile, since Ajai's days were busy fighting the Counter Insurgency operations, Shalini too soon created a routine of her own. There was a car with a local number plate and a local Kashmiri driver at her disposal. She made sure to use it to the hilt, by moving out to Srinagar on multifarious errands.

She shopped to her heart's content. But Ajai always had a worry about her security. Even though the situation in the Kashmir Valley was reasonably calm, yet there was always an element of danger and uncertainty. Ajai would always caution her to not set a routine with respect to timings and routes that she would take.

Meanwhile, Ajai's parents too had joined him in Sharifabad to make the most of the relatively short tenure that he would have as GOC Kilo Force. The social life in the garrison was also quite good, with regular functions happening ever so often, primarily due to restrictions on troops and their families from going outside. A highlight of such functions would be the mouth-watering *Seekh Kebabs* that one officer posted in HQ Kilo Force excelled at preparing, being an expert in barbeque.

In the middle of all this, Ajai got allotted a *Separated Family* accommodation in New Delhi, meaning that he would now have to vacate his Sekhon Vihar flat. However, being the GOC he couldn't afford to go himself due to his professional commitments. So it came upon Shalini to manage the shifting all on her own.

As always, there was a silver lining here as well. She was able to go to her trusted Nephrologist, Col Nair once again in the R&R Hospital for a routine check-up in the middle of shifting.

This was just as well, because by now Abhinav's marriage had been fixed with Sukriti who too joined them for a short while in Sharifabad. Needless to say, Shalini was ecstatic at the prospect of having a daughter-in-law soon enter their lives.

It was almost as if Abhinav's marriage was one more responsibility that she would check off her 'To-Do List' before the inevitable end of her mortal journey of this lifetime.

Of course, this also meant that there was yet more shopping and other planning to be done!

That said, by this time the relationship between Shalini and Ajai had deepened further and was on a different level altogether. The trials and tribulations of the past one decade, instead of taking a toll, had made them appreciate their togetherness even more.

Search for cure had put them both on the spiritual path and as months and years passed, they had learned to see what is really important in life and to appreciate it that much more, instead of getting tied down in the vicissitudes of life and just trudging along.

The companionship with each other was cherished more and more as the days progressed. This was also part of the reason why despite his frequent travels, Ajai made it a point to be back in Sharifabad each evening. Their best moments were those that they spent in blissful togetherness, looking after and taking care of each other.

If one thinks Ajai was the sole caregiver in this relationship, they couldn't be more wrong. This was more so during the current tenure as GOC Kilo Force where due to the very nature of the military situation, most of the operations would happen at night and as the senior most officer responsible for all that happened in Kilo Force area of responsibility, Ajai would get frequent calls throughout the night, at times with news that could be quite stressful. In these moments, Shalini's calming presence by his side would act as a natural stress buster. It was Shalini who gave him the strength to carry on soldiering the way he did.

It had been the same during his previous tenure as DDG DV in Army Headquarters. With the sole task being to go through the worst of the discipline and vigilance cases of all types, it could be very easy for someone to get depressed. But Ajai managed to retain a positive outlook towards life due to his own outdoors passions as well as due to Shalini who kept him grounded through it all and gave him solace whenever he was in need of it.

This, was the nature of their relationship, spurred, no doubts by their connection of past so many lifetimes. Where medical conditions that Shalini suffered from, would have broken down most relationships, Ajai and Shalini along with Abhinav and Sanjana rallied and used that as a catalyst to come closer to each other.

This immense strength and zest for life that Shalini possessed, naturally rubbed on to all those who came in contact with her. For example, the Kilo Force ran a Vocational Training Centre (VTC) for local Kashmiri ladies in and around the Sharifabad Garrison. Over here, they were taught new skills in addition to opportunities to further hone their own existing skills. The shawls, pherans & suits that these ladies made were a big hit and would bring them a decent income as well.

Shalini transformed an already successful VTC into something that functioned at a different level altogether. Her naturally jolly personality soon rubbed off on the young girls that would come to the VTC daily. Shalini came like an angel for them, because apart from learning new skills the girls would also utilize their time in the VTC as an escape from the traditional life back in their homes.

Here, they could get the freedom to be themselves. Thus, they were ever willing to come over even on Sundays and holidays. Shalini understood this instinctively. So she did what naturally came to her – She arranged for a music system to be installed in the VTC! Now the girls, at the end of their classes in the VTC, would close the doors and play latest Bollywood numbers on full blast and dance away to their hearts' content!

It is pertinent to mention that these same girls were born in the days when the insurgency in Kashmir was at its peak and had a difficult childhood and youth. But Shalini being what she was, she handled them beautifully, with great empathy and genuine goodwill from the bottom of her heart. The way those local Kashmiri girls responded to her was something to be seen to be believed!

The girls became very attached to Shalini and Shalini, in turn, took great care of them and helped them gain further skills that would stand them in good stead in future. One such skill she chose to teach her girls was Martial Arts.

Kilo Force established a Martial Arts node in Sharifabad Garrison and employed skilled instructors to teach them the craft. This sowed seeds of excellence in Martial Arts amongst the local populace and many of them went on to represent the State as well as the Nation in various competitions.

Shalini also inspired an upgrade in the designs of the artefacts that were created by her girls in the VTC, making them more contemporary in design. Sukriti too helped in this particular endeavour, being an excellent designer herself. In fact, Sukriti also took a trip to the highly disturbed Old Srinagar to herself learn the Kashmiri art of paper mache work.

Apart from Sharifabad, Shalini also travelled occasionally to the various subordinate Sector Headquarters that functioned under Kilo Force. Her particular interest was the functioning of the many Army Goodwill Schools that these Sectors were running.

The concept of Army Goodwill Schools had a really interesting genesis. It so happened that during the intensely disturbed decade of the 1990s, almost all educational institutions in the Kashmir Valley had shut down, leaving no avenue for young Kashmiri kids to get an education. It was due to this that the Indian Army decided to open what it aptly christened the 'Army Goodwill Schools' all over the Valley for the sake of the future of the children growing up in the shadow of the guns.

Shalini got these schools to do cultural programmes to instill knowledge as well as pride in the greater Indian identity amongst the students. In fact, Ajai was invited as the Chief Guest to the Annual Day programme in the school in Handwara. It was really touching to see the Muslim girl students perform the Durga Pooja. Such is the inherent resilience of the Indian Society, due to which the Indian culture still flourishes despite so many challenges.

Shalini made full use of the Sharifabad tenure to explore the beautiful Kashmir Valley. She visited Lolab, Aman Setu and made many trips to the famous Wular Lake where she and Ajai would often have lunch in the Mess of one of the Rashtriya Rifles Battalions which was deployed in the area. It was a beautiful Mess, overlooking the lake along with guest rooms for the frequent visitors.

Soon after, she organized Abhinav's wedding in Dehradun almost single handedly because Ajai could not take a prolonged leave from his post!

The marriage happened in the last week of Nov 2017 at the DSOI in Dehradun. A couple of months prior to that, Shalini and Ajai sat together and prepared a detailed matrix (in true military style!). It was a document that spanned nearly 30 pages and included each event and the arrangements that were needed to be made for it. In addition, the guest list too was added to it.

Hereafter, all the running around was done by Shalini. She went shopping in Chandni Chowk with Sanjana in tow, she finalised the design of the invitation cards. She basically did all that needed to be done, not afraid to travel to any corner of Delhi or Dehradun for that matter. Sanjana was her volunteer force multiplier for all that was needed to be done in Delhi, while Abhinav kept up with the happenings in Dehradun.

In the midst of all this, Ajai was able to squeeze a couple of days' leave to take stock of things in Dehradun, sign the booking requisition for the DSOI and request the formation commander there for guest rooms for guests coming from out of town.

Shalini shifted base to Dehradun about a month before the wedding date. Meanwhile, Ajai too found a way to come to Dehradun on an official trip. He had been awarded the Vishisht Seva Medal and the investiture was to happen soon. He chose to accept his medal in the Western Command Investiture Ceremony that was fortunately, scheduled to take place in Dehradun that year.

The Almighty, though continuously testing them, was also at the same time, facilitating their journey in His own way!

Finally, Ajai took 11 days of leave and reached Dehradun just before the marriage. Shalini and Ajai had planned for it to be a gala affair!

The scale of the guest list was truly massive – it included all of Ajai's classmates from school, his coursemates including from the Higher Command and the NDC Courses, all regimental veterans and serving officers of Dehradun, all of Ajai and Shalini's friends and of course, the entire extended families! In fact, they even sent a bus to their village to ferry friends and family for the wedding to Dehradun.

For a couple who had announced their marriage anniversary by inviting 100 couples to their three bedroom flat during Higher Command Course, it was merely par for the course.

Once things were set in motion, Shalini and Ajai did the unthinkable – They told Sanjana that now she was the *Director* of the entire wedding ceremony and that they now just intended to dance in the Baraat and enjoy the ceremonies. Needless to say, Sanjana fit into her designated role perfectly and everything went absolutely smoothly.

They danced as if there was no tomorrow!

In the middle of it, Sanjana came over and reminded that it was time for the muhoorat and the Baraat had to be received by the bride's family. But now Abhinav and his friends, who were in great spirits, were unwilling to stop dancing!

Finally Ajai sent Shalini to get their son off his chariot for the ceremonies, but she herself got engrossed with Abhinav and his dancing friends.

It might be pertinent to mention here that Shalini absolutely loved to dance!

Next, Ajai dispatched Sanjana to fetch her brother. Needless to say, she too never came back. Finally, he decided enough was enough and went himself to get the groom. However, Abhinav pulled Ajai too up on the chariot and they all were dancing in total bliss!

Finally, it dawned upon the family that the wedding ceremony had to continue, making them dismount the chariot and proceed further, but not before taking an extra moment to get Abhinav along to the venue.

It was well past midnight when the ceremonies finished. It being a really cold late November night in Dehradun, some of the young guests had lit a sort of a bonfire in the DSOI premises and were snoozing next to it.

The happy family, now with the formal addition of Sukriti to their ranks, continued to dance. Sukriti, Sanjana, Abhinav, Shalini and Ajai kept on dancing to the melodies dished out by the live band that had been requisitioned for the purpose!

They danced till it was nearly dawn. Thankfully, Ajai managed to convince Shalini to find a place and sleep in the DSOI itself while he joined the kids' gang by the bonfire, chatting with them till early down.

Thus happened the wedding of Abhinav and Sukriti. The unsaid part was that it was one responsibility that Shalini had taken care of. Sanjana's marriage would be the next major responsibility that she was still bearing on her shoulders. Thankfully, the Almighty had blessed her with good health for the hectic labours that she undertook for the marriage ceremony.

But now, ill-health came galloping back.

By the time Shalini reached Sharifabad in December, it was the peak of winter. Post marriage, Sukriti joined Ajai and Shalini in Sharifabad to take care of her mother-in-law, while Abhinav was in Dehradun running his nascent venture. Shalini and Sukriti used to spend a lot of time during the day, soaking the winter sun in the glass room, chit chatting and getting to know each other better. They had made a bond with a wild bird 'Bulbul', who used to visit them daily. Such was the bond that 'Bulbul would sit on their shoulders and laps and eat food from their hands.

Even the free birds knew they had a friend in Shalini.

Shalini's health had generally held up well in Sharifabad due to the beautiful weather and the clean air out there. But during the extremely cold winters in the area, Shalini got used to having a kerosene heater in her room for warmth. Despite Ajai's repeated insistence on avoiding too much exposure to it due to the fumes that it emanated, which would get deposited in her air passages, Shalini just couldn't stay away from it due to the bitter cold.

It was a Catch-22 situation all over again, made more precarious with her fairly recent bout of TB. Pretty soon, the inevitable happened and Shalini developed an incessant cough. This, coupled with her already low immunity, resulted in her getting admitted to the Base Hospital in the Badami Bagh Cantonment in Srinagar.

Not one to leave her alone, Ajai also took permission of his Corps Commander and moved into the GOC Kilo Force Hut within the Cantonment and started functioning from there for the duration of Shalini's hospital admission.

His days would begin with a trip to the hospital to be with Shalini. Thereafter he would come back to the Hut and take care of official matters before heading back again to the hospital to be with her. Thankfully, with all this expert medical attention and the loving care by Ajai, Shalini was soon back home in Sharifabad, this time with the Kerosene Heater nowhere to be seen!

Time in Sharifabad passed sooner than they realized and Ajai soon received his posting back to Delhi as the ADG Military Operations (A). This was going to be yet another really hectic tenure for him since it is a very busy post. What made it further challenging was the fact that Shalini's health too had started deteriorating by this time.

As it would turn out, that tenure in Delhi would be the last one for them together. At some level, they both knew it as well. To add to the challenge, Ajai's new appointment in the Army Headquarters would not offer him much free time, at least during the weekdays.

They both made peace with their circumstances as always, and headed to New Delhi in the month of April 2018 with a sense of anticipation and an intent to make the most of whatever little time of togetherness that was left for them as a couple in their current mortal forms.

13

A FINAL, PEACEFUL SLEEP

The Delhi tenure, though hectic for Ajai, was good in the sense that Shalini could once again be close to specialist care in R&R Hospital. What also helped was the fact that they already had that *Separated Family* accommodation in Delhi and thus, administratively, they were quite comfortable right from the beginning.

Further, Ajai's immediate boss as well as the then Chief of Army Staff were both regimental officers from 11 Gorkha Rifles and not only did they know about Ajai's professional competence but also about Shalini's health challenges.

While on one hand the Almighty had thrown yet another challenge to them, but on the other hand, He also put into place circumstances to help them navigate through it all. Sanjana who too was staying with them, ostensibly due to her career commitments in Delhi / NOIDA, but mostly to be able to be there for the mother.

Abhinav too was based out of Dehradun, not very far away and would often drive down to Delhi.

Now it was up to Shalini and Ajai to make best use of it all.

The immediate challenge was to look after the immediate health concerns of Shalini. Her health had been steadily deteriorating towards the end of the Kilo Force tenure and by the time they moved to Delhi, it was somewhat of a major concern.

Shalini had become very frail and the initial few days saw a number of trips to the R&R Hospital. Thankfully, their Separated Family accommodation was fairly close to the hospital and despite his insanely busy schedule, Ajai could also take out time to make the short 10 minute drive from the Army HQ to the hospital.

Her creatinine levels had gone dangerously high, indicating a loss of kidney function. This necessitated haemodialysis, for which a fistula would have to be made. Accordingly, Shalini was prepared for the surgical procedure many times but each and every time, one complication or the other would crop up during the Pre-Anaesthesia Test. Sometimes her blood pressure would be high, or some other issue was discovered due to which she couldn't undergo the surgical procedure.

So, the fistula just could not be made and all this time her Creatinine levels continued to be alarmingly high. To top it all off, Ajai continued to be in office for nearly 12 hours each day.

Without fistula, the process of haemodialysis could not commence.

Shalini was getting visibly weaker and weaker as the days progressed. The only viable option was to have another transplant. By this time, it was possible to transplant a kidney even if the blood groups were not matching, unlike during her first transplant almost a decade ago.

Ajai offered to donate his own kidney, but Shalini just would not agree to it. In any case, during one of the consultations, the doctors simply ruled out another transplant due to the condition of her liver that couldn't handle the stress of a major surgical procedure because of the bout of Hepatitis C that she had suffered from some years back.

Shalini's condition kept on deteriorating, causing much worry and anguish amongst her family.

Finally, it was suggested to go in for Peritoneal dialysis. The family quickly studied about it and consulted the doctors. It seemed doable, and a minor surgical procedure was undertaken to commence the dialysis.

All this happened within the first 2-3 months of them shifting to Delhi, mind you. The extended family stood solidly with them all and enabled Shalini and Ajai to pull through this trying time with his professional commitments on one hand and Shalini's medical issues on the other hand.

Peritoneal Dialysis involved puncturing a hole in the abdominal cavity and placing a soft, hollow tube called a catheter into the abdomen, close to the belly button. The end of the catheter comes out through the skin. A cleansing fluid called *Dialysate* is filled into the abdomen. *Dialysate* contains a sugar that draws waste and fluid from the blood vessels in the abdomen. The solution and the waste is drained and thrown away after a set amount of time.

The procedure had to be repeated thrice a day and took between 60 to 90 minutes each time. Further, it required a sterile environment as well.

It was going to be very inconvenient for Shalini, but it seemed to be the only way out. As always, she took to it with a smile.

Right now was not the time for her to go. There were many, major responsibilities that still needed taking care of. Yet, she knew time was short, so she accepted her fate smilingly and just got on with the task of discharging her own duties towards the family.

It was this fortitude and manifestation that kept her going for her last couple of years before she finally left her mortal body, satisfied that her responsibilities towards her family were well and truly taken care of.

In order to save the hassle of daily trips to the hospital, Ajai got a sterile room made within their house and further, requested his Battalion to send a soldier trained as a Battlefield Nursing Assistant, or BFNA in short, to be attached in Delhi for the procedure to be done at home itself. The procedure was taught to Shalini, Sukriti and Rifleman Adarsh, the BFNA with due care and diligence.

Once again, her transformation was near instantaneous. With the body able to eject harmful toxins, Shalini was once again back to her natural, healthy self.

Then, in the month of July 2018, the entire family made a trip to Bhutan, this time with the newest member, Sukriti also accompanying them. Undertaking this trip with Shalini's condition was a major decision but what helped was the fact that the Indian Military Training Team (IMTRAT) in Bhutan was at that time, headed by Maj Gen BS Raju, a coursemate of Ajai's and thus, the medical setup over there was pre-warned about Shalini's condition.

The family spent a blissful one week or so in Bhutan. They visited Paro where the IMTRAT is located and took a leisurely walk in the market, followed by a meal at a local restaurant. However, Shalini wisely declined to undertake the trip to the famous Tiger Monastery the next day due to the gruelling trek that it involved and chose, instead, to spend the day resting.

They next moved to Thimpu for the second part of their trip. Over there, they took a walking tour of the iconic local landmarks. This time Shalini chose to accompany the family. Even though she walked very slow and got tired easily, she managed to keep up and the slow moving group patiently took in all the magnificent sights and vistas of the beautiful capital of Bhutan.

She especially enjoyed the visit to Punakha Dzong – The Palace of Bliss where the coronation of the King of Bhutan takes place. She took her time to savour the beauty and architecture of the palace. She was also overjoyed to see the thick, lush and green forests enroute and enjoyed her lunch post the visit in a restaurant next to the confluence of the Pho Chhu and Mo Chhu Rivers.

Thankfully, her health kept up throughout that blissful visit, with due precautions being diligently adhered to and they were soon back home in New Delhi, this time with more beautiful memories of togetherness in the picturesque Bhutan.

Challenges continued to be there. The first and foremost amongst them was the danger of infection at the point of incision in her abdomen. This first happened about six months after the dialysis commenced.

The doctors prescribed heavy dosage of antibiotics to get rid of the infection. But hereafter, once every one and a half months, it would get infected despite all precautions and Shalini would have to take copious amounts of antibiotics all over again.

With her body already under so much stress, this abundance of antibiotics ended up messing with her digestive system and her food intake went down drastically. In fact, as the days progressed, she would struggle to retain even the little food that she ate, instead of vomiting it out as it started happening with alarming frequency.

Yet, she carried on living her life with her trademark flourish. Despite having to undergo dialysis thrice a day, their social life was quite busy thanks to a tonne of coursemates, other military acquaintances and of course, their families that were not very far away!

Shalini kept running her household as always, handling finances, planning for and hosting dinners. She even travelled to Roorkee and Dehradun on a couple of occasions, though the travel itself was a bit complicated due to the dialysis.

Shalini, typically, would never shy away from travelling out of Delhi, especially for things that were really dear to her heart. It included the marriage of their ADC from Kilo Force days, Major Abhay that was to happen in Jwala Ji, Himachal Pradesh in June

2019. Despite Ajai's reservations, he did not have a say in the decision because Shalini had already decided that they were going!

The bonds of GOsC with their ADCs are unique, almost like a parent-child relationship. Hence there was no question of not being there for Abhay's wedding. More so, because Shalini had already promised him that they would be there for his wedding!

Ajai tried, unsuccessfully, to convince her that her medical condition would be an impediment for the trip. But what ultimately helped make up Ajai's mind was Shalini's ultimatum that she would definitely be going for the wedding, regardless of Ajai being able to make it or not!

Decision made, now came the time for making the logistical arrangements. The car was sterilized and Sepoy Ravi Kant, the driver who also accompanied them on the appointed day. Ravi Kant was also trained as a standby for the dialysis procedure in absence of Rifleman Adarsh Rai, the BFNA from Ajai's Battalion. They started right after her first dialysis for the day and enroute, found a PWD guest house to do another dialysis. The third dialysis was done at the destination once they had reached their hotel.

As always, Shalini was not one to see her condition as an impediment. A minor inconvenience was the best that her medical condition was considered as, in her zest for making the most of her life!

They spent three days in Chintpurni, Jwala Ji and Palampur and aside from being part of Abhay's wedding, they also caught up with some of their Battalion officers and veterans settled in and around Palampur.

In addition, they visited many of the temples that Palampur and its surroundings are dotted with, in addition to one of the major Budhhist monasteries over there. All in all, it was time well utilized indeed.

As always, the Almighty blessed Shalini with good health throughout this trip.

It was as if she had a pact with the Almighty with respect to her health during her travels.

Two days after returning to Delhi, there was a fresh infection at the point of incision for the dialysis. Once again, she was put on antibiotics, along with which came the usual side effects.

However, something seemed to have changed at this time, because thereafter, the bouts of infection became more and more frequent and Shalini's health started deteriorating fast.

She was unable to hold on to the food she ate and would throw up ever so often, losing the nutrients in the process. She was now more or less confined to bed. She stopped going outside at all, though on one or two occasions she would still muster up strength when she wanted to.

One such occasion was a movie 'Uri' that she was really keen on watching.

Of course, this request of hers put Ajai in a spin with respect to the sheer logistics involved because Shalini just couldn't sit in a chair for the duration of the movie. In a stroke of luck, he found out that there was a theatre in one of the malls in Vasant Kunj that had the luxurious recliners for movie goers.

So off they went for the movie along with Sukriti!

Ajai had already spoken with them and apprised them of Shalini's condition and that she would need assistance getting to the theatre. They were happy to facilitate and helped transport Shalini to the theatre in a contraption that they had handy for people who were not in good health or had some disability.

Needless to say, she enjoyed the movie thoroughly.

She was never one to stop living her life. If she decided to go to Abhay's marriage, she did it. If she decided to go for a movie, she did it. It was as if there was a reservoir of strength and willpower that she could dip into, whenever she wanted.

One more such trip that underscored her tremendous resolve was the one that she and Ajai undertook to Thiruvananthapuram to attend the wedding of the daughter of Air Marshal Chandrashekhar, a coursemate of Ajai's. This time, her health was really not permissible and Ajai tried his best to dissuade her once again. As always, once Shalini had decided to do something, there was no turning back, health issues notwithstanding.

Her reasoning was simple. Air Marshal Chandrashekhar and his gracious wife Komala were very close to the family and they absolutely had go to the wedding of his daughter.

Reluctantly, Ajai booked their flight for Thiruvananthapuram, still very concerned about Shalini's health. He was still not convinced about the wisdom of making this long trip. Yet, he could not push Shalini beyond a point, because at this stage, her every wish was like a last wish and he didn't want her to have any unfulfilled wishes, or regrets when it was her time to go.

His worst fear came through when right after takeoff Shalini told him that she had intense heart palpitations. Alarmed, Ajai asked if he should ask the crew to return to Delhi to deboard them, but Shalini declined, saying that she would be fine. So Ajai just held her hand as she silently struggled with her condition. It finally took about 25 minutes for her to become normal again.

Thankfully, the rest of the flight was uneventful. The hosts had made good arrangements in Thiruvananthapuram, given Shalini's condition. For the first two days, they stayed in the house of Mrs Swapna, the wife of their coursemate Maj Gen MU Nair. The house was big and airy, just perfect for Shalini. The loving fuss of the hosts and the pure Thiruvananthapuram air gave a boost to Shalini's health.

In this duration, they went on to visit the famous Padmanabh Mandir as well as the Ganpati Mandir in Thiruvananthapuram.

Shalini was not one to miss an opportunity to explore!

Thereafter they shifted to a hotel as the marriage ceremonies kicked off. The Reception was at a beach right next to the hotel. While they were getting ready for the evening, Shalini had a nosebleed. No matter how hard they tried, it just wouldn't stop.

Ajai suggested that they skip the evening, but Shalini was not convinced. Thankfully, after a few tries, the nosebleed subsided and Shalini rested for a few minutes before getting ready and joining the rest of the guests for the Reception.

The reception was a gala affair indeed, with a lot of coursemates and other known acquaintances in attendance. And as if magically, Shalini was able to be on her own two feet for most of the evening, hardly ever sitting down.

It was almost as if she was able to draw the energy and power from the happy gathering itself. She was absolutely normal all over again. Frail, yes, but still her old self.

It seemed that even the Almighty had given up trying to hold back this purest of souls over the past few days and had given her a *Pass* to be able to enjoy that one evening amongst friends, many of whom she would not be able to meet again.

She continued to be in good health as they came back to the hotel room quite late in the night. Next morning too she was fine and not to lose such a beautiful opportunity, Ajai took her back to the beach for a leisurely, unhurried stroll by the sea. Later, they even went to explore the local market and did some shopping before returning home to Delhi.

One of the reasons why Ajai didn't push Shalini beyond a point while trying to dissuade her from her desires to travel was because at some level he knew there was a method to this madness. Shalini was striving to close as many chapters in her life as she could, before the inevitable happened. She was saying goodbyes to her loved ones in her own way.

She would make it a point to go and through sheer grit and resolve, *will* herself to stay well enough.

Another such example of this came when she insisted on attending the Reunion Function at the Regimental Centre sometime in the year 2019. There was no point arguing with her, especially in matters of the Regiment because she was really attached to it.

Ajai and Shalini went to Lucknow to join the Regimental family in celebrating togetherness. This time they stayed in the famous Peacock House with Ajai's recently promoted coursemate Lt Gen MU Nair who was the Chief of Staff at HQ Central Command in Lucknow.

This was the time when her infections had become very frequent and she was hardly able to eat. Yet she went and as always, was able to attend all functions and meet all members of the Regimental family who were present there.

This was the last Regimental function that she would attend. In a way, she had gone on to bid farewell to the cherished Regimental family on her own terms.

How Shalini managed to do all this was through the deep dive into spirituality that she had taken over the past many years. She had surrendered herself totally to her Guru, Mata Nirmala Devi. Shalini had been absolutely regular in her practice of Sahaj Yog. She would often tell Ajai that many times while meditating, she would go absolutely blank, as if losing her consciousness.

It was this immense faith that kept her going. She would pray to her Guru, talk with her Guru and lay all her problems at her feet. Through this sheer faith and *dhyan*, Shalini was able to tap into a cosmic reservoir of energy whenever the need arose.

At some level Ajai also realised that Shalini wouldn't go till the time he actually let her go, such was her loyalty and love for him.

Further, one major responsibility was still holding Shalini back in this mortal realm. She wanted to see Sanjana married before she left. Over the past years, Sanjana had become like a friend to her instead of daughter and she had steadily taken over more and more responsibilities without anyone noticing.

Thankfully, Shalini would get to see this dream fulfilled soon enough. Over time Shalini had come to realize that Sanjana's 'friend' Akshat, whom they would often see at home, was perhaps more than just a friend.

Not one to waste time, especially when it was in short supply, Shalini just sat down with Sanjana one day and asked her about Akshat! After initial hesitation, Sanjana too confirmed what Shalini had been thinking. However, she and Akshat were still undecided on marriage.

It was at this point that Major General Ajai Kumar Singh decided to put his imposing military persona to good use!

One fine day as Ajai returned from office, Akshat was home, sitting with Shalini and Sanjana. So as Ajai walked in, he sprung a question on the young man in pursuit of his daughter:

Ajai : *Phir Baat Pakki?*

Akshat (Off balance!) : *Kaun Si Baat?*

Ajai : *Shaadi Ki, aur kya?*

Akshat (Still dazed)	:	*Haan*
Ajai	:	*Chalo phir ho gaya!*

So this is how Akshat and Sanjana finally realized that deep within their hearts they were always looking to get married. It was just that the weight of the decision had kept them in a dilemma. Ajai made them overcome this dilemma by catching them both off-guard and extracting the truth by denying them an opportunity to think or for that matter, overthink!

This was a classic use of interrogation techniques that he had put to good use in the Kashmir Valley in the 1990s, though this time for a more benign purpose!

After offering sweets to the still perspiring Akshat, Ajai told him to speak with his parents whereafter Ajai too would call them up. Thankfully, they too were on board and the match was formally blessed by both families.

Knowing Shalini's condition, Ajai suggested that they do a *Roka* ceremony at a date of earliest mutual convenience. He also suggested that they would do it on a relatively large scale, not knowing about Shalini's health prospects in the coming months. Once again they were in agreement and accordingly the spacious Atulya Hall in the Army Air Defence Officers' Mess in Delhi Cantonment was booked for the function.

Naturally, Shalini was ecstatic with happiness, at being able to check off one more of her pending tasks before her departure.

They booked the venue, which had lavish spaces and a huge hall. Since most of Akshat's family was in Delhi and family on Sanjana's side too wasn't very far away, they decided to celebrate the simple *Roka* ceremony as a sort of a 'mini-marriage' function and decided to invite all their friends and family. Same was conveyed to the groom's side as well.

To ensure maximum attendance and allow the guests to reach back home after the function, they decided on an afternoon function. Once again their entire extended family from Roorkee, Dehradun as well as from their village was in attendance, as was Akshat's family.

Shalini too was fairly healthy and thoroughly enjoyed the event. At the end of the day, it was one more self-appointed responsibility that was off her shoulders.

However, her health challenges continued to persist and even worsen. As her trips to the R&R Hospital became more and more frequent, Shalini's room in the Officers' Family Ward of the R&R Hospital became more or less reserved for her. Yet, even though in immense pain and discomfort, she would still continue to wear a genuine smile on her face.

Thanks to familiarity and good support with Department of Nephrology as well as Shalini's medical history, Ajai could just give a phone call to the Nephrologist who would ensure necessary arrangements were in place by the time Shalini reached the hospital with Sanjana and Ajai's PA who would do the necessary paperwork.

As for Shalini, it was almost like a homecoming!

With such frequent trips and admissions in the hospital, she knew most of the doctors, nursing staff, admin and even temporary employees of the ward. It may sound weird, but Shalini coming to the ward would be almost like a festive event, with everyone rushing to meet and greet her!

They would all flock to her and crack jokes and talk with her. '*Arre Madam aap phir aa gaye?*', they would ask, to which Shalini would smilingly reply in the affirmative!

The warmth that Shalini exuded despite being critically dependent on external support for basic life functions, was something that pulled everyone towards her regardless of their state or stature.

Meanwhile, due to major military and geopolitical happenings in the neighbourhood in the year 2019, Ajai's job became more and more demanding. Shalini would keep herself busy with a variety of pastimes, which included playing games on her iPad, staying up to date with the latest on the Regimental and Coursemates' WhatsApp groups, or even taking care of the kitchen to whatever extent she could.

Ajai would try to take out whatever time he could, but slowly, his days in office started to get longer and longer, mostly keeping him there till nearly 9 pm. Further, despite Saturdays and Sundays being off, he would still need to go to office on Saturdays at least.

Thankfully, on Saturdays, he would go to the office by 10 am and be back home by noon, with the rest of the weekend dedicated to time with Shalini.

Days continued to pass and her health continued to get more and more critical. Then came another news that filled Shalini's world with yet more joy.

In the last week of Jan 2020 came the news that Ajai had been approved for promotion to the rank of Lieutenant General, after having missed the promotion in the previous selection board.

Coming as it was on the heels of a prior rejection, this news was even more dear to Shalini who once again, naturally, decided it was worth celebrating and expressed her desire to *Pip* him with his new rank badges in the office which was done with her and Lt Gen Paramjit, DGMO.

She knew that she wouldn't be able to actually see Ajai get promoted to the rank of an Army Commander, just as she would not be able to see Sanjana and Akshat get married. She decided to make the most of whatever time she had left.

A gala celebration was hosted by Ajai and Shalini in the TA Mess in New Delhi where once again, most of their extended family from Roorkee and Dehradun too joined in. But not content with just that, they also went on to organise yet another celebration in Roorkee itself.

It was here that most of the family members realized, perhaps for the first time, how seriously frail Shalini had become. For the first time, she was seen in a wheelchair, enjoying herself but at the same time, struggling to keep up with the events.

It was a bittersweet celebration for those who realized what it actually was, i.e., Shalini coming home to say her final goodbye to her loved ones, masking it with a celebration of an occasion of immense joy.

For the very few people who knew about Shalini's true condition, the doctors, despite their best efforts, had hit a wall. There was nothing more that they could do to help her beyond what they had already done.

During their periods of togetherness on the weekends, Shalini and Ajai would talk about a lot of things, including the end of Shalini's journey. Ajai told her that when the time comes, she should just break free of her mortal body without any regrets or longings. He told her that she had already done much more than any normal person could even have dreamt of doing in her condition. Her responsibilities towards her family had already been taken good care of.

Ajai also knew that Shalini's major concern was regarding him and the children. He told her not to worry about them anymore and instead, just move on and break free of the cycle of birth and rebirth.

Meanwhile, the world was slowly coming to realize that the COVID-19 pandemic was looming. India too had announced the first lockdown in the second half of March 2020. It was treated as an operational matter in the Army due to the possibility of the Armed Forces being called upon to aid the civil authorities. Hence, the responsibility to deal with COVID-19 came to rest with the Military Operations Directorate, which meant yet more work on Ajai's hands.

At about this time, Shalini seemed to have come to the realization her time to go was nearing as well. It became apparent to Ajai as well, when one day after returning from office, he was changing into fresh, sterile clothes and he saw Shalini looking at him with a wistful smile.

This was the moment he knew. This was the moment they both knew.

Soon thereafter, he suggested that she get admitted in hospital once again because of her inability to digest any food. What was left unsaid was that it might be her final hospital admission. Yet, always one to do things on her own terms, Shalini insisted that it being a Sunday, she wanted to stay home with Ajai and the rest of her family.

Accordingly, she was admitted to the hospital the next day.

As they both knew, this was the last time she would get admitted in hospital. Medical science had done what it could do to keep her going for 14 years since her diagnosis. More than that, it was her staunch belief in herself that had added so many years to her life.

Her burdens had been taken good care of.

Her family was well and truly settled.

Her duties had been discharged.

And most importantly, she had been given the freedom to go happily by her life partner.

At about 5 pm on 01 Apr 2020, Ajai sent out a message to all his contacts asking them to pray for a safe and easy passage into the eternal realm for Shalini's soul.

About three hours later, Shalini finally breathed her last.

A good heart had stopped beating.

The world was definitely much much poorer for the loss of such a pure soul that had lived and breathed and laughed amongst them all for so many years, never letting her own pain come in the way of looking after others. So much so, that she decided to leave her body before the enormity of the pandemic made things worse for her family.

Shalini was finally free of pain.

She was consigned to the eternal flame the next day in Brar Square, with all her loved ones bidding teary farewells to a life that was so dear to them all.

Thus ended the journey of this beautiful soul. Even though she was gone as far as her physical form was concerned, she continues to look out for her loved ones even to this day.

EPILOGUE

Sometime in the month of September 2022, Shalini's brother Atul was in a Court preparing for a case when he suddenly realised that his hands and legs started to freeze and he realized that something was wrong. So much so that after a while he was having difficulty even getting up from the chair that he was sitting in.

He cut short his work and requested his client to drop him home. Once home, he told his mother that he wasn't feeling well and went to his room and lay down in his bed.

He remained there for the next three days without any improvement in his condition.

In this duration, Atul lost all sensation in his limbs and his face too became crooked / droopy. In short, he was more or less paralyzed.

This caused quite a bit of alarm in the family and they rushed him to hospital. He was seen by a Neurologist who diagnosed him with a rare and deadly neurological condition called the GB Syndrome. In layman's terms, Atul's immune system was mistakenly attacking his peripheral nervous system and hence, the loss of control over his limbs.

Such was his situation that the doctors surmised that close to 95% of Atul's nervous system was affected and that his chances of survival were really bleak. In fact, had he not been brought to the hospital for another couple of hours, he may not have survived at all.

Atul spent the next few days struggling between life and death. While the family members were in a panic, he himself was oblivious to it all, being in a different realm altogether.

It was somewhere during this time that he saw Shalini.

Atul had a vision that he still remembers in great detail.

He was sitting on a bench next to a road. On the road was a Fiat car where he saw his Brother-in-Law Ajai. Ajai was loading his luggage in the car, as if preparing to proceed on a long journey. Atul went up to him, hugged him and asked where he was going. Ajai told him that he had to leave for some work.

This was about the time when the file for Ajai's promotion to GOC-in-C Southern Command was being processed with the Ministry of Defence and he would soon receive his orders to move from Delhi to Pune.

Next, across the road, at some distance, Atul saw a big tree with a small hut near it. Outside the hut was a beautiful lady dressed in white. Upon closer examination, Atul realised that it was Shalini, who had now regained all the weight that she had lost towards her last days. Not only was she looking definitely healthier, Atul also noticed the radiant glow of her beautiful aura.

What followed was a silent communication between Atul and his elder sister. Atul signalled to her from a distance, asking why she is not coming closer to see off her husband. To this, Shalini signalled that she was fine where she was. Atul then signalled that he will see off Ajai and come over to where Shalini was.

What happened next was yet another non-verbal communication, but this time with Shalini conveying a message to Atul at the subconscious level. He *heard* her clearly, telling him that he needn't come to her and rather to stay where he was. Shalini then blessed him and told him that he will be fine.

It was from that moment that Atul started regaining control of his nervous system and soon made a full recovery.

Sceptics may dismiss this as a hallucination or even a dream, but fact remains that for Atul, it was very much real even though he himself realizes that there exists no rational explanation for what he had experienced. However, as they say *Absence of Proof is not Proof of Absence.*

There has always been a world much beyond our sensory perceptions and what Atul witnessed was his sister reaching out to him from over there and blessing him with good health and long life.

Even though no longer in physical form, Shalini continues to look after her loved ones to this day. Be it Amit whom she brought back from the brink and later suffered a stroke while Shalini was still alive, to Atul whom she also brought back from the brink, but after she herself had left her body.

Of course, with her brothers taken care of, she also decided it was time for her father to move on!

It so happened that ever since moving to Pune, Ajai had been calling Shalini's parents to visit. However, her father was unable to gather the courage to visit Shalini's home when she herself wasn't there anymore.

Thus, Shalini decided to take matters into her own hands! Her father saw her in his dream one night, telling him that he had spent his entire life working tirelessly for his family, having settled all his children so well and created a fair amount of wealth in the process. She told him that now it was time to do something for himself.

Her father asked her what she meant, to which Shalini told him to go visit her home in Pune!

Now he had no choice but to do what his eldest child wanted him to do.

The next morning, as soon as he woke up, Shalini's father announced that he was going to Pune to visit Shalini's home. Tickets for him and his wife were booked the very same day and soon they were in Pune visiting the *Polo Vista*, which is the official residence of GOC-in-C Southern Command. It was a magnificent abode, befitting a senior officer of the Indian Army.

The best part about it was Shalini's photo at the very entrance of the home, welcoming all that came visiting it. A blissful week was spent there by her parents in the company of Ajai and more of their family members.

Another testimony to the fact that Shalini continues to look after her loved ones lies in the home that Ajai has built post retirement in Dhaulas, Dehradun. He was able to find just the perfect spot that Shalini had always wanted – by the flowing stream, next to a forest and with a clear view of Mussoorie!

Moreover, the construction of the house was entrusted to Abhinav who took a temporary sabbatical from his own business venture and devoted all his time and energies into creating not a house, but a temple in the memory of his mother. In doing so, he himself came of age and matured much beyond his years.

As mentioned in our scriptures, the soul lives on even after the physical form is discarded. Shalini's indulgence in her family's well being continues to bear testimony to this ageless wisdom.

A good heart had indeed stopped beating when Shalini passed on, yet the beautiful, eternal soul continues to thrive.

"REMEMBER ME"

"To the living, I am gone,

To the sorrowful, I will never return,

To the angry, I was cheated,

But to the happy, I am at peace,

And to the faithful, I have never left.

I cannot speak, but I can listen.

I cannot be seen, But I can be heard.

So as you stand upon a shore gazing at a beautiful sea,

As you look upon a flower and admire its simplicity, Remember me.

Remember me in your heart:

"Remember Me"

Your thoughts, and your memories,

Of the times we loved,

The times we cried,

The times we fought,

The times we laughed.

For if you always think of me, I will never have been gone."

– Margaret Mead

ABOUT AJAI - THE NARRATOR

Lt Gen Ajai Kumar Singh, PVSM, AVSM, YSM, SM, VSM, PhD (Retd.), brings over 40 years of distinguished service in the Indian Army. Commissioned into the Eleventh Gorkha Rifles Regiment, he has navigated diverse and challenging terrains across the country.

Throughout his career, he has held prestigious staff and command positions both domestically and internationally, culminating in his role as Southern Army Commander, where he was entrusted with the critical responsibility of defending nearly half of India's land mass.

He is a keen mountaineer, trekker and an enthusiastic sportsman with interests in cycling and yoga.

He has authored various articles on leadership and spirituality. Besides this, he is a motivational speaker and lectures on geostrategic issues, India's strategic culture, life's philosophy and spirituality.

https://en.wikipedia.org/wiki/Ajai_Kumar_Singh